IN THE WORDS OF FTZ4

"I don't think Milwaukee knows the *national* treasure we have in Steve Palec. The capital of Wisconsin isn't Madison; it's Steve Palec. He's a friend—a brother—to anyone who needs one. The guy is just amazing! It's hard to put into words who Steve is and that's why I'm as excited as anyone to read his story. I hope you are, too."

▶ *LeRoy Butler #36*
Green Bay Packers (Retired)
Inventor of The Leap

"Steve Palec is one of the most interesting and remarkable people who I have met in my long career and I congratulate him on his extraordinary accomplishments."

▶ *Allan H (Bud) Selig*
Commissioner Emeritus, Major League Baseball, HOF 2017

"Steve is a great guy! He has been able to maintain his love for music along with a successful business career for many years. That is not easy, but speaks to his passion. He is thoughtful, too. I still have that Stevie Wonder aircheck he made for me many, many years ago."

▶ *Greg Marcus*
President and CEO
Marcus Corporation

"Steve is so Milwaukee in all the good ways that Milwaukee and the Midwest are. Midwesterners are nice people and genuine and that fits Steve perfectly. He's authentic."

▶ *Jessob Reisbeck*
Anchor
WJLA TV ABC
Washington DC

"The real entrepreneurs of the music industry moved to movies. The people who took over were into the spotlight and the money, but not the music. It was like a cancer. The fever and meat weren't there anymore. Steve Palec rejuvenates the realness of what it once was. The meaning of it all comes back through his show. It brings me back to the reality of what the artistry was. He breathes new life into it– life after death."

▶ *REED KAILING*
Musician and Actor
Grass Roots, Player, Badfinger, The Hardy Boys,
Beatlemania (Broadway/as Paul McCartney)

"When I think about Steve's next chapter, I think, *'Who the heck knows!'* There are so many possibilities. He's a perfect example of who, when I think about him, I say, *'I don't know what's next, but it's gonna be good.'* He's Milwaukee through and through. He's proud of and excited about our city. He knows everybody everywhere. He's a hometown guy (who travels to Kentucky for the best bourbon).

▶ *NICOLE KOGLIN*
Fox 6 News (Milwaukee)

"Steve fits in this city. A city of this size couldn't hold Steve's interest for so long if it was not also open to change, growth, and great sports. The city is good for Steve and he's good for the city. He's world-class entertainment–an eclectic person with wide-ranging tastes. You can take him at face value. He is who he is and I don't think that will ever change."

▶ *SCOTT PAULUS*
Director of Photography
Milwaukee Brewers

"Steve Palec is my dear friend; he's a true foodie, a sports enthusiast, and definitely quirky. His eyes see the world through a unique lens. He's lived a colorful life and has worked hard for what he has. I think he's hit a point in his life where he is able to reflect, be grateful, and embrace and enjoy every day and everything about every day when the alarm clock wakes him for the world. He's there for the ride; he's there to enjoy it. And now we can, too, in his story!"

▶ *KATHLEEN O'LEARY*
Executive Director/CEO
Wisconsin State Fair Park

"Everybody in town knows Steve Palec, but they don't really *know* him. I imagine that's what happens to most luminaries with a vehicle. They know that persona, personality, and voice (literal and figurative). He goes so deep on everything he does. You can't *not* be impressed with him."

▶ *JAY FILTER*
Photographer and Creative Director
Winner of International Photography Awards(IPA),
International Fine Art Photography Awards (FAPA)
and Prix de la Photographie Paris.(PX3)

"Following Steve on social media is even better than following Conan O'Brien. He's super fun. It's a testament to his awesomeness. He's an incredible DJ; his show made me think about radio differently. His fan base will follow him anywhere he goes. It's a really special thing that not everyone can do and people will love to know more about who he is."

▶ *JORDAN LEE*
Program Director
88Nine Radio Milwaukee

In Between The Aisles

"Steve plays a major role in the city and county of Milwaukee. He has always been a dynamic factor in bringing projects to the area. He exemplifies professionalism. It's not just a job for him. He has a love affair with the Milwaukee area. It's always clear that this love is what drives his passion for development and he is excited about the impacts he can help make."

▶ *SCOTT WALKER*
Former Governor of Wisconsin (Republican)

"Steve Palec is one of the best storytellers of all-time who has a window seat to some of the more iconic moments in American History. Complete with encounters with important figures from the twentieth century, Palec weaves fascinating tales onto the pages of his book that will be shared for generations to come. A must read for anyone who is a connoisseur of the finer things in life."

▶ *EARNELL R. LUCAS*
Milwaukee County Sheriff (Democrat)

▶

In the Eyes of His Family

"Growing up with other kids, everybody would say, 'My dad is so cool!' I was able to say, 'My dad is so cool!' . . . and mean it. My dad knew more about Rock & Roll than their dads. He was Rock & Roll when Rock & Roll meant something. I had the cool dad. That was not argued by anybody else. I think he needs more light. People need to know who he is. He's talking about these legends, but he himself is a legend. He's made a name for himself."

▶ *JOE PALEC*
Steve's Son

"I would describe my dad as someone who likes to perform. He likes to live his life larger than the average person. He likes to make big gestures. He has also helped me to think critically about things. Things have a purpose. He's given me a good appreciation for history and American culture as a whole and what I can take away from that. He reminds me to enjoy those things that are out there to be enjoyed."

▶ *HALEY PALEC*
Steve's Daughter

"Steve is really complex. He has an exterior, funny-guy persona that everybody loves. His purpose in life is laughter. Everyone thinks he's funny, creative, and clever . . . and he is, but he has a deep side to him. He's fragile. He strives for safety, love, approval, and knowing that he matters. Everything he does is intentional and with the purpose of wanting to make an impression. I'm happy to just be with him."

▶ *ALETA NORRIS*
Steve's Wife

In Awe

Beatles, Baseball, & Bourbon
Appreciating Spectacular *and* Simple Stuff

By Radio Personality STEVE PALEC
(#0 Bestselling Author unless you buy this!)
with #1 Bestselling Author Reji Laberje

Foreword by Green Bay Packer Legend LeRoy Butler

In Awe – Beatles, Baseball, & Bourbon – Appreciating Spectacular and Simple Stuff
Palec, Steve
Laberje, Reji

Editors: Howard Schlossberg, Kimberly Laberge
Cover Design: Mike Nicloy, Nico 11 Publishing & Design, www.nico11publishing.com
Interior Layout: Reji Laberje

Photo Credits–Front cover photos by and used with permission of Jay Filter–jayfilterphotography.com. Back cover first and third photos in Miller Park by and used with permission of Scott Paulus–ScottPaulus.com; remaining back cover photos courtesy of Steve Palec including with Les Paul, "Steve Palec Was There" WKLH Marketing Series by Steve Eichenbaum, with Aaron Rodgers, Live Remote for WQFM, and with LeRoy Butler. Interior Photos: Steve Palec Emoji (page vi)–courtesy of OnMilwaukee; Steve Palec author photo and In The Studio photos by and used with permission of Steve Olson; Reji Laberje author photo by and used with permission of Kimberly Laberge; all other photos in book courtesy of and used with permission of Steve Palec, Aleta Norris, or OnMilwaukee unless otherwise noted.

Categories:
Humor & Entertainment/Radio/General Broadcasting
Arts & Photography/Music/Rock
Bographies & Memoirs/Regional U.S./Midwest
Biographies & Memoirs/Biographies/Baseball

www.stevepalec.com

Dedication...

This book is **not** dedicated to my wonderful wife, kids, dog, radio friends, commercial real estate colleagues, musicians, athletes, fast-food chefs, bourbon distillers, or the TV stars I admire. You'll hear plenty about them in the stories and acknowledgements where I can give them the space and words they deserve.

I dedicate this book to laughter.

I wouldn't want to live without it.

I'm in awe of its power.

▶

Love at First Leap

Since that frigid December day in 1993 when LeRoy Butler made a spontaneous leap into the arms of fans, the Lambeau Leap has become a Packers tradition. It declares that nothing gets in the way between Packers players and their fans. In all of football, nothing symbolizes a greater connection between players and fans than the Lambeau Leap. To the fans who welcome every player with open arms, we thank you. Here's your chance to experience your own Lambeau Leap right here, right now. Make it legendary.

IN FROM THE START

Foreword by LeRoy Butler

"If I had some more time to
spend, then I guess I'd be
with you, my friend."

▶ FROM: *If I Needed Someone*
BY: *The Beatles, Rubber Soul*
(Capitol Records [North American Version], 1965)

*T*HE best friendships, to me, grow organically and not in a forced way. Steve Palec and I have broadcast together, judged the Sporkies[1] side-by-side, enjoyed sports, and—ultimately—even been in one another's weddings. But, it didn't start out by my being brought in to "meet" Steve. I crossed paths with him and thought, *'This guy is the white LeRoy Butler!'*

He was so much like me and sometimes opposites do attract, but other times you gravitate toward people who are like you. We connected immediately as friends. He's funny. Everybody likes him. Artists and athletes both say good things about him. Yes, athletes, too. He does Rock & Roll Roots on the air, but he could do sports just

---

[1] *Wisconsin State Fair's annual food competition.*

as easily. He loves sports and, anything he loves, from bourbon to baseball, he learns.

Steve could do a lot of things. I could Google any random subject and he would have a thoughtful answer for it. More than forty years in the radio business and as a household Milwaukee name, so he knows *a lot*. It goes beyond music and sports, too. He knows the community. He knows people. You need a person for flowers? Steve knows where to go. You want landscaping? He's got a guy. Your nephew needs a birthday gift? Steve has just the thing. Anything! It's amazing. I'm not making this up. He doesn't just *know* people. He can connect them and make things happen and never for a "thank you," or recognition, but just because he thinks it's what he's supposed to do.

▶▶ **He doesn't just know people. He can connect them and make things happen and never for a "thank you."**

Steve is *so* connected, one of the *most* connected people in all of Wisconsin, but you wouldn't know it. He never acts bigger than the personality he is on the air with or spending time with in person. Some of the people I've met in the media aren't friendly and open like Steve. They're guarded. It's hard to be around that. Everybody wants to be near Steve Palec, though. He's a good guy. He's one of the only people I'm still close with from my days doing a lot of media. He's humble. He approaches stars and non-celebrities in the same way.

I only have a few true *friends* in my life. I have a lot of associates, but not a ton of friends. It's sometimes hard when people recognize you. Not with Steve. He wasn't starstruck with me. He doesn't treat me like a celebrity. (In fact, I feel like I should treat him like one!)

I remember one day when I was in the studio. The Packers had lost and, on those days, everybody is down, especially around me. I was already retired, but I would hear clichés from people wanting to comfort me all the time. *'You can't win 'em all.'*

Instead, Steve came up to me and said, "Well, LeRoy, look on the bright side. At least it's not your fault, anymore."

I laughed for twenty minutes straight. He knew what to say. He didn't avoid me or give me a line, but talked to me like family.

As an entertainer, he is amazing. Grown men love him, women adore him, and young people find him funny. He connects with all people. You can let your hair down, put on your party dress, and be free with him. He's just a free-spirited guy. There's no filter–just Steve being Steve. That's why I love him. Our wives have had to break us up from talking and talking and talking and talking. He's a brother to me in every way.

Steve, LeRoy, and FOOD! Clockwise from top left: backstage at the Sporkies, enjoying a bite in the "Palec Pub," and a friendly food fight over lunch at Stella Van Buren in Milwaukee

Probably the most flattering experience I ever had, short of playing in the Super Bowl, was being asked to be in Steve's wedding to Aleta. I blushed purple. I was like a freshman cheerleader being asked to the prom by the star quarterback!

We both know what finding that true love is all about, especially later in life. It was a good moment. Years earlier, a friend of mine was going through a divorce. I've been through a divorce. Steve, too. This guy was really in the dumps, though. So, we got the bourbon flowing and opened up with him.

"I went through it," Steve said. "I came out better. I realized what I did well. I also realized my mistakes and faults."

It takes a true man to own his mistakes. Steve did that to help this guy out.

"Divorce doesn't make you a bad person," he said. "Mistakes are mistakes and you can learn from them and change."

To this day, that friend—now remarried and doing great—talks about how guys don't get in each other's business like that. '*Thank Steve for me,*' he's said more than once.

4

When you have a good friend, you can open up. For me, that good friend is always Steve. He doesn't judge. He's just easy. And that shared history and openness is part of why finding his wife was emotional.

Aleta *is* the quintessential Steve story in a single person. If you know how a guy treats his wife, that's how he is in his life.

▶▶ **Aleta is the quintessential Steve story in a single person.**

"She's meeting THE Steve Palec?" I said. "I need to know how you found her!"

Well, he laughs and jokes so much that I thought he was going to tell me it was on Tinder or something, even though it wasn't true. Instead, he got serious. I never heard a guy tell a story like that. He got tears in his eyes. He was sentimental and soft. He could barely talk and this is a guy who's on the radio!

"God is good," I told him. "All the time, brother."

Football thrown as a ceremonial first pitch at the start of Steve and Aleta's wedding

At left, LeRoy and Aleta's stepmom on the day of the wedding; he's just one of the family

Below, LeRoy snaps a selfie mid-vows at Steve and Aleta's wedding

Next Page, Top – Steve later returned the honor when he stood up in LeRoy's 2019 wedding to Genesis; here they are before the ceremony

Next Page, Middle – Steve with two members of the bridal party at LeRoy's wedding

Next Page, Bottom – LeRoy and his groomsmen (Steve at the back on the right)

I've had some great friends and teammates in my life – Brett Favre, Donald Driver, Frank Winters ... but with Steve? He's the only one I could get that deep into conversation with about the women in our lives. It was a powerful moment. We hugged. It was a Hallmark card! Those are the moments that need to be told. No one knows that two guys can embrace over the fact that they love their wives so much. He loves Aleta and I love my wife, Genesis. We let it out and it was easy. And then we just as easily laugh together or give each other a hard time.

This book is a big deal.

I don't think Milwaukee knows the *national* treasure we have in Steve Palec. Sure, we've had great bands and brands, but who helped catapult them? Who gives them a platform? Not just on his show, but behind the scenes, helping people out and connecting them?

He'd probably be all weirded out over me saying so, but some of this stuff—his real heart—it just needs to be told.

His life inspires.

With a *leap*,
~ *LeRoy Butler*
Inventor of the "Lambeau Leap"
Green Bay Packers Strong Safety 1990-2001

IN THE STUDIO
A Prologue

"After years and years of
writing story songs I've
learned one thing. If you're
writing a story song you
better have a darn good
ending. And if you don't then
you better have a good moral
to the story...."

▶ *FROM: The Bottomless Lake*
BY: John Prine, In Person & On Stage
(Oh Boy Records, 2010)

I WALK into the studio early Sunday morning, inspired. It's more of
an "audio lab" where I tell stories. It's much larger than most
people expect. A big, arched table winds its way through the room. I
make my way around the massive table to the side of the room with
paintings of Bruce Springsteen and the Beatles. Over here, in
addition to a telephone and many microphones, there are nine
computer screens, the news on a television on the wall (with closed
captioning, of course; can't interfere with the audio), and—hung

opposite the TV—an unmissable clock, bright red, just like the on-air light beside it. It glows above a window that peers into the next studio.

This whole *room* is exciting for me. I get to be a different person here, or maybe I'm just the most like myself here. I've had to be a chameleon in so many other parts of my life. In one of my roles, I work in commercial real

▶▶ **I get to be a different person here, or maybe I'm just the most like myself here.**

estate in a tall glass building with secure elevators overlooking the water. In another role, I'm a simple married man with a suburban Milwaukee home in a quiet neighborhood where one of my greatest joys is just sitting in my recliner with my dog, Luke. I'm Aleta's husband and lucky for that. She's my perfect fit. I'm a fervent fan of the Brewers, Packers, Admirals, Bucks, and Badgers. And I'm a Milwaukee lifer. But in this place where I was born to work—in the studio—I get to be an artist, a professional, a passionate music lover, a walking book of trivia, and (if I'm lucky) a friend people invite into their living rooms or cars for a few hours every weekend. Here, I get to play the soundtrack of my life, the life of a first-generation American who has tried to encompass all that America is through the signals of FM radio.

Before coming in here this week, just as I've done for the last thirty-two years, I worked to put together a road map. When I put together subjects—*themes* for my weekly

radio show, *Rock & Roll Roots with Steve Palec*, I start writing down those songs I know, then I research and find some more. Sometimes, I find so much of intrigue, I'm tempted to do a one-subject show, but that only happens maybe four or five times a year. Instead, I like to force myself to be creative and find those three to four "articles" that will be the pillars of my three-hour airtime on Milwaukee's Hometown Rock Station, 96.5 WKLH.

I don't typically work with a producer. I hear it in my head, so that's what I "produce." I think it would be harder to work with somebody else. Except for answering phones, which I usually don't do, I don't really have a need for a producer. I begin with a "Root-Salute Artist," throw in a couple of unique topics, such as: genres of music; featured instruments; lyrics about specific subjects; or the geographic demographics of different artists or songs. This week, ninety-seven audio cuts are what I pull up on my computer screen. Overpreparing is the recipe for this program. I line up more than I'll ever have time to use and I continue to add or change things as I go, all the way up until the next weekend programming takes over.

I try to look for the kinds of knowledge and tidbits that most people would never think to search for. I want my listeners to feel like they are getting all of the inside stories at a concert, except this is a multi-artist concert of my choosing. I want there to be a mix of comedy, encyclopedic knowledge of Rock & Roll, and instrumental and musical information, too. Each feature is there to bring some new joy to the unseen listeners in my audience. I spend several days in preparation, to create a four-hour show, just to be able to put on a three-hour show. So, yes, overpreparing *is* key.

▶▶ **I try to look for the kinds of knowledge and tidbits that most people would never think to search for.**

This morning, I've suited up in a Pappy Van Winkle[2] t-shirt. While I'm in casual clothing that represents one of my favorite bourbons (another of my passions), this is a long way from chill time. I'm about to work out. Radio may be relaxing for those who get to hear it, but make no mistake, I need to be at the ready in this place. I run back and forth between stacks of CDs, my cell phone for research, a digital sound board, CD player stacks, computer screens

---

[2] *Pappy Van Winkle is a rare, limited edition bourbon distilled at the Old Rip Van Winkle Distillery in Frankfort, Kentucky.*

with audio cuts and samplings, a set of headphones, and a microphone set at a level to reach my voice way up in the air for my six-foot-three-inch frame. There is no sitting. I run back and forth in the studio. I'm a sound scientist in here, driven, thinking, manipulating the perfect formula for my audience's listening and connecting pleasure. I've been described as looking like an octopus in front of a microphone.

I need to have multi-tasked focus in the studio . . . keep my gears grinding. When a song comes on for the listeners or a commercial break to pay the bills, I can't be the stereotyped radio DJ from WKRP in Cincinnati. Unlike the hit TV show's legendary Doctor Johnny Fever, I'm not sitting back and having conversations, listening to the music, chatting with people, or waiting for my next obligation to speak between songs. I need to be *on*, even when my voice is not. When that *On-Air* red light goes on, it should be catching up with me. My brain needs to hear it *all*–layers, words, cuts, cues, and music.

The show is live and I'm following along with it as it broadcasts across the air. I dig through my next possible cuts while listeners are unassumingly turning up the tunes in their cars and homes and offices. I try out different songs. I've had to get good at listening for what I need to hear in fast forward and learning to find the exact cue, sound, or stopping point I'm looking for, prior to selecting the next song. Sometimes, just before my cue, at the last second, I'll change my mind and find a cut or sound bite that is a better fit or flow for the show. I like to stay on my toes to keep it interesting.

▶▶ **I like to stay on my toes to keep it interesting.**

Volume is all over the place in here. I was raised on analog sound. It's richer and without isolating various tracks, it allows ambient sound into the mix. Today, digital recording is pristine and doesn't always have the same balance the way the real world sounds. That's why I use vinyl, tape, CDs, and actual noise from the studio, and mix them together with digital on air. The attention to detail is worth it.

So, volume gets blasted up and pulled down in the room–to draw my "hear" where it needs to be, sometimes out loud in the studio and other times through my headphones. I also look at what's happening outside and on the news. Today, on this snowy day, I

slip in a couple of extra cuts: *"Oh the weather outside is frightful!"* Then I mix in my work of reading the weather. When I get to the commercial break, sometimes I'll even answer a listener's email that comes in.

I always cross off the used cues on my paper and on the screen. I have the roadmap that I completed before the studio time; it's my list of songs, artists, and cuts, but I don't know what I'm going to play next, or what I'm going to say. I know the contents of the loose outline I created and I consume my options between performance moments. I keep gum and a bottle of water nearby, but usually don't get a chance to partake in either during my audio marathon.

Sometimes, I have to run out of the studio for a second . . . and I mean a *second* . . . to grab something when inspiration strikes, or to ensure the recording is going well in the other room. I have this whole building to myself this morning, but I don't mind.

Steve: Are you aware of how much it meant to those of us in the radio industry to have songs like *Nights in White Satin* and *Tuesday Afternoon* that allowed us to leave the studio for a while?

Justin Hayward – The Moody Blues: (Laughing) We were just lucky that our stuff was recorded so well that the FM medium was just perfect for it. When FM radio came along, ours were the albums that were the favorites really because they were recorded so well. Unlike a lot of other British records at the time that were just done in mono and even if there was a stereo version, it was drums on the left and vocals on the right.

Enjoy these ⌐ *snippets from the interview archives.*

15

When I get home after the show, I'll need quiet–pure silence for half an hour at least. I'm actually an introvert . . . something most people don't realize; I do get emotionally energized by this solo work, but it's physically exhausting at the same time because of how much I pour into it. Mental energy is a big deal, too. This morning, I have one moment when I play six clips all at once. I slide a lever up, click something on my computer, press play on a CD, and my hands need to be as swift as my voice is strong. Nothing in here is simple, but it's my job to make it feel that way when it pours out of the speakers that are playing my show across Southeast Wisconsin. I've only missed doing one live show in all the years I've been on the air. It was because of an ice storm and I even *tried* to get out of my driveway, but couldn't.

▶▶ **I do get emotionally energized by this solo work, but it's physically exhausting at the same time because of how much I pour into it.**

Rock & Roll Roots is kind of like a themed magazine set to music. I have three articles and I need to weave them together with smaller inserts and features. It's something I'm proud to say I do well. It all flows together. I could just present a chunk at a time, but I want to make a fluid, three-hour production.

Here's what a listener might hear on *Rock & Roll Roots*:

Steve: This is Rock & Roll Roots. Morning! I'm Steve Palec. *"What'll you do when you get lonely. And nobody's waiting by your side...."*
   -Layla; Song by Eric Clapton
Steve: We've all heard this song, *Layla,* numerous times. It's an impassioned plea from Eric Clapton to resolve his unrequited love for a woman who has had a lot of songs written about her–Pattie Boyd.
"Something in the way she moves. Attracts me like no other lover...."

-Something; Song by George Harrison and The Beatles

Pattie Interview: I find the concept of being a muse understandable.

Steve: It would be amazing if only you had one song like *Something* written about you.

"You don't realize how much I need you...."

-I Need You; Song by The Beatles

Steve: George Harrison met Pattie Boyd on the set of the movie, "A Hard Day's Night."

Society Reporter: What do you call that haircut?"

George Harrison: "Arthur"

-A Hard Day's Night; Movie Cut

Steve: They married. And George's good friend Eric Clapton eventually fell in love with Pattie and tried to convince her to leave George.

Pattie: He gave me a kiss at a party. George came over.

-Fight Sound Effects

George Harrison Interview: People thought we should have a fight. It wasn't like that.

"Take the dawn of the day and give it away. To someone who can fill the part of the dream we once held...."

-So Sad; Song by George Harrison

Steve: Pattie did finally leave George. It was the end of that marriage. But not the end of songs. Eric Clapton's *Wonderful Tonight* is about . . . you guessed it."

Eric Clapton Interview: I think of my ex-wife whenever I hear that song. She's had some knock-down songs written about her.

"It's late in the evening, she's wondering what clothes to wear. She puts on her makeup and brushes her long blonde hair...."

Steve: Clapton was literally waiting for his wife to get ready. Here's Eric Clapton on Rock & Roll Roots."

"We go to a party and everyone turns to see. This beautiful lady that's walking around with me...."

-Wonderful Tonight; Song by Eric Clapton

Having done the show for decades, there have of course been moments that were important, too. There have been wars, and elections, and positive news, and major events, and sporting endeavors, and natural disasters. I am a responsible citizen who is cognizant of what's going on around me. When there are tornadoes and storms, that's the hardest, because all of the alarms are going off and I'm worried about lightning, but I need to get that news out to listeners. Most people don't realize it's a live show. It's live! I do my duty to try and weave in the pertinent information that everybody should know, whether it's a tragedy, a celebration, or an act of nature.

One day, phone lines began lighting up when the Sikh shooting in Oak Creek[3] happened. I couldn't find anything on the news. It wasn't being reported yet. I finally saw a few tweets from legitimate sources and I realized it was an unfortunate, true event. I had to break the news of the situation on the air. It's important to honor times like that to respect the power of this little room. It's amazing that I'm handed this 50,000-watt station to just do what I want.

▶▶ **It's important to honor times like that to respect the power of this little room.**

On the air, I do live with some fears, including profanity, playing the wrong cut, hitting the wrong button, or dead air. But I enjoy being on that edge. I'm constantly asked if the show is taped. It just sounds that way. I once played James Blunt's *You're Beautiful.* He says "fuckin' high." I jumped high enough to dunk over Giannis Antetokounmpo to hit the "dump button" on that. I've worked hard to earn my station's trust.

IT'S SO MUCH FREEDOM.

THEY JUST LET ME GO!

I'M STILL IN AWE.

---

[3] *On August 5, 2012, a mass shooting occurred at a Sikh Temple in Oak Creek, Wisconsin. The hate crime claimed the lives of six people, including the temple's founder, and wounded four others, before the white supremacist perpetrator took his own life.*

"This is *Rock & Roll Roots*, I'm Steve Palec," I slide in as my on-air light comes up. I've been told I kind of dip my body when I'm talking into the mic, like I'm reaching down into my soul to grab my voice. I go to a spoken clip and silently lip some of the words I remember setting aside for this moment. I may not know it until I choose it, but I've done my homework and these pieces are stamped on my brain. I drop in the occasional laugh, appropriately timed "Hmmm," or a question to my listeners.

If I play two songs in a row, I'll fluidly slide down one lever and another up at the same time. When I first started, we would play, like, four songs in a row, *sets* of music we called them, and I'd try to blend them together–segue them. I lived to find the perfect segue songs. It's exciting when you get one that fits just right.

When I think about sets and themes and segues, I realize that I've kind of lived my life like my show. I have a lot of stories, or "articles," as I call them on my show. I know the articles I've wanted to work into my big plan–family, career, and community.

Steve: Your songs, as phenomenal as they are, could be frustrating for those of us in radio because they are eight, nine, ten, eleven minutes long. You even covered Paul Simon's *America* and tripled the length. Were those choices conscious?

Jon Anderson – Yes: Oh yeah because we wanted to put on a show. We never thought we were going to write music for radio. We actually started expanding music right at the very beginning of the band Yes in 1968. Of course we did *America* and *Something's Coming* from "West Side Story" into long form pieces. And I just had the idea that we would put on a show and the audience would sit or stand there and listen and we should take them on a musical journey. And that's how Yes music evolved. It was never created for the radio.

▶▶ **When I think about sets and themes and segues, I realize that I've kind of lived my life like my show.**

I know the features that will bring joy–the athletes, artists, and adventures that have played in my life and become a part of my own story, just like a song does for the person who hears it over the chapters of his or her existence. I overprepare. Always. I want to know all there is to know about the things I experience. I try to know my cues, but sometimes the figurative sirens are going off and I need to be the one to keep my head and just face the situation. I work through the transition to the next moment.

And, when I get it just right?

It's so much freedom.

I can just let go!

I'm in awe.

And I never take the experience for granted

**"There goes the last DJ
Who plays what
he wants to play
And says what
he wants to say
And there goes
your freedom of choice
There goes the
last human voice."**

▶ *The Last DJ, Tom Petty*

▶

IN THE BEGINNING
Can Anybody Hear Me?

"Davy, hear that?
War drums."

▶ *FROM: Walt Disney's Three Adventures of Davy Crockett*
BY: Buddy Ebsen as Georgie Russell
(Disneyland Records, 1958)

I WAS very young . . . seven or eight years old, I think, when I had my first defining experience. My Mom, Sophie, was down the hall asleep. It had been more than twenty years since the bombings of World War II kept her awake at night in her London home. She was outgoing, had a great sense of humor, and was interested in the life around her.

My Dad, Samuel, was with her. Dad was a Jewish Lithuanian, though we weren't really raised with a lot of religion. He'd escaped two concentration camps, in Dachau and Dunaburg, as a teenager, saw his own parents murdered before his eyes, and survived alone afterward on bread . . . when he could get it. He ended up in a third concentration camp at Stutthof, where he spent the rest of his days until Victory in Europe. The experience left him bitter.

I don't blame him. Today, PTSD is a real thing that gets recognized and cared for. That wasn't the case, then. And, while respecting and honoring a Holocaust survivor is commendable, living with one was truly difficult.

I had a *Dennis The Menace* comic book in which the titular character went to visit Pearl Harbor in Hawaii. I read that comic over and over again and, for some reason, I just loved it. I wanted to know even more because real history fascinated me, but we couldn't ask our parents about the war. Not even the war in the Pacific. Not even the fictional war from the movies.

Our house was not the war. It wasn't welcome there. We didn't speak about it in any context – romanticized, fantasized, or realized. And it was so far removed from my reality that I couldn't wrap my head around the idea of war at all, especially the one that affected my parents.

▶▶ **Our house was not the war.**

It wouldn't be until decades later that I would visit Pearl Harbor–alone. I didn't talk to a single soul there; rather, I just took it all in. I was somber and reverent. It was one of my few bucket list items . . . to visit Pearl Harbor like Dennis the Menace did and maybe understand something from history about which I could never ask.

My war-born parents came—though my father didn't ever assimilate—to America, to Wisconsin, to Milwaukee after World War II. They were uncelebrated survivors to their first-generation American kids, me and my brother, Andy.

Brothers Andy (left) and Steve (right) Palec

Andy and I didn't have a close relationship, either. I really mean that. We didn't have a *bad* relationship, just not much of one at all. We were kind of opposites, my brother and I. We looked different and had different interests. He was studious where I was more oblivious. He was serious and I was a goof most times. Sometimes we shared a room and other times I was on my own. I don't really remember a lot of details to be honest. Each of our memories are our own. To me, it was like our family consisted of four separate lives under one roof. Today, Andy and I are helpful to one another in life (we actually both ended up in real estate). We're cognizant of our shared history and who we are to one another, but we don't really hang out or share childhood stories and nostalgia from our early days.

My mother really was extraordinary, if you could see her exuberance through her formal British manners. She was social, humorous, and fun. She valued her relationship with her parents, sisters, and brother and she made friends easily. She was strong, and had to be, not because of the war, but because she chose a difficult life with my father and it was the '50s. It had only been four decades since women received the right to vote and they still were held back by societal limitations.

In those days, the combination of a damaged father and proper mother meant that the whole house was mostly quiet. The exception was when Dad was mad, so we just kept our distance, free-ranging ourselves into adulthood, each in our own way.

When I was that little boy, I remember the moments when they were all asleep. I remember because those nights have always stuck with me, without being too esoteric about it. It's not logical, but—when I would lie in bed—it's like I could feel myself and my senses leaving my body. With all the awareness of my young mind, I knew it wasn't my imagination. Something was really happening to me. It was a sort of out-of-body experience.

I had been a worrisome headcase when I was young, and I was sick a lot, so I had this really skinny frame. Well, on those nights, I would have to use all the strength of my scrawny body to hold myself down and force my small weight into my bed. I remember being very fearful, but I wasn't incapacitated. I was so tired, but I would lie there trying to hold every cell of myself together until I would finally fall asleep. It happened so often and so powerfully that, to this day, I still don't like to lay fully parallel. I never told anyone about the experience, no matter how often it occurred. In my home, there wasn't really anyone to talk to who would understand. But it did happen and it's made me very open to not dismissing the unbelievable or strange claims that people sometimes have. Oh, I'm still skeptical, but never dismissive.

In my adult retrospection, I often wonder how much of our brains we really use and I can't help but think that maybe I shouldn't have tried so hard to hold myself down.

Was that dying?

Or maybe the opposite?

What would have happened if I had just let myself go?

Each morning, I came downstairs. Not a lot of conversation took place. I got good at reading the situation in a room. I wasn't sure how even my well-intentioned words might be received, so silence was easier. The television, a staple at the end of the day and one of my certified babysitters, wasn't on before we left for school. We didn't get a morning paper, either, but the radio was filling the air. Often, it was WBBM, the Chicago All-News Station, or it would be Milwaukee's WISN Radio morning drive time with Charlie Hanson and Shaky. Hanson was a brilliant radio host who used his own voice to create the alter ego and sidekick, Shaky.

Because the tension was so palpable in our house, with me just wanting the mornings to get by, it was Hanson's creation that got my days started. It broke the awkward silence and served as the constant in our alley-facing kitchen. These were my windows to the world: the voices from the radio; the television screen at night; and the view of the alley into a life that never quite felt like my own. Life wasn't in my house, it was out there. That's where my world existed–in speakers, and screens, and streets that I wanted to make my own.

To me, my friends included '60s sitcom characters: Jethro Bodine, Theodore Cleaver, Hank Kimball, Opie Taylor, Charlie O'Casey, and Gomer Pyle. I was as close to them as I was to the kids in the neighborhood and to my classmates. It probably explains the wall I kept around me. My TV friends didn't interact with me and, in turn, I liked them without favors or intimacy. I expected much the same for people in my "real" life. I was glad for acquaintances, but I didn't require anything else.

Steve: When I was a kid, there were some girls that put together a group that would lip-sync all the Herman's Hermits songs. They auditioned the boys in the neighborhood to be their lead "singer." I got chosen because, and I will never forget these words, "You look okay, but you're no Peter Noone."

Peter Noone – Herman's Hermits: Only one of us could be Peter Noone. At that time there were two big records in the charts. "I'm Into Something Good" from Herman's Hermits and "Eve of Destruction" from Barry McGuire. Fortunately, we were right.

Sometimes, my parents felt obligated to take us somewhere away from the windows of our home. It was usually just a trip from a AAA TripTik. We'd travel someplace like Springfield, Illinois, to see Lincoln's birthplace; it's about as far as Dad would go. We'd stay at '60s-style resorts. I had no social skills beyond sports in the neighborhood, so it was always a little uncomfortable. The adults got to do their thing and we'd have an organized activity time. I remember the counselor singing *Love The One You're With* around a campfire and I couldn't relate to the lyrics. Those trips weren't really memorable for me, so I'd come back to my windows, and speakers, and to the alley where I tried to figure out how to make my life based on those views.

My parents, meanwhile, were very aware of current events and politics. Those rare instances when there was communication, it would be cerebral and I'd pick up on the events of the world. I saved the newspapers from man landing on the moon and other important events. We could actively and positively interact as a family when we were discussing social issues.

Being British, Mom measured up to the stereotype of being a bad cook at even the best of times. She did love candy, sweets, and chocolate, and those were always around. Perhaps that explains my lifelong adversity to the food pyramid. She was pleasant enough drinking her tea, but with Dad I never knew what I'd get, so I looked out toward the alley, ate my "home-cooked" cereal, and listened on. With Mom careful in her interactions and Dad in his own world, I heard the news and the sports and the music; they drew me in. Those mediums became a love and then a passion. Those who shared them became family.

I remember as a kid really enjoying basketball and even wanting to go to a basketball camp more than anything. Dad thought it was the most frivolous thing he'd ever heard. I may as well have wanted a Ferrari. Also, my entire childhood, I wanted a dog to be my companion, like pretty much every young boy for all of time. I really believe my Mom would have acquiesced. My Dad thought this was as foolish as the idea of basketball. I would leave hints (like dog food lying around the house) thinking my Dad wouldn't have to buy the food, so maybe that would make it okay.

As an adult years later, the day I bought a house. I also bought a dog named Addison. Addison was a Keeshond and he needed a companion, too. So, I eventually bought a second Keeshond named Lena. By the time I had my son, Joe, I had both dogs. Getting ready for a walk with my son one day, I hooked the two leashes to Joe's stroller while I grabbed his bag, and the dogs took off. I chased them down the road and it was only their lack of symmetry that allowed me to catch them – thank God. In that moment, there was no time to have feelings; I just acted. And, because all was well, the moment became comical. Maybe Dad was right? I guess I still disagree, though, because I can't imagine being without a furry companion. (Today, my best pal is Luke, my Goldendoodle!)

Boyhood me, though, whether it was money or means, usually figured out a way around most things, but basketball and a dog never happened.

My other (and probably largest) early desire was a radio. I wanted one so badly. I would actually take the newspaper, find an ad, cut out the *picture* of a transistor radio and glue it to a piece of cardboard. I did this from when I was about five years old and, up until I had the real thing, I walked around with that handmade craft as my "radio."

When I used to make my way to school, I would do a newscast or sportscast in my head . . . **Every. Single. Morning.**

I'd learned from what I'd heard at home and, as embarrassing as it sounds, I was playing it in my mind and sometimes even saying it out loud. *'Good morning, I'm Steve Palec,'* I'd say to myself.

The thing about growing up in America with two parents from two different countries is that we didn't really have roots or past examples that were shared with one another or our community. Even with my Mom's parents and siblings around, we were out of place in Milwaukee. My family wasn't a part of it. The city was still developing the melting-pot culture it has today. We had no concept around how families or kids should be in the urban Midwest. Sometimes I envied the kids who were told, *'You're going to be a plumber, like your dad!'* Not that I wanted to be a plumber, figuratively speaking; it's just that we didn't talk about dreams, or the future, or what we would grow up to be one day. Nor did we talk about how we should even come to have those ideas and discussions.

Mom was a secretary on and off, mostly to be social and because she happened to know how to type, a real business skill in the '50s and '60s. She needed to make some money of her own beyond cash for the basic necessities doled out by my father and to share a few extra coins with us kids. (Dad didn't believe in allowances.)

Dad was a carpenter, but didn't really have any educational direction or desire. Also, in Wisconsin, in the winter, so many of the trades came to a complete standstill in those days. He was laid off almost every year, so not having a job was a thing, too. I heard all the gloom and doom. But when he was earning money, he contributed to the household and right when we needed it, minus the dues he was forced to pay into the unions–something he would bitch up a storm about. Work (*labor*) was meant to put food on the table and nothing more. And he did work really hard; it *was* labor. His specific type of carpentry was being a "finisher," doing drywalling and other interior work. He also did roofing which he hated because it was brutal. He pushed through to get a job done, but there was never any joy in it for him–no sense of accomplishment, or pride, or fun. In fact, I can't think of anything my Dad found joy in; maybe that's why it's something I so desire in my own life.

▶▶ **In fact, I can't think of anything my dad found joy in; maybe that's why it's something I so desire in my own life.**

Neither one of my parents was necessarily working in his or her *vocation*–his or her calling. They were *just jobs*.

While I certainly had no thoughts about a radio career ever actually happening, I knew that I wanted to be bigger than what went on in my house. I wanted to be about more than surviving. I had no constraints about whether my daily productions for an audience of just me was working well; it was something other than "work" to me, though. I practiced my production every day because I liked it.

When I was around seven or eight years old, my parents acquiesced at last and got me my own transistor radio to replace my cardboard creation. I listened to it all the time. I listened to everything I could. And, at home, I would listen to vinyl record albums on this behemoth of a contraption—a giant piece of furniture, really—that I convinced my parents to let me pull into my own room.

One of the first records I remember putting on was Walt Disney's *Three Adventures of Davy Crockett* from Disneyland Records. I'm not even sure I know how the album came to be in my house, but it was tangible recorded sound, so I devoured it. Buddy Ebsen voiced George Russell and kicked off with his storytelling:

"The first time people heard of Davy Crockett...."

I listened over and over and over again as a kid. It wasn't just a reading of the story. This was two great actors—Fess Parker and Buddy Ebsen—in a fluid tale from start to finish. There was music and spectacular sound effects. You'd hear water splashes, bushes rustling, and a layering of sound, instruments, and voices. There were subtleties in the volume, too.

You could always hear the voices no matter what else was happening in the recording and that truly interested me. I thought that was so cool how all the different sounds played together, sharing the space. As an impressionable sponge, I listened to the message, the well-acted story, the sounds, the music–all of it.

"Davy, hear that?" George would say. "War drums...." (and the war drums would actually play as if they were off somewhere in the distance). *How did they do that?*

Sound has layers; I was fascinated with the realization. That album affected how I heard everything and still hear it today. Hearing became something more than physical for me. The *Three Adventures of Davy Crockett* affected how I listen, how I regurgitated what I'd heard, how I changed sound, an understanding of volumes and frequencies (though I didn't know them by those words, then); and it changed how I tried to hold people's attention with layers of interlacing soundwaves.

▶▶ **That album affected how I heard everything and still hear it today.**

It changed everything.

That album was so impactful that, years later, I even sought out Buddy Ebsen's daughter, Kiki Ebsen, and helped to fund one of her CDs. She had become a musician and I read a story about her in the LA Times when she was working on her fourth album. At the time, she couldn't get a label. This was during the infancy of crowdsourcing campaigns and I jumped at the opportunity to help out the family of one of my inspirations. As a boy, though, the horse hooves, the water streams, the voices, the distant drums, the rustling in the bushes, and the instruments of a child's story record would help to shape my entire life.

As a kid who just wanted to play ball, watch television, listen to music, and soak in those traditional American pastimes, that specific concept of family life felt so far from what I actually experienced as normalcy. Being different and having a different kind of family and home was difficult. I didn't bring friends over to hear my parents' strange accents or take a chance that Dad would have a blow-up in front of them.

Right or wrong, I remember being embarrassed by my parents. We'd be going to the community pool and my Mom would say, "Steve, go get your swimming costume." That was the last kind of thing I wanted the other kids to hear, so I kept my home life and my activities separate. (Although, starting with Beatlemania in 1964, British accents became cool!)

Not everything was permeated by my Dad's doom and gloom or my parents' different ways of speaking. Neighborhoods were a big deal in 1964 and the neighborhood I lived in was vibrant. I could buy cigarettes with a parental note. We played all day with all kinds of kids. Sports were unorganized, so you could pretend to be anyone. Ice cream tasted like heaven. Really. It's not the same, today. We'd collect Coke caps with Packer Players' pictures on them; those are so valuable to collectors today. I got beat up . . . and I got my first kiss. I liked the latter more.

It was a more innocent time with regards to what was out in the streets for public consumption, but it was also a time when kids both did and didn't figure out things on their own.

I had freedom to roam, but I didn't get a lot of advice, direction, or social skills. I had to discover life in my own way. I learned to go downtown and it was completely different from my own streets–exciting. I was living on the northwest side of Milwaukee at the

> ▶▶ **I had freedom to roam, but I didn't get a lot of advice, direction, or social skills.**

time, but—as I aged up to my pre-teen years—I'd head to the downtown area once in the summer and another time in the winter.

It was a whole different world downtown. I had a few must-stops with friends when they joined me. We went to the Milwaukee Public Museum, the auto repair shop (because they had these great stickers that we would put on our bikes), and to the Army/Navy surplus store to discover cool stuff for a boy that you couldn't find anywhere else. Some of my favorite downtown trinkets, though, came from our favorite place – the Moon Fun Shop, just a few doors down from the A&W Root Beer shop.

The Moon Fun Shop was sort of a precursor to Spencer's Gifts. The store had a combination of all sorts of goofy tricks and the kind of nonsense gimmicks that a kid would love, like fake poop and Chinese finger cuffs; all of this was, oddly enough, alongside an extensive display of pipes and smoking paraphernalia. The place was a slice of pure nostalgia.

On one of my downtown road trips, I learned a lesson I'd rather not have learned. The Beatles' "Hey Jude" album had just come out and I was going to buy it on one of my downtown trips. The album was a U.S. release that compiled a number of singles that had already been released. But buying an album, or even a 45, was a big deal back then. I saved up, bought it, came back on the bus, and realized at the transfer that the album had been stolen from me. It was so impactful. It has residual implications to how I'm protective of things and how aware of my surroundings I am. I beat myself up over it and had no tools to deal with my disappointment, but I steeled myself by deciding that something like that wouldn't happen again.

My parents knew about my downtown trips, but weren't involved or protective the way you would expect today. Helicopter parenting, as it is known, didn't really exist at that time. It forced me to know who was around me, things to avoid, and landmarks to look for. I carry those things with me still today as I take in my and other cities.

We'd make our way back to the neighborhood, our domain, paying attention to stops and transfers to get home safely. To our bikes, we'd add the new stickers we'd collected from our adventure, or maybe go to the gas station to get even more STP decals.

In those days, Milwaukee was made up of a lot of working-class neighborhoods. If you wanted money, you went and made it. And, without a lot of it, we took in what our city had to offer. Of course, there was Lake Michigan's sandy lakefront, our personal ocean that never ended. There was Capital Court Mall, which was kind of a town square, with a Gimbel's and JC Penny. There were a lot of parks and a public pool at Dineen Park.

My bike was maybe my most prized possession. It allowed me freedom to explore. I could just *GO* . . . safe, fun, and free range. Kids have so many advantages today, things I couldn't have begun to comprehend in the '60s and '70s, but neighborhoods? Those aren't one of them. That's a beautiful gift that I had growing up.

Milwaukee in the '60s was like living in a silent movie with subtitles . . . until February 9, 1964. That's when The Beatles were on Ed Sullivan. Suddenly, the movie of my generation had a soundtrack and we blasted it in our homes and hearts and travels. While I realize that the soundtrack matched up across the whole world and not just my city, I felt like every song lined up to my neighborhood, my experiences, and my life. It only strengthened my desire to be a part of this thing called radio.

|| ◄◄ ► ►► ||

I remember one guy in my neighborhood had a reel-to-reel tape recorder and I got to record myself on it. So, even at a young age, I was able to

▶▶ Even at a young age, I was able to shape my voice.

shape my voice. It was my community and not my parents that helped me find my unique sound. In fact, I couldn't even do a British accent. Not then. Not now.

When I listened back to the recording of myself, I thought my voice sounded strange. It intrigued me to an idiot-savant level. I heard this uniqueness, something that was different than how I thought I would sound, and I had to figure out why it was the way it was. I discovered, in a very rudimentary way, that I was not hearing my voice in my own ears, but rather facial bone vibrations and distortions. I realized that I could have my own voice and it didn't matter what others heard in their ears, what I heard in mine, or what the recording sounded like. I could never control what each individual person's ears were able to hear. Because of that, instead of working to change or adapt to what I thought I *should* sound like, I decided to use the information I'd discovered to just be natural and accept what I could not change.

Later in life, I would find myself with a group of people around a campfire and one guy had a guitar and did a "Margaritaville" singalong. I was in a great mood and having fun, so I sang at the top of my lungs. I realized that, regardless of how I could sound as a speaker, my singing voice should be outlawed. I could control my tone and even do some impersonations, but could not carry a note.

"Are you sick?" the guy asked before he just stopped playing.

But day after day, week after week, year after year, I practiced using my voice as a speaker. It became muscle memory. By the time there was a hint of a vehicle by which I could actually bring my voice out into the world, I'd been privately training on those walk-to-school productions countless times. The vehicle for my debut didn't formally introduce itself to me until middle school.

I had always been the kind of student who would either be bored in class or—when it was something that interested me—be all in.

There was no in between for me. I distinctly remember sitting in a math class from 10:00 to 10:45 A.M. and I'd struggle. I'd try to get by as minimally as possible. Anyone sitting next to me probably thought I was a lump of coal. I could move to English or History, though—something that caused a spark—and I'd be a different person. I'd become outgoing and I'd volunteer and participate. One of my "spark" classes was Speech.

I remember one Friday hearing that we'd be talking about radio the following week; I lit up. Monday was going to be scholastic. We spent other days learning about the business, the mechanics, and the history of radio. I discovered that I loved radio for *all* that it was–more than just as the welcome voices at home. On Thursday, we were told that we would culminate the week by doing a broadcast on Friday.

▶▶ **I remember one Friday hearing that we'd be talking about radio the following week; I lit up.**

For our broadcast, we talked about all of the different roles of a radio production: the news anchor; the salesman; the sports broadcaster; and so on. My role was to be a newscaster. That night, I thought, *'I don't have to worry or be up all night thinking about this. I've done this every morning for all of my life.'*

The next day, I woke up, grabbed my cassette player, and turned on the radio. Nixon was president at this time and the station played what I'd learned was an "actuality," or, a clip of an *actual* event. I captured it. I also captured a sports actuality and a third clip. I don't even believe I wrote a script. I knew the top stories–my top three articles. I knew what to do.

I can still picture my Speech Class that day. Mr. Frost, my white-goateed teacher (pretty forward for that time!), wheeled in this huge reel-to-reel on a cart the size of a café table. "Alright, class, we're going to start our broadcast," he said as he pushed "play."

You could hear that thing *clunk*:

One of my most studious classmates was assigned the role of station manager. In a

mumble, the words tumbled out, "....brought to you by Samuel Morse Junior High School."

CLUNK.

Susan, our "program director" went next. She read the script in a very upbeat and preppy way. She was going for the "A" (but didn't have any sincerity).

"This is our presentation on this day of the various parts of the radio curriculum!"

CLUNK.

Next came the host of the show. With a script in hand, in front of a big bulky microphone, he nervously played his part as one long monotonous sentence: "Good-morning-I-am-your-host.Let-us- begin-the-news-of-the-day."

CLUNK.

"Okay, Steve. Newscast," Mr. Frost directed.

People saw me carrying up my little tape recorder and whispers began. My years-long secret show was about to go public.

"Good morning. A crisp forty-two degrees at 9:05. I'm Steve Palec. Here are your top stories. In Washington today, President Nixon announced new initiatives in Vietnam." And then I hit my first actuality. "Locally, Milwaukee had two murders yesterday," I bellowed as I continued with my second actuality from the scene. "And in sports, it was the Bucks over the Baltimore Bullets," followed by a clip of Lew Alcindor (better known today as Kareem Abdul-Jabbar). "In Milwaukee weather, temperature will fall to thirty-five today and the same tomorrow. That's your news. I'm Steve Palec."

There was total silence. The class had their jaws on the ground. There was no clunk. Mr. Frost forgot to turn off the tape recorder. Instead, we sat there for ten seconds that felt like minutes. Finally, he jumped up and stopped the recording.

CLUNK.

And that was my first broadcast.

All of my practice had paid off. I blew even myself away in discovering that there was this thing I could do and do well. It was no longer a play I rehearsed by my lonesome.

It was a revelation to me. My classmates' reaction to me wasn't some magical guarantee of success, but it became my moment of realization that I had something special. I could be my own window to the world . . . and build one for others.

I knew and studied everything I wanted to do to pull off that newscast, not for the grade, not to impress anyone, not to make my parents proud, not even to own that day . . . but for my life.

For the first time, people were listening.

IN PURSUIT

Just Ask

"You can't get what you want
till you know what you want."

▶ FROM: *You Can't Get What You Want*
BY: *Joe Jackson, Body and Soul*
(A&M, 1984)

P RIOR to my really getting into playing and listening to music, it was spoken segments that intrigued me. The classroom newscast may be how I was able to connect with it for the first time, but I was truly obsessed with sports much more than music. I wanted to be a sportscaster. Sports could have taken me to TV or to radio play-by-play. I was fascinated at the importance of this specialized media that was included in the news and on TV.

My sports affinity, paired with media, made my broadcasting desires big enough to drive me to learn how to type, still at an early age and when it wasn't a common skill, especially if you weren't a young woman. Learning to type wasn't enough, though, even with my one Speech Class and my daily practice. I needed more. I needed to know what it was like to be ON the radio.

Milwaukee lost the Braves in 1966 when they moved to Atlanta, so aside from the Braves T-shirt I had (my favorite, by the way), baseball wasn't in the forefront, even as the White Sox played some games in Milwaukee. My uncle took me to a ballgame in the late '60s and the grass was the most beautiful thing I'd ever seen. I was hooked for life.

> ▶▶ **My uncle took me to a ballgame in the late '60s and the grass was the most beautiful thing I'd ever seen.**

I was also amazed when I wrote letters to national sportscasters asking for autographed photos . . . and they would send them! I had an 8x10 from famous NBA broadcaster Chick Hearn in my bedroom. It wasn't the typical pin-up, but it was mine.

Then, there was my favorite sportscaster of the day: Eddie Doucette. Doucette was a Milwaukee disc jockey (DJ[4]) who, at the time that the Milwaukee Bucks were formed[5], was approached because he could convey the excitement necessary for this new expansion team. As sports radio entertainment went, the announcer to take the job would have to compete against the '60s' Green Bay Packers[6]. Ted Moore play-called those glory years, including announcing for the famed 1967 Ice Bowl on New Year's Eve. Because Moore came to Wisconsin in 1960, at the early onset of the Packers' NFL domination, he was a beloved household name and voice.

Doucette was up to the challenge of becoming the original voice of the *new* hometown team, though, and I was an instant fan. (He would remain their play-by-play announcer from the 1969 season and through the next sixteen years.)

---

[4] *Radio Trivia: while the term "DJ," meaning "disc jockey" eventually came to refer to compact discs, or CDs, (before vinyl came back!) the term was originally used in 1935 by radio commentator Walter Winchell to describe the people who played phonographs on-air.*

[5] *The Milwaukee Bucks were founded in 1968.*

[6] *The '60s were considered the Green Bay Packers' dynasty years. They won championships in 1961 and 1962, as well as in 1965, 1966, and 1967, all under legendary Coach Vince Lombardi.*

As fate would have it, Milwaukee ended up getting one of THE best play-by-play announcers I'd ever heard. He brought so much excitement in his voice and terminology. Much

▶▶ **As fate would have it, Milwaukee ended up getting one of THE best play-by-play announcers I'd ever heard.**

like other great broadcasters from history would eventually become known for, his vocabulary itself earned its own recognition: *The Doucette Dictionary*. Doucette was "The King of Phraseology," "The Word Wizard," and "The Sultan of Sweet!" He blew me away. I listened to him and to Ted Moore of the Packers like they were the Bible. For me, they were. It was scholastic as much as it was fanatic.

I used to call in to Moore's talk shows as a little kid. I was this prepubescent boy with a high squeaky voice and I surely wasn't very articulate, yet. Nonetheless, I was kind of training myself vocally and I was well-versed in sports, so I could carry on an intelligent discussion on the topics they discussed. The fact that I was a kid probably made for a good gimmick. Today, there is a station for everything, but at that time it was finite and it was magical. I couldn't believe I could dial a number and be on the air!

I'd call in again and again. I wouldn't give up until I got through. I did it all from the lime green rotary phone on the wall in my kitchen. It was flexible for only as far as the cord would uncoil and stretch without pulling out . . . *and* we had a party line. If someone on the party line was using the phone, I would freak out. I called consistently and I would get on consistently. It became a part of my life. My streaks became obsessive. I remember the stress of keeping the streak going. If I was on day fifty-two, for example, and I hadn't yet made my day fifty-three call-in, my biggest fear was that my parents would begin fighting loudly. *'If Dad is screaming at Mom, how can I call in to be on the radio?'* I kept up the streak, though, eventually, growing it to the point that I was on the radio seventy times.

Gino Salomone (now a film critic known by his first name to even A-list movie stars) was a neighbor kid a couple of years younger than I and he lived across the alley. He was witness to my calling streak. The driveways between our garages were connected diagonally and the two of us would play full-court basketball from his house to mine. The garages didn't exactly line up, but if there had been a league for diagonally played sports, I would have dominated.

Gino was first generation from Italy.

I couldn't understand his parents.

I was first generation, too.

He couldn't understand my parents.

In these ways, we understood each other.

Gino kind of looked up to me if for no other reason than I got him his first Playboy. Every night, if we were shooting hoops, I would run inside to call the radio show and keep my streak going.

I remember saying to Gino, "I think I now called the show seventy times. Maybe *you* should call in and say, 'That kid has been on so much, you should have him on as a guest.'" (Apparently, I understood the power of marketing oneself at some basic level, even then.)

Gino called in for me and Ted Moore *('Ted Moore, himself!')* said, "That would be a good idea. We should do that."

The appointed day came about and Ted Moore (it didn't feel right to call him by something other than his full name) had told me to be at the studios by 4:45 P.M. for the 6:00 P.M. show. My mom went to my uncle's house to listen, so I was on my own to make my way to 200 North Jefferson. The studios were in the Third Ward[7] before there actually was a Third Ward.

I put my summer and winter Moon Fun Shop excursions to work; I knew the streets and buses well. I got out of school early that day, took a bus from 86th and Capitol and then walked . . . in the dark.

---

[7] *Milwaukee's Historic Third Ward is today an upscale creative district with trendy restaurants, art galleries, theaters, and eclectic and creative stores and shops.*

It was winter in Wisconsin, so of course the sun had gone down by then. Getting to the building was a total blur to me.

How I didn't freeze up, wet my pants, or do something somehow even more embarrassing was beyond me. It was my first time in a studio and I was so excited, while wanting to not act like a fool at the same time. I was impatient because, once a week, he had a journalist, Oliver Kuechle, there in the studio with him. This was that night and I remember watching fifteen minutes of the hour I was there get eaten away by this other guest.

Finally, Ted Moore had me on. My uncle used a cassette recorder over the speaker to record it, but I honestly don't remember the contents so much as the actual experience. All I know was I did the show and then, by 7:00, it was over.

I'm indebted to that man.

"Young man, I think you have a bright future," he told me. "Enjoy your evening."

Then, I walked again–this time on the clouds, because I was pretty happy for my time with the legendary broadcaster. I knew the general direction I needed to go, somehow found my way to Wisconsin Avenue, then to Fond du Lac Avenue, and once more back to Capitol where I could take a bus home.

I learned that I could do some of these cool things that interested me if I simply asked . . . and most people didn't think to ask at all. I wondered if I could repeat my on-air success.

About a year later, in junior high school, radio would be one-upped by television. I was about to get a chance to test my "just ask" theory. My art teacher, Mike Moynihan, a cartoonist for the unconventional and underground Kaleidoscope[8] magazine (and a relatively progressive guy for the time), would be the man to give me the opportunity. At the beginning of the semester, there was some money that was earned and shared by the class and Mr. Moynihan wanted to use it to have an album playing while we worked. The class

---

[8] *The Kaleidoscope was an underground paper published out of UW-Milwaukee after being founded by John Kois, radio DJ Bob Reitman, and The Shags bandmember John Sahli. It regularly fought censorship as part of the Liberation News Service and Underground Press Syndicate and was considered journalistic scourge in its four years of operation.*

got to pick out three albums. I heavily lobbied for the Beatles' Abbey Road. The other two were class picks. The fact that he wanted to have music playing proved to all of us teens just how cool he was!

I was thrilled when Mr. Moynihan decided to teach a film section in his class. We were going to get to film on a Super 8 camera if we wanted to be a part of the project; he knew not everybody was going to be engaged, though it was a perfect fit for my interests. You could choose to be part of the teams making the movie and I was all in from the start.

Television was another passion of mine, alongside radio and sports. TV stations, before videotape, were either live, had a network feed, or, for commercials, ran actual 35-MM, thirty-second films. Stations would simply throw away the commercials or promos when they were done. Those discarded reels were kind of like STP stickers to me. I loved to collect them! I'd go to the stations and ask them for their extra commercials. I would just stare at the actual filmstrips. I remember I had one for the Bob Newhart show, and on the side of it that would be the audio, I'd look at the white squiggly lines that represented the words and music and study them. This was what sound looked like and it fascinated me.

Where radio had Eddie Doucette and Ted Moore, television had Hank Stoddard, on Channel 4, WTMJ. Hank Stoddard anchored sports for WTMJ, Channel 4, at 10:00 P.M. As my class's film section got underway, I sat down and I wrote a letter to Hank Stoddard: "I'm a junior high school student at Samuel Morse and we're doing a study on film. Could I come to the station and film you doing the sportscast?"

I'm not even sure there was much more detail than that in the request, but he responded, "I'd be happy to accommodate that." In fact, he reached out and told me to come to the station in a few days.

This was a TV station. TV to me WAS Hollywood. It felt like I had just reached the Mt. Olympus of Broadcast. This studio was *on* Capitol, so getting there after school meant taking just one bus.

▶▶ **It felt like I had just reached the Mt. Olympus of Broadcast.**

I walked in and I couldn't believe it. I found myself in this incredibly intimidating situation. I had the guts and desire to be there, but was scared to death at the same time. I walked up to a welcome desk and told the receptionist I was there for Hank Stoddard. (Even those words added to my intimidation: *I* was there for *Hank Stoddard!*) He couldn't have been nicer, even though I was pathetically shy. It was more than a feeling of being star struck. That would have been easy enough. But Hank Stoddard wasn't just a celebrity to me; this was the guy I saw from the box who led me to the world! I didn't know how to respond when finding myself face-to-face with him.

He asked me to go with him to the Pfister Hotel for an event he was emceeing.

'I'm suddenly tagging along with Hank Stoddard! And I'm in Hank Stoddard's car!'

I occasionally would go downtown to a museum or the shops that my friends and I visited, but this was the Pfister Hotel where baseball players, politicians, and stars stayed. My host for the evening was to be emceeing a dinner there.

We stepped into an elevator and were greeted by the Mayor of Milwaukee. It may as well have been the President of the United States for all my nerves. This was a stomach tumbling roller coaster and my head was spinning. I remember having the sudden thought that I needed to remain anonymous because I believed Mayor Maier probably had the authority to deport my parents.

"Hi Hank."

"Hello Mayor," he nodded back.

I remained silent. Stunned.

'WHAT? What is this goofy kid disconnected from the outside world doing in an elevator with the mayor and Hank Stoddard?'

Hank had to say a couple words at the start of the dinner, kick it off, and share a few stories of the day in a professional and classy manner. I still emulate him when I work as an emcee today. It's not intentional so much as it was how I saw it done and I didn't see any reason to mess

▶▶ **I still emulate him when I work as an emcee today.**

with his successful formula. He left the people there with a better feeling than they had come in with and that's something I would always remember.

After his emceeing duties, he took me back to the station. I still hadn't filmed anything!

"Make sure you're standing far enough away that the whir of your 8-MM camera isn't picked up by our mics," he told me.

Then, I filmed him doing the 10:00 P.M. newscast and, in awe, absorbed the full studio scene until the 10:30 finish. I would later edit. (Editing in those days meant cutting the actual film, lining it up to the right place between the frames and splicing it together with tape. And for the music? I had the audio on a cassette and had to sync the sound live when playing the video.)

I stepped outside of the studio and realized that I didn't know how to get home. It was too late for my bus. We had only one car, which Dad drove. Asking my host for a favor would have been out of the question. I hadn't thought this through.

Hank spotted me as he was leaving, though, and actually drove me home. I told him to drop me off on the corner near my house. I didn't want to take this experience home.

This was all my own to indulge.

In flight

Steps Beneath The Veneer

"What the people need is a
way to make them smile.
It ain't so hard to do if you
know how."

▶ *FROM: Listen To The Music*
BY: The Doobie Brothers, Toulouse Street
(Warner Brothers, 1972)

*E*VERY group has that one guy who they indulge. He's bigger than everyone else, in the best way, like he won the genetic lottery. He's different–admired. When I was in high school, most of my friend group was a year older than I, so my group's "guy" was even cooler to me, this skinny kid who assumed at this point that he was going to be working in media. Hell, I would put on a T-shirt and was so scrawny, it would look like it was draped loose on a hanger. I was *not* the lottery winner. And, besides being skinny, I had sinus issues later, and, well, I saw the world a bit askew.

The guy we called "Papa Bear," a fit swimmer named Rick Schmidt, who even in high school had a Grizzly Adams look about him, was our group's wild man, adventure leader, lottery winner. I fell into his group by pure chance because his brother and I were the same age and he liked me okay enough. The group partied hard, with Rick like the sun at the center–people just gravitated around him. He pulled us along and we willingly followed, getting together to make trouble, especially if one of us managed to get a hold of a car.

"If Rick walks off a cliff, will you just follow him?" my Mom chided me in her British inflection.

Well, it wasn't a cliff, per sé.

But I followed.

Every time.

One of those rare times we did manage to get a vehicle, Rick said, "I got an idea."

Oh, we didn't know what the idea was, but gravity won . . . and we were in orbit with him. Seven of us got into the one car. This was the day of bench seats and no seat belts, so we just crammed in together. Papa Bear drove us to the airport, up to the outskirts of Mitchell Field[9] and he took the car right up to the fence. You could do that sort of thing then.

"I've done this before," he said. "We're gonna go lay on the runway," and, with that, he was out of the car and halfway up the fence before the rest of us even had time to think about the insanity of this whole plot he'd just suggested.

▶▶ **We're gonna go lay on the runway.**

We all got out of the car after him–Papa Bear leading his cubs.

Now you have to know that this hanger-like kid wasn't exactly the most athletic guy in the mix. There were some things I just plain sucked at–things like climbing fences. But Rick and the rest of the guys jumped the fence, so that's what I was going to do. Somehow, I managed. I climbed up and got myself over the barbed wire without losing anything valuable in the process. Then, I kept up with the others as we made our way out to a sort of crossroads on the airfield.

---

[9] *General Mitchell Field, originally Milwaukee County Airport, is Milwaukee's International Airport. In 2019, the new name, "Milwaukee Mitchell International Airport," was assumed to keep out-of-state travelers from confusion by including the hub city's name.*

There were lights for taxiing, taking off, and landing. Rick explained the different lights and what would be happening.

Then, we laid down ...

on our backs ...

in the middle of a runway ...

waiting for a full-sized plane to land ...

and hoping it didn't land ...

on us.

Too late to turn back now. Rick's gravity held me down to the ground. Part of me thought, *'Okay. So, this is where I die.'* But the part that was in for the adventure, the part that brought me there to begin with said, **'I'm invincible!'**

As a plane began to come in, we could hear its engines. They groaned louder. My eyes opened wider. My breath came quicker, or . . . maybe . . . it just stopped completely for a moment. I don't remember which.

"Whatever you do," Rick said, "DON'T. MOVE."

Like I could.

I closed my eyes–squeezed them so tightly shut that I was trying to keep out the whole experience. There was no joy in this–no exhilaration. I was in a moment of sheer terror with a tiny portion of hope that I'd actually get out of this alive. I didn't even care what the experience was like for the rest of our group. They weren't even there with me in my head. In that moment, it was just me trying to get through and I wanted it to be over.

First, I could smell something. *'Fuel?'*

Then, the ground shook.

The plane went over us.

I felt the heat–the fiery breeze.

My heart was pounding.

Light bled into my eyes ...

even while they were squeezed tightly shut.

The moment seemed to last forever, though it was mere seconds; fear does that to a mind.

The second the plane passed, Rick was back on his feet. "We have to hightail it out of here," he told us and just ran!

He, the athlete, ran for the fence while the rest of us, barely able to rise from the anxiety-induced paralysis that held us to the runway, followed before the colored lights and sirens behind us could catch up. I don't know how we managed to make the run back or how I got over the fence a second time (and—for a second time—sparing the goods) and into the car. It was all as much a blur as the fuel-laden fumes of our flyover jet.

Sometimes I wonder what the Papa Bears of our post-9/11 world are making their groups endure today.

This was high school. Friends were crazier. Girls were cuter. Music was louder. Ideas were bigger. And the biggest idea for me, one of radio as a real vocation in my life, became clearer and stronger than I ever realized it could.

Except for school and my unique family's interactions, I was pretty much raised by television and radio. I had no anecdotes, either told or observed, about who I should be or how to make it happen. I think it served me well. I felt like I had a broad view of life and the world and I would take that with me into every experience. I was tolerant of different perspectives. I was open to what was going around me–everything from current events, to music, to sports. These things would serve me throughout my life.

The downside, though, was that I picked up things from television families and historic interactions that left me with a slightly off-kilter idea about the real world and how to behave in actual-life scenarios. You don't realize how skewed entertainment's representations of the world are until you try to use them in your life. Those odd thoughts about how interactions and relationships worked outside of my home or the television came to the forefront on my first date.

Unlike most people's first date stories, I couldn't even tell you who I was with. I couldn't remember her name, what she was wearing, why I asked her out, or anything else about her if you asked me today. It's because, unlike so many other moments in my life that I wanted and worked to hold onto, I was not fully engaged when I was on that date. And I should have been! This wasn't a couple of kids hanging out after school. This was formal. I had asked someone to go out, saved up, planned, and we were going to a very nice dinner.

I had no idea how I was supposed to act; I only knew I was supposed to go to dinner. I took her to the Milwaukee Public Natatorium. It was a former public bath-turned-restaurant . . . and then aquarium. I heard it was "the thing" to do because there was a dolphin show as part of dinner. Dinner and a show! I felt pretty suave for seventeen. This was special. But when we got to the restaurant, that feeling of cool

Photo Courtesy: OldMilwaukee.Net

drained from me like the former baths. I was a combination of nervous, excited, intimidated, trepidatious, and proud. Plus, every raging hormone that could accelerate one's emotions was surging through my body and turning all of those feelings into an internal whirlpool of confusion. That whirlpool—stronger than all the other pools around me—destroyed the moment!

I was trying to do everything right, according to how dates went on television episodes of *My Three Sons*. Dad hadn't told me anything. My brother had nothing to share on the subject. My date and I got seated after walking through the restaurant, deeper and deeper, past other tables and couples, well past the dolphins, to this crappy, last-minute thought, folding card table next to the kitchen This was an expensive endeavor for me and I knew from all I'd seen on television that being seated right next to the kitchen was an insult. I had saved for this and I was upset.

Do I say something?
Would it matter?
Did I screw up?
When James Bond wants a good table, he slips the host some money.
Should I do that?
How much?
Would they laugh?

I don't remember much else about the evening. I came to the realization that I had spent the entire time, right up until the meal was served, thinking about all these questions that I didn't speak. I was having a private debate in my head again, but—for my date—I was totally and completely . . . *silent*.

Much like today, in high school I could be in a full room of people with no sense of timidity, but at heart? One-on-one? I was an introvert. A few people in my life have recognized the trait in me and it's true. In my dating days, a girlfriend once shared that she didn't see deeply into me. She realized how very little she got from the "real Steve." For most of my youth, I didn't recognize it in myself. It would be another few years before I heard Paul Simon's "Something So Right" from his *There Goes Rhymin' Simon* album (Warner Brothers).

"They've got a wall in China.
It's a thousand miles long
to keep out the foreigners.
They made it strong. I've
got a wall around me you
can't even see. It took a little
time to get to me."

On that first date, I just sat with my own awkwardness without actually understanding it. I never forgot the overwhelming sense of embarrassment I felt, not just for being seated by the kitchen on this date that

▶▶ **I may look like the veneer is complacent, but— underneath—steps are being taken.**

was supposed to be significant, but for my own silence. To this day, if I can control an event to at least some extent, I do. I recognize that some things aren't controllable. I can have great tickets to a great ball game, but can't make the team win. That much I've seen happen in my life. I work hard, though, at directing the elements of an experience that I can control. I may look like the veneer is complacent, but—underneath—steps are being taken. I try to ensure embarrassment doesn't happen for me or the people I'm with. And I don't just try to avoid embarrassment, but encourage engagement. If everything is going as it should, then people are free to enjoy the event. They're able to be relaxed instead of anxious. After being detached from a moment that should have been a memory, I realized I didn't want to leave such feelings up to chance. I didn't want to leave *awe* up to chance.

With that lesson in mind, later in life, during a peak time in my dating endeavors, I used to have the same date with women every time we went out. In the period of time between getting divorced and meeting my second wife, my commercial real estate career came first in my life. From 7:00 A.M. on Monday to 6:00 P.M. on Friday, I lived what I considered to be one fluid, packed workday. And I continued to work on other things outside of the office at night for both my real estate career and radio show. I didn't go out on weeknights at all. Work was my main focus and main priority. Then, on Friday nights, I had an all-out collapse at home to do nothing. I was spent.

But, I had some disposable income, a "cool" radio show, and I was in my early thirties. I had the opportunity and the desire to make Saturday nights special before my Sunday radio show and going back to my Monday-to-Friday work marathon. During that time, I was in tons of offices and I met a lot of people. I never forced it, but if I met a woman of interest, I'd say, "What are you doing Saturday?" I wasn't slimy or insincere. This wasn't a numbers game for me or notches on a headboard. There were guys who behaved that way and I wasn't judging them. To me, though, this was just my night out on a Saturday and I innocently asked for someone to be with me. If it could be a woman who was interesting or smart or beautiful, that just made the night and the conversation that much better for my weekly escape from the grind. As a result, I actually had a lot of dates. That said, every single one of them was the exact same date over and over and I never tired of it. I called it "scare and comfort."

I picked up my date at 6:00 P.M. We had a 7:00 P.M. dinner reservation, so there was some time to kill. Our reservation would be at a different place I selected each week. (I learned all the great spots.) I'd take the woman for a drink to use some time before dinner. This was the "scare" part of the date. We would get into my car and start driving. We typically began in a downtown area and made our way, block-by-block, to a much more desolate location. The neighborhoods grew worse as we drove–dilapidated, even. Then, there were no houses around at all. We would arrive at an abandoned train yard and, as far as the eye could see, were train tracks. One set ended at an old, broken down train car at the end of the track. There were no other buildings, no lights, no signage, and no semblance of safety. I can only imagine my date's thinking:

'This is fine. Actually, this is getting questionable. Um, just how well do I know this guy? Come to think of it, this is really bad. Did we just stop in front of an abandoned train? Get me the fuck out of here!'

The "abandoned train car" was actually a very little-known severance package. Although, I guess that doesn't sound much better. The railroad company that owned the track and car during the '40s, the epitome of train travel days, was itself a company at the epitome of travel. It was luxury and the bar car was the entertainment pinnacle for its trains. Part of the severance package with some of their long-time employees was that they left a train car for them and it was turned into a bar. There was no advertising, publicity, marketing, or signage. The guy who ran it may as well have been from 1940 and time in his bar car never went a day past 1959. He spoke perfectly, sat you down, dressed in era, played songs from The

Frank Sinatra/Dean Martin/Las Vegas Rat Pack overhead, and served the kind of ornate martinis and cocktails you would expect from the Golden Age of Hollywood.

My dates probably feared that this real estate guy from the radio had some hidden, dark agenda. Then, they walked into the equivalent of a movie set. They'd be ecstatic! From fear, to relief, to ecstasy. Maybe I shouldn't tell this story. Come to think of it, my Saturday nights were the Stockholm syndrome of dates.

But I had a purpose.

After drinks, we'd have dinner and there was never a lack of something to talk about following that emotional roller coaster. Conversation always flowed. I'd finish the night at a comedy café with which the station had a partnership. We got to drink free and see top-level comedians and, if we were spent from talking, the show took the pressure off of going deeper than this simple night out was supposed to be. For a good year, the planned excursion kept me from sitting home alone or sitting by kitchen-side card tables and it kept me in the moment every time I went out. I'm not sure how my dates may have interpreted the nights, though.

Scare and Comfort, AKA Stockholm Dates, and certainly dating after a first failed marriage, were far from my mind as I made my way through my high school days. I still hadn't figured out my own path, much less with whom I would be in a relationship.

If you'd asked my parents who I was as a teenager, you'd have gotten very different answers. My Mom would have said I was creative, goofy, and fun . . . like her. But she didn't ever tell me she loved me or get playful or emotionally affectionate. Not that she didn't feel those things, she just didn't express them. Her description of me being goofy amongst other, less-reliable traits, would not have been meant as an insult; it would just have been her observation.

Dad, on the other hand, would have said I was skinny, weak, and not serious enough. He would have been right, too . . . and it definitely *would* have been intended as an insult.

Neither Mom's nor Dad's likely descriptions of me actually led to any kind of identity growing up, though. *What even was an identity?* I didn't have a path. I envied those who did.

I had a lot of freedom. I wasn't told when to do homework, what school was supposed to accomplish for me, or where I should go and what I should do in adulthood. I literally had no goal. For that matter, I didn't know I should. I just did the things for which I had both ability and affinity. And, when I did those things, whatever they were, I

▶▶ **A** *love* **of radio, rather than a goal or decision to make a career of it, is what drove me to pursue opportunities within the medium.**

tried to know as much about them as I could. A *love* of radio, rather than a goal or decision to make a career of it, is what drove me to pursue opportunities within the medium. I kept my cassette recorder with me, even through high school, capturing sounds.

Somehow, before I was even a teenager, the *Meet The Beatles* album ended up in our house. It was the same year that they came to Milwaukee. Not that I could have done much about it at the age of eight, but I wish I'd known then that it was a moment that would never happen again. It would be another ten years before I would get a chance to see my first Beatle live–George Harrison, but without John, Paul, and Ringo by then.

Steve: We're about the same age. Does February 9, 1964 resonate with you?

Billy Bob Thornton: Ed Sullivan Show. Beatles! I remember it very clearly. Watched it on an old black and white Zenith laying on a hardwood floor on my stomach. Me and my brother. It was a transformative moment as it was for everybody.

Meet The Beatles started my musical journey. Not that I lost my love of sports, but I really cherished that album, so music became mixed into my radio aspirations. I listened to that album so many times. I read every word of their lyrics. I looked at every song. It became the soundtrack for my life. The Beatles always kept me satisfied until their next album. They grew musically while I grew as a young man. Our journeys were paralleled. I learned to understand music as art beginning with that release. For me, the definition of a song as a piece of art is when it could be performed without any technology. I didn't know it then, but that's what I've come to understand through my years of absorbing music. Not that studio trickery can't be art, too. It can be amazing and enjoyable. But, if someone can read a song's lyrics as a poem, or perform it live without an engineer, or even let someone else interpret it—another musician, or singer, or even the listener—then it is art.

Before the time of The Beatles' rise to a never-before-seen hyper super-fandom, my Mom's family moved over from London: her parents, sisters, and brother. At family gatherings, there would always be music. *'Put on some music'* someone would say. I had a few older cousins hip enough to put on the good stuff. It may be a bit cliché to say that The Beatles gave me a love of music, but they did and that love carried beyond their work to albums of every genre.

I began looking at other albums for any number of reasons. I loved the Herb Alpert and the Tijuana Brass album because of the cover art. *Whipped Cream & Other Delights* was entrancing to me because, well–I was just like every other red-blooded American boy at the time that album came out. Musically, I loved it, sure, but I found myself just staring at that album and didn't know, at the age of nine when I first saw it, why it fascinated me so much. A woman covered in cream on a blank background. In the words of artist and humorist Gelett Burgess, "I don't know much about art, but I know what I like." I knew I liked that album art. Other than the occasional National Geographic issue, I couldn't remember a visual drawing me in more than the *Whipped Cream* album cover. When Herb Alpert used to perform songs from the album live, he would apologize to audiences: "I'm sorry. We can't play the album *cover* for you."

▶▶ **"I don't know much about art, but I know what I like."**

As an adult, years later in radio, I thought, *'What ever happened to her?'* I tracked down the model, Dolores Erickson. She shared that she was pregnant at the time of the famous photograph and the whipped cream? It was actually shaving cream. Nope. Didn't ruin it for me either. At the time I finally spoke to her all those years later, she was just a nice woman with a great side gig for some extra income: autographing Herb Alpert album covers.

There were other albums I loved for the way I related to their songs; I appreciated story albums and great comedians; I sometimes just enjoyed an interesting or eclectic mix that found its way into my home, like the *Superstars of the '70s*. Actually, my brother had better and more varied musical taste than I did in those days. He introduced me to Jethro Tull and Emerson, Lake & Palmer. *Superstars* was a record company loss-leader album; it was designed to get you to buy the entire LP from the various artists who were featured on it. I can remember *every one* of the different types of sound that could fit on those ridged black discs holding some intrigue for me.

I didn't dislike any particular song or genre. Even in those things that I wasn't passionate about, I could find something that deserved my admiration and I would try to share those thoughts with others.

By the time I was a freshman attending John Marshall High School, the British Invasion and free love Rock & Roll led to albums coming out once a week . . . actually, more like twenty a week! It was such a thriving time for music. Today, so many of the new albums of my childhood are the well-known classics. The degree by which spectacular music was being released in the '70s is unmatched in any time since.

As my love for music grew equal to my love for radio, I considered myself old enough to embark on what you could call the seed of a career; not just a job to put food on the table. I was smart enough to learn from my "just ask" lessons with Ted Moore and Hank Stoddard and put them to use. I decided to write a radio station a letter. Actually, I wrote a letter to *Every.Single.Radio.Station.* in town:

"I'LL DO ANYTHING. I'LL SWEEP YOUR FLOORS. I'LL GET SANDWICHES. PLEASE. CAN I BE A PART OF WHAT YOU DO?"

I got two answers back. One of them actually had an opening for a janitor, so they literally wanted me to sweep the floor. I would have done it, too, if that was the only answer I got. It was the media equivalent of working in the mail room, I guess. I didn't have to find out, though, because the other response I got was from the University of Wisconsin-Milwaukee's (UWM) radio station, WUWM.

They said, basically, "Hey! The door's wide open. Come on in. Hang out. We'd love to have you."

They meant it and I did just that all through high school, heading to the WUWM studios almost every day, getting my first training from then-student Dave Edwards, who retired as General Manager from an NPR station in 2019. Then, I leveraged that relationship for my next connection in music networking. I was a semi-shy kid, but wasn't afraid to ask for things. Now I had access to the UWM radio station, but still wasn't "IN" radio. ON . . . but not really *in*.

And then one day, I found myself digging through the racks at a Hampton Avenue-based independent record store called Record Head. It's actually still around today and I occasionally look through the racks of (now) CDs to brainstorm ideas for my radio show. In 1971, it was shelves and shelves of vinyl. I was in that store all the time and, as a freshman with little to no disposable income, I got music with whatever I could scrape together . . . far too slowly for my tastes.

One day, I asked the owner, Scott Heifetz, "Hey, who does your radio commercials?"

Once a week, he had been advertising new music on WQFM and WZMF. The stations did the commercials for him. "Do you think they'd let me do the commercials for you?" I asked the owner.

"Sure. If they're good."

Because of my access to the studio at WUWM, I put together commercials for him and—just like that—I had my music fix arranged . . . and any other albums I happened to want. It was a service trade; his commercials for my vinyl addiction.

One of the albums that came home from Record Head became one I loved and memorized; it was George Carlin's *Class Clown*, which contained the famed, "Seven Words You Can Never Say On Television" routine. (Most of the words are still moderated today.) With a desire to embrace the irreverence of the late, edgy comedian (even by some of today's standards), I brought the album into school.

My social studies class was a place where we often discussed politics and current events, in addition to history. I loved it. It was one of my engaged classes! I challenged my social studies teacher, Miss Sally Gunnerman, by asking if we could play the routine in its entirety during class. She was not a crusty, leathery, bitter, trampled-on teacher who was hanging on, waiting for retirement; rather, she was young, idealistic, kind, and positive.

"This is important cultural commentary," I said. "Could we play it in class?" I was braced for a "no."

She saw the request as inquisitive and surprisingly took the calculated risk by saying "yes." It was a time when teachers were trusted more openly than today. That's both good and bad, I suppose, but on that day, it meant that she chose to allow the George Carlin album as a shared offering from a media student. All seven unmentionable terms bounced through her classroom as we listened to the full performance, a recording that today can actually be found in The Library of Congress. The album was followed up by a discussion about free speech and creativity. It wasn't just comedy that Carlin addressed; he encouraged us to consider the weight that words can carry. Miss Gunnerman believed we assign too much value to them and they shouldn't affect our core beliefs.

The absolute effect of Carlin's sarcastic creativity caused a change in my own sense of humor. That was probably a pivotal moment in my ability to take chances. Had that teacher put a stop to my request without explanation, I don't know if I would have turned out to be the person I am today. I am impressed by her courage! And today, I know how to take something to the edge, but also know where that edge is–not by sheer instinct, but by logic.

Pushing to play that album was just a tiny flicker of my rebellious side. I wasn't trying to cause shock so much as I was trying to connect and find my own voice through these artists who made their ways into my ears. I wasn't going to be the kid talking about free love and LSD. Yet. Even while I began to identify myself through media, though, I still had slightly skewed ideas about what "work" was supposed to be and how, why, and where to get a "real job" that wasn't *frivolous* (as I'd been told radio was).

My freshman, sophomore, and junior years of high school had me regularly at the WUWM studios and I had carte blanche to go there all summer long too; I took full advantage of that opportunity! Then, it was the summer before my last year of high school. I grew six inches and, as a result, I was in pain all three months. For all the pain, I wished I'd grown a full foot.

Relative to that, there was a Jefferson Airplane song called "White Rabbit." It was in the psychedelic era of songs and it had huge drug connotations. It starts by saying, "One pill makes you larger, and one pill makes you small, and the ones that mother gives you, don't do anything at all." Something about that song always gave me pause before taking any pills. By the time I was a senior, I had hesitant thoughts about doing "hard drugs" despite a drug-infused culture, world, and industry. It was the industry and not the lifestyle of it that allured me.

I was doing commercials for Record Head and other local businesses. I'd spent hours and hours going over my *Superstars of the '70s* album on the large, furniture-sized record player in my room. I treated that collection as if it were a textbook to learn about music. I had been practicing with my voice since my walks to Ralph Waldo Emerson Elementary School. I'd learned about radio production in Junior High. I had experience in the studio, on-air engagements with some of the top names in the area, and I was now doing newscasts.

I was ready.

My on-air opportunity to play MUSIC arrived and, just as I do today, I practiced what I had prepared. I played the songs I knew and studied for that moment, songs from the *Superstars of the '70s* album. Some were and some were not the coolest hits for the day, but it was what I practiced and I was going to play The Allman Brothers' "One Way Out" or The Doobie Brothers' "Listen To The Music" on a talk station with confidence. Radio *was* my confidence.

At that point, I didn't just have three years of real studio time under my belt, I also had enough credits that I didn't need to be at school full time. I thought I needed to have one of those real jobs going into my last year of high school, so I applied at Barnaby's Pizza as a busser. But it seemed I had already uniquely and singularly qualified myself for just one art: talking to unseen people through a microphone. As a result, this simple enough bussing job for a seventeen-year-old was not one for me. (Plus, there was the little matter of the fact that they didn't want me!)

So what was for me?

I looked in the classifieds and saw an ad for a telephone solicitor for a company selling timeshares at a lake property. Talking to people I didn't have to see? I could do that. I got the job and worked four-hour shifts in what can only be described as a boiler room. We made call after call after call following a script: "I'm calling for Dutch Hollow Lake. Am I speaking with the head of the household?" We would try to set up appointments and they would get a free trip if they took a sales visit.

▶▶ **I got the job and worked four-hour shifts in what can only be described as a boiler room.**

For some people, this telemarketing was their full-time work. For me, I considered the work to be more training for the radio. Even though I abhor rejection—something I got in spades during the job—I considered every call to be a practice for doing commercials. I would work on articulating an emotion in my voice as I spoke. I also learned to respond and think on my feet in a live scenario. Because it was summer, I asked for a double shift. I would work in the afternoon and at night. I did the work all summer long, and then in my senior year, I went to school in the morning and, either in the afternoon, or as a double shift in the afternoon and evening, I would be back at work making calls . . . and I still squeezed in time at WUWM whenever I could.

Then, Dutch Hollow Lake timeshares went under like so many other companies in the era. I don't know what prompted me as a senior in high school to my next idea, but, after the company went out of business, I went to the unemployment office and said, "I lost my job. Can I apply for unemployment?"

It turned out that, between the double shifts in summer and most of the time that I'd put in until they closed, I had enough on-average hours to be considered full-time.

I filled out the paperwork and they said, "You're seventeen. Aren't you in school?"

I said I was available for full-time work as long as it was second shift. They rubber stamped it, put it in, and somehow, it was approved. I began getting checks. At that point in my life, it was more money than I needed and now, without the double shifts, I actually had time to spend it. I went to Record Head every week for the latest releases. My buddies were looking at these great albums and I would walk out with several. David Bowie, The Rolling Stones, Led Zeppelin, Pink Floyd, Paul McCartney, and the debut album of an eclectic new and unheard-of group named Queen all came out in 1973. I had my own money *and* the deal with Record Head for doing their commercials. I was getting *all* the new releases.

▶▶ **David Bowie, The Rolling Stones, Led Zeppelin, Pink Floyd, Paul McCartney, and the debut album of an eclectic new and unheard-of group named Queen all came out on vinyl in 1973.**

By the fourth week of unemployment, I got a notice that I needed to go into the unemployment office about finding work. It was the '70s–not exactly a high point for the American economy. I got in line with all of the fathers, and mothers, and other adults looking for jobs and realized that, with second shift-only availability and as a seventeen-year-old, I was not going to be getting unemployment much longer. After six weeks, when jobs likely and hopefully went to some of those I stood in line with, the checks were cut off.

By the way, they were nice enough to say that they could ask for all the money back . . . but they didn't.

"Just go away," they said. And I did.

Because I wasn't living the typical high school life and schedule, I somehow became friends with a lot of graduates from the year before me. In my high school senior year, one was a freshman in college at the University of Wisconsin-Whitewater. There were about eight guys and I would hang out with them. They all had a little disposable income and they all had cars. I wasn't really a car guy. Some were fascinated by them, but they never did much for me. I just had my 1964 Ford which I'd bought from my boss at the telephone center. It cost me $300. I bought it, brought it home, and faced my parents, who were thoroughly pissed about it.

"Did you even think about insurance? Maintenance?" I hadn't, but I had wheels now to be able to hang out almost nightly with my new crew.

Paul Reamer, who would eventually become my roommate, had me over on campus and we were hanging out. I asked one of my buddies to borrow his ID. I only needed to be eighteen[10] and I was still a bit short of that. He said I could, but we got pulled over on the way back and the officer knew that this group of guys in the car going back to Whitewater were probably drinking. He asked for IDs and I gave him my friend's ID. We all got tickets! This guy, who wasn't even with us, actually got a ticket for my irresponsibility. We somehow managed to stay friends, but he was not happy about it and I didn't blame him. I screwed up. There are some things I just couldn't fix. I took a lot of flak for a few years for that move. In the moment, I had panicked. I could have said I didn't have an ID with me, at the very least, but I didn't do the right thing and I felt terrible.

Another time, this group thought it would be fun to go out to see an adult movie. We drove all the way down to Illinois so we wouldn't be seen, and we were wondering if we had to be eighteen. The grungy place showing the flick didn't even care how old we were. We just had to be members of their "club" and they were all too happy to sell us the memberships. We had to pay to see the movie and, if you're wondering, no, it was not fun to go with a group of guys to watch an adult movie.

---

[10] *The legal drinking age in Wisconsin was just eighteen until the year 1986.*

Then, it was 1974.

And winter.

Then spring.

Then graduation.

High school graduation really held no sentimental value for me. So much of my life was built around media and looking to these non-high school activities that it made the world I actually lived in feel less real or like something to which I could not connect. Homecomings, prom, and graduation were all supposed to be these special events—milestones. Most came and went without pause and here I was at the pinnacle of youth accomplishments—the completion of high school.

My younger brother had skipped a year ahead in school and was graduating right alongside me. As a much more engaged and studious kid, it may have meant more for him, but I didn't know if that was the case. We didn't have deep discussions. At any rate, my parents had no traditions in terms of those typical finish lines in American childhood . . . for either one of us. They came to the ceremony, but there was no pomp and circumstance about it or big celebration to follow.

▶▶ **My parents had no traditions in terms of those typical finish lines in American childhood.**

I distinctly remember being a part of a pretty big graduating class in 1974. The ceremony was held at the Performing Arts Center, which had only been around for about five years at that time. It would eventually become the Marcus Performing Arts Center, a respected institution of downtown Milwaukee.

I'm not proud of the way I left high school. I had a plan and it was so stupid. There wasn't even any semblance of comedic value or logic to what I was going to do. I went to a pet store and bought a mouse with the intention of letting it loose during the ceremony. It was so dumb! But, it got even worse. I forgot to poke air holes into the box that held it. I opened the box and it was dead. I felt so much guilt that I shoved the box back under my seat and hoped no one saw. I look back with wonder on that rodent's fortuitous demise.

Can you imagine?

For as smart as I could be at that time—on my career path, in basic academic tests, and in knowing my industry—I was totally inept in terms of my occasional judgment, or lack thereof. It was like something out of one of the sitcoms that I'd looked at to learn about life. If I had succeeded in my stupid joke, it could have had horrible results. There could have been a panic; someone could have gotten hurt; I might have ruined the moment for others in so many different ways. That mouse dying saved me. I don't know if it's right to call death a divine intervention, but its death kept my life on track. I would have been notorious for idiocy.

When it all came to an end, I realized that I spent my childhood with one foot in Norman Rockwell's world of American pastimes, innocence, and joy. The other foot was in Rock & Roll, opportunism, and anarchy. Maybe my Norman Rockwell paintings would have been drawn by graffiti artists.

Airplane runways, bad dates, and George Carlin.
The Beatles, *Whipped Cream & Other Delights*, and Record Head.
Strange jobs, a crappy car, and crazy friends.
Nobody really knew me because I still didn't know myself.
Dumb mistakes I made and dumber ones I was saved from.
I still never heard or said "I love you" with anyone.
They weren't typical high school memories ...
but they were mine.
These experiences would carry me into adulthood.

▶

In the Dorms

The Need To Turn Life Up

"There've been moments of despair, times I could not care, I was the lonely one. Then you showed myself to me and I found I needn't be another lonely one."

▶ FROM: The Lonely One
BY: Dave Mason, It's Like You Never Left
(Columbia Records, 1973)

*C*OLLEGE brought me into an adulthood that put the full dichotomy of who I was at the forefront and I didn't deal with it very well. I found myself always in crowds and always feeling lonely at the same time–disconnected, disengaged, and disinterested. My memories from the short stint as a

Steve: *The Lonely One* means so much to me. It's so powerful and I wore out copies of the vinyl.

Dave Mason: Well thank you. I haven't played that song in many years. That was a cool track and I got Stevie Wonder to play harmonica on it which was great.

university student aren't many. They are broken up into a few remarkable moments at the beginning of the school year and a handful of events that, while not necessarily related to college, just happened to occur during that season of my life.

College was a bridge for me from who I was to who I would become, but—as I embarked on that part of my journey—I was just idling. As a broken-out, skinny freshman living in the dorms, the only place where I had true confidence of any kind was on the radio. My diverse tastes in music didn't earn me any cool points, either. Helen Reddy's "I Am Woman" and Olivia Newton John's "Have You Ever Been Mellow" weren't exactly college anthems. I was so happy to have cut my teeth on Top 40 radio. The diversity it welcomed was tantamount to the freedom I have today.

Steve: I love hearing *Romeo's Tune* on the radio. Does that song have the same affinity for you as it does for me?

Steve Forbert: Probably more, Steve! It's my calling card and I sing it almost every show. I still relate to it as if I'd written it a week ago. I miss the old Top 40. When something was really good in its style, it rose to the top of that mixed bag. You heard Frank and Nancy Sinatra one minute and then you might hear Motown, then country. It was a lot of variety of very good things.

Granted, I liked everything I heard on the air for one reason or another, so music and airtime became the events that I would recall all these years later. They are, after all, what made the moments and the days that helped shape me and my future.

Day One – Bob Reitman was a Milwaukee area radio personality who began as a poet and was already a legend . . . a GOD . . . in the eyes of those of us on the lower rungs of radio by the time I arrived at UW-Whitewater. Reitman used to put together poetic shows that touched on singular subjects, like "rainy day music," or "songs about war," and so forth.

As a freshman on campus, I walked into the college radio station on my first day. I felt secure that I would eventually end up there, but I didn't know it would happen as quickly as it did. One day, weeks later, some friends from campus were getting together to go to a concert in Milwaukee. We decided we didn't want to be late, so we left really early and found ourselves in downtown Milwaukee at 5:15 P.M. – long before the concert was to start. We stopped in at a small restaurant to get a bite.

On the other side of the restaurant, there he sat: it was Bob Reitman. We all knew who he was, of course. There were four of us that came to the restaurant; three guys and one girl, all from the University of Wisconsin-Whitewater Radio Station, WSUW. We sent the woman over to him because we figured she was the most likely to be well-received by an essential stranger. She was able to get Reitman to motion all of us over and we eagerly went. When he showed us how approachable he was, the floodgates opened up. We all had a great conversation flowing between us.

In the course of our music gushing, he said to me, "Have you ever heard of Patti Smith? You need to hear her. I'll send you a cassette."

I wrote my college address down and he actually sent me three cassette tapes! As a freshman, to get those tapes in the mail meant a lot to me. I was in awe then and I learned to be a person of my word to anyone I met, regardless of their status or what they may be able to do for me in return. I was just a college kid who really looked up to this guy. That moment made me admire him all the more and, later in life, we became true friends in the small world of the radio business.

▶▶ **I learned to be a person of my word to anyone I met, regardless of their status or what they may be able to do for me in return.**

Day Two – Throughout high school, I had already gotten to experience the UW-Milwaukee radio station. After graduating, I wanted something different. In retrospect, I have few regrets, but that was one of them. I often wonder what would have happened if I'd have found a way to go to a major market somewhere warm. I wasn't a great student with top grades, but a different city for my skill set may have changed everything. Then again, *because* it may have changed everything, maybe I should be grateful that I did choose UW-W. It's a great life, after all.

I had my high school buddy, Paul, already at UW-Whitewater to be my roommate. We got the paperwork fixed on the first day so that we could room together. We bought a bunch of carpet squares and put them into our dinky little dorm room. It felt classy to us. We had great music . . . *and* carpeting! Wow.

When I met with the WSUW Station Manager on my second campus day, he heard of my experience and gave me my pick of slots! I was on the air the next day. My own programming included the student-run airtime and a half-hour weekly show. I did essentially a comedy show; my half-hour long audio assault. I don't know whatever happened to those shows. My buddies thought they were hilarious and, at least in memory, they really were. My friends also loved the fact that I could help them do their own on-air shifts and obtain college credits. I was given freedom and trust that nobody else at the station seemed to get and, really, I felt like I had just lucked into it. Sometimes, though, I took that freedom a little too far.

▶▶ I was given freedom and trust that nobody else at the station seemed to get and, really, I felt like I had just lucked into it.

My biggest claim to fame, or—rather—infamy, came from my eighteen-year-old brain's lapse in judgment. (Some things still hadn't changed.) It was toward the end of my freshman year and I'd already felt pretty comfortable calling my own shots. I thought it would be a cool idea if, on the first spring-like day we had, we began spreading the word that, at a certain time, for all the dorm rooms that were facing the quad area, everyone should open their windows, put their radio speakers in the windows and *blast* WSUW out onto the campus. It was basically an unsanctioned live concert. I got a wrist slap from the radio station and from the school, but I must admit that it felt pretty good that, on that day, instead of the maybe eight people who listened, there might have been eighty!

That moment gave me my first awe-invoking glimpse into what I call the "Good Morning Vietnam" feeling of radio. The movie "Good Morning Vietnam" is loosely based on Adrian Joseph

Cronauer (masterfully portrayed by Robin Williams who would win a Golden Globe as Best Actor for the role). Cronauer was a DJ on the air for The American Forces Network and his broadcasts were blasted out on Vietnamese beaches and battlefields. The DJ positively affected the lives of the troops through his entertainment. To this day, I am humbled and honored when someone tells me I was a part of their day . . . far away.

Dating Days – Or, not dating, as it were. The truth is, in college, whether you're seeing someone or missing out, it's an event either way. It was my first time away from home and I wanted a relationship. There was one girl that all the guys in my dorm just gawked at. We called her Little Queenie after the Chuck Berry song, but none of us ever had the guts to approach her. We had nicknames in our heads for a few of the other exceptional beauties around campus, too.

Two to three weeks into the year, I went into the shared, open showers on the dorm floor. A presumed-gay classmate of mine was in there. I was a bit naïve then and it was a different time. I didn't judge him, but wasn't sure how to act around him, as if it should have been somehow different than how I acted around anyone else. When he asked if I had a girlfriend, I tensed up at why he might be asking. Immediately (and stupidly) I thought, *'Say yes!'*

I told him that I did.

A year later, one of the nicknamed beauties was in a bar and we ended up talking. She said, "I noticed you the first week and had my friend ask about you, but he said you had a girlfriend." What if I would have been honest, engaged, and not quick to judge? I'll never know.

Radio Days – I got my very first "rock star" interview.

"You're great on the air," a couple of the entrepreneurial guys at the station had told me. "Let's leverage this."

I was moldable clay at that point. Between the three of us, we came up with a *syndicated* radio show. It was the first time I'd hear that term in my career, but far from the last. We decided to start a syndicated interview show called *Spotlight*.

"I got you an interview with Frank Zappa in Madison," he told me.

I was eighteen! I had no idea about how to articulate my language for interviews yet, but thirty-six hours later I found myself face-to-face with the "Don't Eat The Yellow Snow" legend, feeling like I was doing pretty much just that. I had a couple of his albums and I basically winged it, talking to him with a tape recorder.

He wasn't interested.

My questions were dumb.

It was a disaster.

I'm not sure where the recording of that show is, either, but that's okay. I got no pleasure out of the experience, even though I should have. I learned to never ever again go into an interview without doing my homework. It's one thing to be put into a position to have to think on my feet or talk to a stranger, but—given the opportunity—I never wanted to relive that moment. I wanted my interviews, from that point on, to *feel* off the cuff, but I vowed to always give some thought to where I would take an interview if it hit a lull. If, organically, I had interviews that went into other areas than what I had planned, but they kept moving, I wouldn't have a problem with them. But I never again knowingly sat down to an interview without preparation. *Spotlight*, our little syndication project, was never given the spotlight. It went nowhere, but I did get other interviews.

▶▶ **I learned to never ever again go into an interview without doing my homework.**

Concert Days – In 1974, George Harrison, was on solo tour. I found a friend who took me down to the concert. It was the first time I'd ever seen a Beatle put on a live show and I realized I never ever wanted to miss out on an opportunity to see one again.

I got to see another Beatle, Paul McCartney, later. To this day, he still is down-to-earth and cooperative. He's nice to everyone. His voice, to me, is the same as it was all those years ago when I first heard him on *Meet The Beatles* at those childhood family gatherings with my Mom's family. Getting to hear him live was and is a treasure. I get to hear back the soundtrack to my own life and the lives of so many others. I've listened to hundreds of outtakes and sometimes there are mistakes, but he still has a voice as pristine as it was in the era of *Beatlemania*. Almost always, hearing him live is like listening to an album. He gets it. He's not self-indulgent.

Every. Single. Song.

Every. Single. Time.

Many years later, I wasn't going to miss an opportunity to see McCartney once more and I had the wherewithal to not only buy the ticket, but to go online and discover that there was a VIP experience you could add. I bought the opportunity to sit in the front row and have dinner with peers doing the same; Paul McCartney and his band came in for the soundcheck they did before each show. I knew it was going to be spectacular, but I didn't *really* know. I had no idea what a Paul McCartney soundcheck was going to be like. It was a mini-concert! There were maybe forty of us sitting on chairs that were set up on the field at Miller Park during what turned out to be a forty-five-minute sound check! It felt like I was at a backyard concert with friends.

McCartney was a perfectionist. He would stop, adjust, reset video, and play with his sound. It was an exceptionally hot day. He was out there for so long. The crowd waiting to come in was supposed to be seated already, but they were outside the stadium for forty-five minutes. I tweeted the experience and, to learn when they could come in, people waiting in line began to follow my feed. The sound check turned out to be the best concert I'd ever seen. The show after the soundcheck was just as fantastic. The temperature was still in the nineties that night and it was humid, but he played for almost three hours, barely even stopping to hydrate.

My Whitewater concert experiences weren't quite as intimate, but catching tours was part of my "job" as a hopeful syndicated radio host, after all. The main concert promoter at the time was *Daydream Productions*. I called Randy McElrath who was with them and said, "I'm with WSUW. I'd like to review your (Kenny) Loggins and (Jim) Messina concert."

I had no *real* outlet, but they said "yes," and gave me a first-row seat at a time when these guys were at the height of their popularity. It was my first time in the front row of a concert. I was reviewing it in my mind, but my attending didn't really have anything to do with the review and, at the end of the day, I didn't even have a chance to talk about it on my show.

I confessed to Jim Messina years later. It felt really good to get that admission out to this guy who had given me multiple three-minute increments of joy through songs like, "Your Mama Don't Dance." Messina was moved. I had felt guilty about it for so long and let him know how important his music had been to me.

"I have to say that to hear how our music affected you all these decades later makes my heart feel good," he said.

In 1974, a well-known music critic of the time, Jon Landau, famously wrote, "I saw my rock-and-roll past flash before my eyes. I saw something else: I saw rock and roll's future and its name is Bruce Springsteen."

The Boss came to Milwaukee on October 2, 1975. I went with a buddy who was open to going, even though this Springsteen guy wasn't really well known yet. Two to three songs into the show, our friend and idol Bob Reitman took the stage.

He came out and said, "I've been told we're going to clear the theatre out. Leave in an orderly fashion and come back in...." (I don't remember how long to be honest, but we had to vacate for a while.) It turned out there was a bomb scare and the area needed to be swept for safety. My buddy and I left; *how on earth would we kill a couple of hours?*

Steve: What do you remember from that night?

Max Weinberg: That was the strangest show I'd ever been involved in. The record company had planned a party for us at the Pfister after the show. We just ended up having it in the middle of the show.

There was a Greek restaurant across the street. It was small and family owned and, to their amazement, they were filled in about two minutes! The place was just packed; it was a sit-down restaurant with menus. Gyros were the cheapest thing on the menu. To buy an entrée with a drink at a sit-down restaurant was not part of the plan or budget, but we didn't really have a choice. They took the gyros off the menu.

Meanwhile, it turned out that Springsteen and the E Street Band had gone back to the Pfister Hotel and started drinking. He wasn't the guy who showed up polluted for something he took as religiously seriously as his music, but it was a unique circumstance, so they moved their after-show party to the pre-show party. We got the rest of the concert later that night. It might have been the most incredible show I'd ever witnessed.

Steve: When I was at the restaurant, what were you doing?

Gary Tallent: I am guessing we figured we weren't going back. We weren't polluted, but we had a few laughs and, all of a sudden, we were supposed to go back. I thought, *'Okay.'* The show was a little more loose than they tended to be.

Steve: Well said, Gary, because every time the band has been back to Milwaukee, Bruce always says, "Are you loose?"

Gary: We WERE loose that night.

Days Gone By – I walked away from college with a few lessons: be true to your word, push to the line . . . but not beyond it, never judge, always prepare, and don't miss opportunities to experience something great or, even more importantly, share that experience with someone who needs to hear about it. The lessons of my time at UW-Whitewater, though, didn't always come through wins. Some were demonstrated and others were from my own hard-earned wisdom . . . and occasional missteps.

Overall, I was lost in college. I typically skipped most of my classes, basically skipped the dating scene, and ultimately skipped out on the remainder of the experience. I only attended for a year.

I was dispassionate, disappointed, and dissatisfied.

▶

In the Locker Rooms

Finding A Seat At The Press Table

"You want a better kind of
future. One that everyone can
share. You're not alone, we
all could use it. Stick around,
we're nearly there."

▶ *FROM: It's Coming Up*
BY: Paul McCartney and Wings, McCartney II
(Columbia, 1979)

*I*N the '70s, few radio and television networks had an exclusive, on-
site coverage reporter for all of the different teams and games,
which satisfied my own pursuits. My experience with interviewing
during college, combined with my love of all sports, served me well
to become a "stringer." That's what they called the freelance
reporters who attended the games and called in their coverage to the
different media outlets to which they were contracted. I wasn't
exactly Hank Stoddard or Ted Moore; I didn't have my own Doucette

Dictionary; and I wasn't yet into full-time radio; but these became my sportscasting days.

I was resourceful enough to realize that not every station had people to cover games, so I got myself credentialed by the Milwaukee Brewers, the Milwaukee Bucks, and Marquette University. I provided coverage to various radio stations and NBC. There used to be somebody at every stadium and that's how they would get the updates in thirty-second increments on the phone in the press box.

"Let's go to Steve in Milwaukee...." they would say.

Then, after the games, I would get audio clips from the different players in the locker rooms–winners and losers.

"WHAT YOU SEE HERE

WHAT YOU SAY HERE

LET IT STAY HERE

WHEN YOU LEAVE HERE"

It's strange that a steam- and stink-filled room cluttered with dirty equipment and uniforms, filled with loud voices and noise, and exposed to extreme emotions and language would have such a decree, but words like those are posted on many athletic locker room walls that I went into over the years.

The first time I went into a locker room, it was like having a backstage pass at a concert. This was a cathedral to me. The first few times I went in as a reporter, I couldn't speak. I didn't want to stick out like a sore thumb. There used to be an unbelievable demarcation between print and other media. As a stringer, I was second class. Print was exalted. Newspaper was THE journal of history . . . *and* sports. I had a feeling from day one that I was on the B-Team. Because of this, and the fact that I was this little guy in a roomful of comparative giants, it took a while to blend in.

I got comfortable pursuing sportscasting. I was at all of the local teams' home games, including the Milwaukee Does[11] professional women's team. I went to the first ever Does game. They were obviously much more careful about my going into that locker room, but the same rules applied.

I was doing what I loved and it helped pay the bills. I was so poor back then that I would take apart couches for spare change in order to be able to get enough money for a McDonald's burger, but—at the games—I got to eat free, a practice long since abolished by pro teams, as reporters now pay for their meals. Nonetheless, my lifelong love of fast food and stadium eats may have begun there!

The first check I got as a stringer was so exciting. When I saw *my* name next to the NBC peacock, I wanted to frame the check– but I needed the money. Every day, I would call in for my credentials until I was known enough to get full seasonal credentials, which included a parking pass to the same lot as the players at County Stadium where the Brewers played at that time. I would come out after I was done and kids would ask for my autograph, thinking I was a player!

▶▶ **When I saw my name next to the NBC peacock, I wanted to frame the check–but I needed the money.**

As a stringer, I sat at a press table, could actually eat in the press room, and was looked at as serious and trustworthy. If they were looking closely enough, my buddies could spot me on TV. At a Marquette game, there was a loose ball, coming right at me, and the players were coming right behind it. There was a grizzly, older print writer on my left and a TV personality on my right. I remember feeling the ball graze the tips of my hair. One player sailed into the air over me; the older writer practically had a heart attack; the TV announcer ducked and covered. I sat there .... frozen. I never moved! The player jumped over the press table—full spread—and cleared us all. All my buddies got a good laugh at that moment.

---

[11] *Years before the WNBA, there was the not-as-successful Women's Professional Basketball League. The Does played in Milwaukee Arena for two of the league's three seasons before disbanding.*

I got to talk to the players, be heard on radio and television, and eventually even work as the sportscaster for WAUK (a Waukesha, Wisconsin station). My most memorable interview was when the Brewers were playing the Red Sox and Hall-of-Famer-to-be Carl Yastrzemski was, to me, just a photo in a book. By the time I met him in a locker room, I'd had ten years of childhood admiration built up to that moment. I couldn't believe I was seeing the actual human being in person, much less being able to ask him a question.

Steve at a Milwaukee Bucks game press table

Yastrzemski was sitting in front of his locker, smoking a cigarette. I asked some innocuous question he'd probably heard as many times as he'd had a hit. Before he answered, he blew his cigarette smoke right into my face. I didn't react. Instead, I just asked my next question. Then, he did it again. Three questions, three answers, and three giant hits of tobacco-infused exhales that are probably still in my lungs to this day. I'll never forget it. It was like wearing a badge of honor to be a guest in that sacred space. If I'd chosen to react, I inherently wouldn't belong. There are certain rules and acceptances that go along with being welcome in sacred spaces (like locker rooms). If you want to stay, you'd better figure it out. If the smoke were reversed, it would have been my last trip.

> ▶▶ **There are certain rules and acceptances that go along with being welcome in sacred spaces.**

With my hard-earned smoker's badge, I was welcome, initiated, and lucky enough to be a part of stories I wouldn't have been able to cough up if not for holding back the cough that day. I'd been part of the beat-writers covering The Crew for a couple of years and I felt comfortable when we came to the strike season of 1981.

The Brewers were a great team in competition to go to the World Series. They had a playoff series with the New York Yankees and the Yanks sent a scout to Milwaukee. This was in the days of scouts writing reports on pencil and paper. They would then type them up, copy them, and send them off. My girlfriend of the time had parents who owned a print shop. That's where the scout happened to take his report. They made copies and so happened to keep an extra copy for me so that I found myself after the next game in the Brewers locker room holding the scouting report.

After the game, you'd usually interview the manager while the players showered, and then you'd speak to the team. Brewers' General Manager Harry Dalton was in the locker room and I asked him, "How much do teams really scout each other."

"All the time. We all pretty much know everything."

"How valuable would it be to you if I had the report?"

"Are you shitting me? Would you share it?"

"Sure."

Dalton took it up to the offices to make a copy while I was standing there. By this time, all the interviews were done and here I was standing there like I didn't belong–the young stringer from the B-Team! All the reporters were gone while everyone remaining was wondering why I hadn't left. I had never been more energized. I dipped a toe over that line from being a disconnected reporter to being part of the team. At the same time, I was so embarrassed standing there when all of the other reporters were gone.

The Brewers finally won a game against the Yankees and I'd like to think I had something to do with it.

I did get a few more insider insights over the years with the Brewers. I got to see many sides of Manager George "Bambi" Bamberger. He was a complete dichotomy. Bambi was kind, outgoing, and friendly, but every fifth word out of his mouth was the F-bomb. He couldn't put together a sentence without it. I'll never forget his last game when he retired (mid-season). I felt a kinship to him. Hanging out with another radio reporter after the game, Bambi came up to us and signed a ball to each of us.

▶▶ **Bambi was kind, outgoing, and friendly, but every fifth word out of his mouth was the F-bomb.**

Another time, after a game chock full of the tried-and-true baseball tradition of throwing at batters, I found myself in the visiting team's locker room. Ninety-nine out of 100 times, I'd go to the Brewers locker room first, then—if needed—the visitor's locker room. Their team's manager was absolutely railing at the Brewers and I was recording it. Everyone was talking about the throwing at each other.

In the Brewers locker room, I rewound my tape and began playing it for Bamberger. Steam was coming from his ears when he shouted, "STOP YOUR BOX! I want to say a few words."

I wanted to have him wait while I fast forwarded, but he was going, so, I lost half the tape of the other manager. But, again in that moment, I felt like one of the team.

Sometimes, that team feeling even carried out to the parking lot. Milwaukee Brewer Dick Davis was "Straight Outta Compton" (literally). We became buddies. Not to make light, but I was in my twenties and it was the '70s: I loved smoking pot. Dick Davis didn't know anybody who had weed, so I would meet him in the parking lot after games or we'd hang in my apartment.

Once in his car, he asked, "Do you have any pot? Just grab an envelope from the back for it."

Fan letters filled the back seat of his car. There was one letter from a little kid written in crayon; Davis was spelled wrong; there was a backwards "r" on Brewers; the whole adorable package!

"Just throw the weed in there," he said.

I felt so awful putting pot into this envelope from a little kid. It highlights what the era was like, though.

One of the best things I took from my sports reporting days was further training in how to read a room. It has served me well in business and in life. You can feel, if you're attuned to it, the culture and attitude of a team that believes it's their year. I'll never forget the Kansas City Royals and the way they talked to others in 1980. There was a magic in them that translated to their performance. The 2018 Brewers had the same spark when they claimed the National League Central Division. Those locker rooms are exciting and energizing. You do not act the same way when the players are bummed, angry, or in a mood. It's not always based on wins or losses, either. You had to read it and, once you learned the skill, you had it for life.

▶▶ **One of the best things I took from my sports reporting days was further training in how to read a room.**

I was having fun as a stringer, but I needed to earn more money than my sports reporting alone could do. I began working at a bank warehouse during the day, smoking pot, and literally living for the night. I still had the dream of radio, though, and that dream kept me from going off the rails at an age and time when others did just that.

I remember that the song "Casey Jones" from The Grateful Dead was considered an anthem to drugs, but—for me (and them)—it was actually the opposite. Those lyrics, "driving that train, high on cocaine" were so scary to me . . . scarier than even the "Helter Skelter" label of the infamous Tate-Labianca murders. I wasn't sure why and I'm grateful for it, but hard drugs, like heroin, which were gaining in popularity, just never had a call for me.

I credit songs like those, as well as Jefferson Airplane's "White Rabbit," with helping to prevent me from going too crazy or getting too experimental in an era when the field I worked in was filled with that sort of thing.

Steve: People were worried about social unrest and the draft and you brought so much fun and comfort during that period. Thank you.

Mickey Dolenz: Well, thank you. That's an interesting observation. I want to say it wasn't coincidental. I don't think the producers and creators of the Monkees actually sat down and had that intent. There is in interesting statement from Timothy Leary in which he writes about the Monkees. He says, "Yeah, you thought it was just some silly goof off." It was the sort of release from exactly what you are talking about.

At the warehouse, we would have very competitive music trivia contests at the start of the day and do some menial tasks throughout the work hours. After work, I would take in the occasional game and then smoke and drink at night. At the same time, I still had this dream that I had to do more in radio.

The warehouse district where I worked was the Third Ward before it actually *was* the now fashionable "Milwaukee's Third Ward," and, as rough as it was then, there was this tiny antique center down there. People were working there during the day, including one young and beautiful woman. We'd all run to the front of the building to watch this beauty go into work each day and we'd watch her go to her car again at 4:00 P.M. at the end of the day. It was the only time we ever saw her. She was striking.

It was a rough neighborhood with an even rougher bar on the block. We were in the bar one day at lunch for burgers and beers when one of the guys saw that the woman was walking down the street . . . and it was neither 9:00 A.M. nor 4:00 P.M. This was my chance! She wasn't on her way into work when she needed to be in a rush. It wasn't the end of the night when a guy walking up to you might have felt creepy in that neighborhood.

I walked up to her on the street and she was friendly enough, but I was failing at coming up with anything I could think of to impress her. I was beside her and looking at her, rather than in front me, when I walked smack-dab into the side of a building. I went down like a shot deer–folded like a pancake. There was blood coming out of my nose and mouth and she took pity on me. This was my one shot, so I used the pity to ask her out. We went to an Electric Light Orchestra (ELO) concert. It didn't go much further than that, but our first meeting has kept the memory of that particular date request fresh in my mind all these years later.

But working in the bank warehouse was my first, full-time "real" job. I had started as a delivery truck driver before moving to the print shop. Within the warehouse, there was really no adult supervision.

▶▶ **With all of us guys, it was basically a five-story playground.**

With all of us guys, it was basically a five-story playground. The top three floors were record retention. There was no reason to go there except that I had a buddy up there. The freight elevator took you to those three floors. I was heading up to the fifth floor when one of the guys with me on the elevator asked if I knew what a kick-plate was. Apparently, it's a plate between floors designed as a safety device. If you put your foot over the edge, it will kick your foot back manually. It was pretty cool. He showed me the way the kickplate worked and we went back down to the first floor. The next day, I was by myself on the elevator and I began having fun with the kickplate.

I tried it on the second floor . . . cool.

Third floor . . . same thing.

Fourth floor . . . no kick plate.

My foot ended up caught between two chunks of concrete. In pain, I had to manually stop the elevator and reverse it slowly to pull my foot out. My foot was throbbing. I finally got back down to the bottom floor and it felt even worse. I realized I'd better take a look at it. I started to take off my shoe and saw that my shoe was filled with blood. I left it on and called my supervisor at the main bank building. He told me to walk it off. He was an old Marine.

He finally said, "Well come over here."

I limped the four blocks away and, when he saw what I was dealing with, he decided to drive me to the hospital himself. He was steaming mad. It's a blur how I got checked in, but the doctor said I'd broken my foot. This didn't please the Sergeant any more. I had taken him away from his comfort and work. I came out an hour later, on crutches, in a cast. Apparently, this helped. He'd thought I was kidding! The bank subsequently implemented a policy of steel-toed shoes in the warehouse.

Probably fearful of a lawsuit, even though it had been my fault, they told me to take a few *months* off. Because I was in an apartment complex that had a pool and I had an equally jobless neighbor in his thirties, this meant a summer of a lot of pot, great parties, and no cares. There's always something in a system of checks and balances, though. I had my entire life free for three months, but every time I smoked pot, my foot throbbed and, I didn't know it at the time, but the break was so bad that it broke my big toe at the root of the nail. It grew back in four pieces like a fork and was pretty gnarly for about the next ten years. I'll never be a foot model. That was my payback.

Gratefully, I hadn't been injured before I got the opportunity to enjoy one of the great perks of being a radio guy and stringer. While trying to break into radio, I was applying any chance I could. I had convinced a daytime station to allow me to provide recorded sportscasts they could use. As such, I was accredited with every area team. I had legitimacy, even though it was a shoestring operation with hardly any ratings. At the same time, at the epitome of good ratings and popularity, was the television show, Happy Days.

The cast of Happy Days had a competitive softball team that played in L.A. They were actually pretty good and they became a travel team that played exhibition games in Major League stadiums before the "real" games by the pros. Milwaukee was ideal, seeing as it was where Happy Days was to have taken place. They played in County Stadium before a Brewers game against a team of media and sports All Stars–led by the legendary Bob Uecker. I got to be on the team. It was one of the coolest days of my life. They had uniforms for us and I got a bat with my name on it. Years later, I reminded Uecker that we were once teammates. It sounded good to say those words.

Steve: Do you have any memories of Milwaukee?

Randy Bachman (Guess Who and BTO): Of course. We did a lot of good gigs there. I think of Laverne and Shirley. In the mid-'70s, BTO hit it big and I went to the Excalibur factory in Milwaukee. I ordered a four-seater Excalibur which is on a 454 Corvette frame. It was just as an expensive luxury and I love that car.

Steve: You don't still have it, do you?

Randy: No, I lost it in a divorce where most guys lose most of everything.

We got there in the afternoon to play and County Stadium was sold out. I played a lot of softball at that time, but even spelling my own name would have been hard in front of 40,000 people. For this game, each hitter was afforded only two strikes. It was my turn at bat. I was sweating profusely, trying to hold onto the bat. Henry Winkler was pitching! Let me say that again–Henry Winkler was pitching to ME!

Their team may have been for fun, but they were *really* good. They played a lot and he pitched *fast*. I was as nervous as could be.

FIRST PITCH.

FIRST SWING.

FIRST MISS.

Ugh. It took all of three seconds for me to have a "long" talk with myself. *You're not going to strike out in front of everybody. Get a hold of yourself. You are standing across from The Fonz, one of the coolest, most popular guys in America. Don't screw this up!'*

I focused and made eye contact with the pitcher. He looked back at me. I didn't know if I should feel fear, determination, or admiration.

Expecting another fastball, I was swinging before his lobbed pitch got to me. He must have felt pity for me. I struck out. I played a lot of softball and usually played first base, but I got assigned to right center. I was so nervous. A fly ball came to me. Catching it should have been no problem, but I had self-doubt creep in. *'Don't mess this up. I wish it wasn't coming at me.'*

The right fielder out there with me happened to be Ron Swoboda. He wasn't just a TV sportscaster on Channel 12; he had been a part of the 1969 World Series-winning New York Mets. As I was waiting for (and fearing) the ball coming down, Ron—like a leaf in the wind—flew in front of me, caught it, and we trotted into the infield together, like equal heroes. It was the third out and I got to bask in the moment with the World Series legend. Then, I did get up to bat one more time and I didn't get a hit, but at least I made contact and to me? That felt like a home run!

▶▶ **It was the third out and I got to bask in the moment with the World Series legend.**

The rest of the cast was in the game and we all had dinner afterward. It was cool enough to be there with the local media legends. Even more surreal, though, was the fact that I was sitting there having dinner with the guys from Al's and with Marian Ross, herself. They were down to earth and fun and she was every bit the cordial Mrs. Cunningham she portrayed on the show.

That day, August 18, 1979, held me in total awe and the memories still elicit that feeling today. It was like being a part of a real family while I sat with this one from a show. *As for me, back in the real world, I was itching for a turn at a show of my own.*

My Day As Bob Uecker's Teammate

OnMilwaukee Article
As Originally Published Online
January 27th, 2019
By: Steve Palec

The legendary Bob Uecker turned 85 years old on Saturday. We were teammates once. Yes, THAT Bob Uecker – the voice of the Brewers, Mr. Belvedere, the Miller Lite front row spokesperson, author, "Tonight Show" guest, Harry Doyle in "Major League," "SNL" host and World Series champion.

We were teammates for one day on Aug. 18, 1979. I was a member of Bob Uecker's All Stars, the softball team that took on the cast of "Happy Days" at County Stadium on a Saturday afternoon.

I've actually only talked to Bob once. And it wasn't even that day. Decades later, we were at an event and bonded as ex-ball players reminiscing about the old day(s). He couldn't have been any nicer and humored me and my hyperbolical recollection of one event, given his many accomplishments. The fact is I'll never forget that day in 1979, much less the time in the 21st century I actually talked to Ueck.

Still not yet even a full-time broadcaster, I was a part-time sportscaster at WAUK back then and finagled my way onto the team. My roommate at the time was WQFM newscaster Ric Schroeder who went on to a long stint in Los Angeles. Prior to the game, he interviewed Uecker and asked about me. Bob, who didn't know me, said, "I'm not sure how he'll play, but he looks good in the uniform."

At that time, "Happy Days" was in the apex of its 10-year run on TV. Not only did they play softball regularly as a group that genuinely liked each other, they were good! And, of course, as witnessed by playing at Wrigley the day before, major league teams across the country were happy to have them visit. And a huge crowd at County Stadium didn't hurt Brewer attendance numbers. True to form, the superstar cast of the show was just as enamored as folks are today to spend time with Mr. Baseball.

While I didn't actually speak to Uecker that afternoon, he did motion for me to enter the game as a batter after a few innings – a tight game I may add.

There were 49,172 people there that day, some of whom were there to see Texas Rangers pitcher Fergie Jenkins face off against the Brewers' Jim Slaton at some point in the proceedings.

But first, I had to face The Fonz.

Henry Winkler was the pitcher for the "Happy Days" cast, and he had struck out Mike Hegan, who just three years earlier had become the first Brewer to hit for the cycle.

Winkler was throwing heat. I swung and missed at the first pitch. Two strikes and you're out. I did not want to strike out so I stepped out of the box, gave myself a pep talk and looked at The Fonz with determination in my eyes. I was going to jump at the next pitch. He must have felt sorry for me. He lobbed a ball in ... unfortunately AFTER I had already begun my swing in anticipation of his blazing speed. I might have been able to hit it if I had the foresight to swing again on the same pitch. But I struck out.

As embarrassed as I was, it was easy to be distracted by a dugout full of amazing teammates that included Fuzzy Thurston, Bob Reitman, Larry the Legend, Robb Edwards and Jonathan Green. It was easy to be blown away by playing against Ron Howard, Anson Williams, Donny Most, Tom Bosley and Al Molinaro. And as I entered the game in right center field, I ran past who I thought looked like Mike Stivic from "All in the Family." I wasn't wrong. Rob Reiner was playing for the "Happy Days" cast.

Uecker had enough misplaced confidence in me to put me in the outfield without knowing that I always played first base given my depth perception was compromised by having no depth perception, So, of course, with two outs in a close game, a fly ball came my way.

Already intimidated and awed by my surroundings, I immediately began to regret my birth. But while the ball made its way down, our right fielder Ron Swoboda, who aside from being a Milwaukee TV sports anchor at the time was also previously a hero for the New York Mets in the 1969 World Series, effortlessly drifted next to me and made the catch. Beaming with a giant smile, I trotted into the dugout from the outfield with him side by side.

The seven inning game ended in a 2-2 tie. While the somewhat incrementally better major leaguers played their game, Uecker's All Stars and the cast of "Happy Days" mingled in a makeshift clubhouse and enjoyed dinner. I sat with Marion Ross. If you're gonna sit down for a meal, it might as well be with Mrs. C, right? She was wonderful.

Just a few years ago, I shared Sporkies judging duties with Anson Williams and Donny Most at the Wisconsin State Fair. I reminded them of that other time we ate together. Most, who you'll remember as Ralph Malph, immediately recalled his triple in the second inning that he tried to stretch into a run. He was thrown out at the plate and tagged out by none other than our catcher, Bob Uecker.

Looking back, that was an amazing day. In all the years since, I've never taken for granted the chance I had to be in the presence of that group, especially Bob Uecker.

For in all those years, like you, I've seen him, heard him and marveled in how lucky we are to have him.

Steve Palec (top row, fourth from the right) as Bob Uecker's (top row, second from the left) teammate

IN AT LAST

The Early Notes Of A Career

"And something is
happening here, but you
don't know what it is.
Do you, Mr. Jones?"

▶ FROM: *Ballad Of A Thin Man*
BY: *Bob Dylan, Highway 61 Revisited*
(Columbia, 1965)

*B*EFORE eventually getting a morning show, I was lucky to land my first full-time radio job working overnights—2:00 to 6:00 A.M.—at WQFM. I was glad I got the position because it was such an influential station at the time. In retrospect, it was really difficult on my body to be working those hours, but it was a perfect fit and timing for my career. On the overnight shift, it was easy to take chances. I had some leeway to make mistakes and I was on a legendary Milwaukee rock station that was part of the culture of my generation. I wanted to learn and was blessed to have the shift that allowed me to do so.

I loved it.

I loved the lifestyle.

I loved the availability I had in my life.

I loved the experience.

These were great times for a young man in the world of (Sex, Drugs, and) Rock & Roll.

Overnight callers are a unique breed. The highlight in my young mind may have been the two female art students who offered to spend time with me. I feigned fascination with their interests and asked if there really were nude drawing classes.

They said "yes," and I quickly found a sketch pad . . . satisfying that rarest of rock star milestones.

One of my unfulfilled bucket list items, though, was going to a party at the Playboy Mansion. There were a couple of guys who could have gotten me in. Milwaukee Native, Kato Kaelin, who I met once pre-OJ days at The Silver Spring House, a Milwaukee area watering hole, was one of them.

I also had the opportunity to interview Bill Maher by phone, who might have had the pull. We hit it off and he asked that I come backstage when he visited Milwaukee. But that was in 2019, post Hugh Hefner days, so I've crossed that visit off my list without accomplishing it.

Steve: With all the musicians you've had on both of your shows, is there someone you really want to get?

Bill Maher: I still want to get Paul McCartney or Ringo on. I see these guys get interviewed all the time and it's the same questions that we know the answers to and they know the answers to. I'd love to run by Paul my theory of why John Lennon didn't want to stay in The Beatles. I don't think it was about Yoko. I think it was about the fact that, at a certain point, he never got an A-side anymore. Can you imagine writing a song as great as *Strawberry Fields Forever* and it's the B-side because *Penny Lane* was more commercial? A song like *Revolution*, but it wasn't the A-side because *Hey Jude* was. I think that's why The Beatles broke up. It was a competition and John Lennon kept losing.

In the early days of Summerfest[12], the station got to broadcast on the festival grounds 24/7 from a trailer. We moved all the albums—actual vinyl—to this Summerfest grounds "studio." As an overnight guy, there was *nobody* around. It was so absurd, but also kind of cool. Even though Monday through Friday was my overnight show, I did get to do a Sunday afternoon. I could actually see human beings on the grounds! The life and activity were amplified after working the abandoned overnight shift. I loved the on-air interviews, admired the artists, and enjoyed thinking on my feet to make the show as entertaining and fun as I could.

---

[12] *Held since 1968 in Milwaukee, Wisconsin, Summerfest is an annual music celebration which currently boasts more than 800 bands on eleven stages over the course of eleven days in the end of June and beginning of July. It is attended by nearly one million music fans and has been certified by the Guinness Book of World Records as the World's Largest Music Festival since 1999.*

George Thorogood was playing a show one night following my rare day shift, so he was brought into the trailer studio. It was invigorating. I was surrounded by people and had a rock star next to me. A girl came up to us; she was thinking about dying her hair pink. In 1980, this wasn't very common. I remember that Thorogood talked her out of it; I wouldn't get to interview him again for several decades, but his time with me at Summerfest was one of many great memories of interviewing artists during the world's largest music festival. I'm in awe when I recall some of my favorite moments.

Steve: What do you think of when I bring up Summerfest?

George Thorogood: I remember the first time we did it, we were asked to play with Southside Johnny. We were on the grounds and I didn't know how the system worked....people paid to get in and then they could go anywhere they wanted. As we were walking onstage, they just opened the gates and the people standing there had been standing for a long time and they came RUSHING in really fast. I thought there was a fire. They were rushing in to see us. It freaked me out, Steve. It really freaked me out.

Moments like the live Summerfest show made me realize I was more ambitious than just doing overnights. About two and a half years into my time at WQFM, I felt I had learned enough for a next step and I got antsy to start climbing the ladder. *How could I elevate an overnight show into a career?* I put together a proposal that said WQFM, a live big-time station, should have a production director, and it should be me, of course. A typical hierarchy in a station would be the general manager of the station, followed by the program director, under whom is the production director and the on-air talent.

A production director would organize, cast, and sometimes record all of the non-live commercials and promo announcements that would be used during programming. At the same time, Andy

Bloom, who was on a similar career arc as I, recommended a research department to maximize ratings. The station had budgeted for one new full-time position and it went to Andy. I liked Andy and actually I'd work with him years later before he moved to Philadelphia to run what became the second-ever radio station to syndicate Howard Stern. I wasn't fired; rather I just wasn't moved up as I desired. So, I used the ideas that I had created, an already great proposal, to talk to another local station–WZUU.

WZUU was a really unique radio station at the time. Their morning show was hosted by the late Larry the Legend (Johnson). And make no mistake, he was a legend. Larry was from Tennessee and had a southern accent. He did things on the air that were new and fresh. He shared news of the day, interviewed major movers and shakers, had call-ins, and even included investigative reporting. He ran quite a show and took the showmanship to the street too, as he drove a Rolls-Royce and made countless personal appearances.

His newsman, David Haines, had a compelling on-air style to grasp the attention of listeners. But he also pushed the line with his lead-ins. Following an overnight murder in the city, for instance, he said, "Hot Lead in the Head and Now She's Dead." (He got in trouble for that one.) Larry wasn't only dominant on the air, he was the VIP of the station for everything that aired with the exception of "The Greenhouse with Jonathan Green." Jonathan had been a staple at WTMJ and had great segues, knew the intro of commercials, and was seamless and brilliant. He would fluidly flow from a statement to the first word of a commercial, tying them together. I use his tricks to this day.

WZUU's belief at that time was that FM radio was permeating life–in homes and cars. Why was talk and sports play-by-play only on AM? They went after the broadcast rights for the Packers and Brewers.

It was a great time on a great station, and they needed a production director. Using my youth-learned "just ask" philosophy, a meeting with WZUU landed me the job. I would never leave a company unless I understood the benefits of leaving *and* my current employer had opportunity to meet the expectation. I spoke to my higher-ups at WQFM and they understood and weren't able to offer an equivalent opportunity, so I gave them notice; unheard of in radio. I left on good terms.

I showed up for my first day at WZUU at 9:00 A.M. on a Monday, as directed.

I met the receptionist and the program director, who took me into a room and said, "Here's your studio. Good luck. "

"Part of the Team!" Steve (back row, second from left) represents WZUU on a company basketball team

I had no idea how to run the board–much less anything else in this studio!

Luckily, the mid-day jock, Bill Shannon, came down to help. He couldn't have been nicer.

He gave me a fifteen-minute crash course, showed me what was expected, and said, "Larry will be here at 10:01. He will want to record commercials. No fuck-ups."

This whole station was basically Larry's!

Larry's parking spot.

Larry's own secretary.

When I walked into the studio back then, it wasn't as sterile as the room I work in today. There was carpeting on the wall and everybody smoked in those days–myself included. There are probably cigarette filters still rotting today that smell better than the carpeting on that wall did. Today's décor is a welcome change.

To the average person taking in a recording console and board covered in buttons, levers, and lights, they may as well be looking at a space station with labels in a foreign language. In that way, studios haven't changed much in the forty-five years I've been working in them. After using the equipment for a while, though, a person can learn what needs to be lit up and used and

▶▶ **Studios haven't changed much in forty-five years.**

what doesn't. I probably use only a tenth of the buttons.

On that starting day at ZUU, I walked into that stanky, smelly studio with its intimidating board. On my first day, first assignment, in the first minute, I was with an equally intimidating guy who had an intolerable attitude about slowing down because he overbooked himself. I was glad to be on "Lombardi Time," as it's called, for famed Packer coach, Vince Lombardi.

The experience brought me back to my first times in professional locker rooms. I had one foot in awe and one in intimidation. I got comfortable being uncomfortable until I felt steady in my footing. Before that footing came, though, I'd sway between confidence and uncertainty, taking it all in and just getting through it. Something in a studio causes you to say, "No choice. I gotta nail this."

The heavens shone that day as I sat before a board I had never touched before. I was able to record Larry the Legend . . . without any fuck-ups. I the spent the next six months in fear of him before I got my comfortable footing. Finally, I got to the point that we could laugh together and I could even start making (light) fun of him, like guys do when they work together. Well, not to his face. Eventually, I even got to tap into some creativity. I started a contest using movie clips and Larry would play it in the morning.

All of the non-live, non-music pieces were sold by the station's salespeople. It didn't matter what it was for; those commercials paid the bills. Copywriters would put together short scripts when necessary and the ads would be prerecorded to be played during the otherwise live programming of the station. I had been managing a lot of the commercials at the time when our copywriter sent me a script for a very . . . *unique* . . . product.

One of our sponsors was Lift-It, an antimicrobial toilet seat handle. It was developed by a Southeastern Wisconsin man and it was a folded plastic handle with blue adhesive that could stick to the bottom of a toilet seat. It was affordable and could apparently prevent germs. The product was just this handle that people could grab to "lift it" (the seat of the commode) without touching the germs of the actual toilet. (How the germs managed to stay off of the handle, too, is a mystery, but, like I said, it helped pay the bills.)

How do you make a commercial out of that?

Our copywriter wrote a commercial script that had God explaining to someone how to use the toilet seat handle. I literally laughed out loud. I thought the best way to play it would be to take it completely seriously. I used some of the technology we had to

▶▶ **A new category was created called the "Special Judge's Award."**

add some reverb and echo so that I could create a "God-like" voice telling a "Moses-like" character that he had to use the Lift-It handle to lift the toilet seat. When the commercial started airing, it freaked out anyone who heard it! It so happened that the Lift-It radio ad aired around the same time when, once a year, the advertising community held its local, regional, and national Addy Awards. My friend, Jay Filter, happened to be the chairman of the awards process. These awards were a big deal. Hundreds and hundreds of entries came in to ultimately be recognized in an equally huge awards ceremony. As a nod to him, I entered the commercial for WZUU. When the judges heard the spot, they broke out in laughter and disbelief. But what do you do with an ad for the Lift-It, exactly? And so, a new category was created called the "Special Judge's Award."

At the local level, it WON! Then, it moved onto regionals, and WON! Finally, it went to nationals, and WON! Yes. I became the winner of a National Addy Award for playing God in a toilet seat handle commercial. The Lift-It image ad

▶▶ **Yes. I became the winner of a National Addy Award for playing God in a toilet seat handle commercial.**

ended up in a national magazine and they even did a full-page story on me for it. I received a beautiful plaque that was proudly displayed at ZUU for all to see.

I spent three years at WZUU.

The station ownership also had a New York station that had moved from last place to first by changing into a Top-40 station with a Morning-Zoo style format. Larry was moved off of the mornings onto an AM channel and we became Hot-Rocking Z95, a replica of the New York plan.

Everything was reimagined.

Every song had to be put on tape.

Every promo was newly recorded.

I spent a full week with the format guru, Scott Shannon, who was, at that point, the hottest commodity in radio, nationally. He hired new staff and worked

▶▶ **He had me do (or redo) everything.**

with me in the studio ("Do this," "Do that." "Find this," "Find that."), and he had me do (or redo) everything. He liked me well enough, though.

"Steve, I can see you have talent. You gotta get back on the air," he said to me.

It was around that time that my old station, WQFM, was making a change in the mornings. They had gone as far as they could with their old programming and they knew that the demographics were changing. They courted me to come back and be on the air, so that's when I went, beginning my stint as a morning radio show host for the first time ever. I had been in awe of Larry, Jonathan, and Scott and even won a national award. I was in at last–ready to tackle the show, the events, and the appearances that encompassed the life of an early 80s DJ.

The Show – I had to fill a four-hour show; it was created new every day. I played a lot of music, but also felt obligated to do two to three unique things every hour. When I wasn't on the air, I *lived* to find ideas for the show. Reading the newspaper one night, I saw a picture of two guys wearing fish neckties.

▶▶ **When I wasn't on the air, I *lived* to find ideas for the show.**

It struck me as so funny, so I called the company that made them and said, "This is pretty cool. Do you want to come in and talk about these?"

They were thrilled. These two guys had just started the company and these were their Ralph Marlin Fish Ties. They offered to give some away. They brought in a box of about forty of them and we were giving them away on the air. It was a good idea, but it wasn't catching on, yet.

A few weeks later, our NBA basketball team, the Bucks, under Head Coach Don Nelson, were in the playoffs. Nelson was known for being a bit disheveled. When he got in trouble for wearing shoes that had a logo on them which was not approved by the league, he covered the logos with tape. Subsequently, I thought it would be funny to give him a tie. I went to his office and I left it on his desk. I didn't think much of it. It was a long shot. I was going to be at the game that Sunday, way up in the nosebleeds.

Don Nelson came out–wearing the tie!

The television announcers focused in on the tie and it became a phenomenon. They sold millions and millions of the ties, then sold the company down the line. The ties are still sold today and it was Don Nelson who ignited the trend. Rewind, though, to the Sunday game. I thought it was really cool that he wore this tie that I had given him. I went to bed early and woke up at 4:00 A.M. to get to my morning show. I picked up the morning paper, all too happy to see a picture of Don Nelson, but with a caption that said, "WKTI's (Bob) Reitman and (Gene) Mueller Give Don Nelson a Fish Tie."

I wasn't going to put up with it. I loved Reitman and Mueller and I had total respect for them, but—for the first time in my professional career—I was angry beyond logic.

I called them that morning and *screamed* at them. *"How dare you!"*

I came to find out later that, parallel to WQFM talking about the playoffs, WKTI had been collecting good luck charms for Nelson from their listeners. The tie was thought to have been part of a box they had dropped off. It was quickly forgiven. Besides, I did have a lifetime supply of fish ties and I watched with pride as they grew their business.

Someone said to me once, "You could have invested, leveraged the publicity stunt to compensation, called in favors!"

Without even thinking, I said, "I won't run out of creative ideas. It wasn't contrived. It wasn't the first and won't be the last."

The Events – We never really had the luxury of budgets, so my approach was one of "guerilla marketing," so to speak. One of the spontaneous ideas I ran with was tied to Ronald Reagan's second inauguration. I found a travel agency offering an inauguration travel package and called them up on the air. I was being sarcastic about the package to be funny, poking different holes in what they were offering. I said that I bet we (my cohosts, Keith Harmon and Fred Mudd, and I) could find our own way to get there. Keith and I worked it out with the station for flights, invited listeners to give us ideas, called our congressman to get party invites, and even hooked up with a Baltimore radio station to be able to broadcast back to Milwaukee. All of this was done on the air.

The on-air broadcasts were hilarious. I remember that we wanted to see if we could get high in the Senate office building. No, we didn't. Not because we thought better of it. It turned out there was a snowstorm and, apparently, Washington, D.C. basically shuts down for

▶▶ **We guys from Wisconsin just didn't get why the city would shut down for snow.**

so much as a forecast of flurries. Don't get me wrong. This one turned out to be an actual storm. We guys from Wisconsin just didn't get why the city would shut down for snow.

We went to "Taste of the Country" at the Smithsonian. We got an invite to the inaugural ball and had to get tuxes. The congressman from Wisconsin wanted nothing to do with us once we showed up. Kevin Hermening, a recently rescued U.S. Marine, formerly one of the hostages held in Iran for 444 days, was there being honored–and he was cool with us. Understandably, we weren't exactly the biggest deals from the Dairy State that night. Just being there was so surreal, though. I was on top of the world. I even got hit on by a senator's wife. (No. I won't tell you which one.) I never did see the president . . .

Keith Harmon, Fred Mudd, and Steve at the Reagan inauguration

Another of my favorite promotions happened organically. One morning I wanted to thank our listeners with a free lunch. A local hot dog place said they would provide the food and we packed the restaurant. A glimpse at that power led to our "office dinners." Each

Wednesday, we'd pick a restaurant and each Thursday we'd pick an office. The nomination calls were entertaining, but it also killed two hours every week (and got us free meals).

We also took the morning show on the road to New York City, where I got to act in a soap opera and check off a bucket-list item by going to see Saturday Night Live. I'll never forget then-cast member Robert Downey Jr. dancing offstage to musical guest star Mr. Mister.

The Appearances – There's a great Albert Brooks comedy routine about DJs in which he says: "They physically don't hear people booing them!" There's truth to that. We don't have to see and hear our audiences, so we can only hope we're entertaining. It's kind of cool to be asked to introduce people in front of an actual audience, though. I always felt some trepidation about it, because I have a high sense of awareness and I see everything going on, including those who are oblivious. That awareness can really kill self-esteem, so I didn't want to do bar appearances. I would do on-air remotes But, unlike a lot of DJs who made lots of money and met lots of people, I didn't want to just hang out. I liked the studio best. Nonetheless, the concert-intro opportunities were there and sometimes—either because I was obligated or because the group was one I admired—I took on the "introducer" role. I don't say "emcee" because that would imply some respect, control, and planning. These were not things common to the role.

There is still a sliver of how it was back then, though. Management and event planning have generally improved in the decades since I began. It was so disorganized then. No one was in charge. Sometimes, they would tell you the band had changed their mind. The stage wasn't really thrilling for me. Sometimes, the band meets are complete letdowns, too. Twisted Sister, a band I really had no interest in at that particular time, was one I introduced. It was such a mess. They wondered why I was even there. I had almost no notice before being told I'd have to mention the record company, the band, and all of the other necessary details.

I was already nervous when the band's lead singer, Dee Snyder, put his hand on my shoulder and said, "Three beats in, make the intro." *Now I have to count the beats, too?* Dee was pretty nice about it, though, and it was the first time I got to talk to 10,000 people in person all at once.

Another time, I was asked to be in a wrestling ring to announce the wrestlers before each fight. I'm not talking Olympic-style, Greco-Roman wrestling. These were body-bouncing, chair-throwing, rope-jumping wrestlers! I'm pretty sure those guys could have killed me with a finger. They were huge! When I arrived to what I assumed was this casual sporting venue, I got yelled at because I hadn't gotten a tux. (Nobody told me! I was in jeans. Isn't that what people wear to what was then WWF, now WWE?) It was a really unique venture. The spectators were casual, but the show was a formal event.

The promoters were adamant: **"DO NOT AD-LIB. DO NOT MOVE OFF YOUR MARK."**

The fight was a huge, scripted, live show. Everybody needed to know where everybody else was supposed to be, including the radio guy who showed up in blue jeans. You couldn't have some local disc jockey throwing everyone else off.

For the first couple of bouts, I read the script. My movement was drilled into me. (**"DO NOT DEVIATE AT ALL!"**)

I read *exactly* what was on the paper, verbatim. At one point, I introduced Jesse Ventura and **THEN** the challenger, in that order. I read it word-for-word, but—for some reason I still don't know to this day—the future Governor of Minnesota *RIPPED* into me. If it was part of the show, I didn't know it. If it was acting, he was in the moment. I was certainly convinced. I defended what I'd done "wrong" in my announcing job! Maybe they wanted me to react, but to me, he seemed sincerely pissed (and did I mention, he was HUGE?).

It seemed my radio career was growing fast. As for working appearances, though, I was grateful that event was a one-time stint, and I didn't really do more unless there was someone I wanted to help out or an event I really wanted to attend. *One thing I did yearn to do was advance my career.*

IN WEDLOCK
A Marriage And A Mentor

"You can't always get what
you want, but if you try
sometime, you just might find,
you get what you need."

▶ FROM: *You Can't Always Get What You Want*
BY: *The Rolling Stones, Let It Bleed*
(Decca/UK – London/US, 1969)

*I*N the short stint I'd had at WZUU, I met an intern who seemed like the woman who could complete the other half of the relationship I had been yearning for from the time I had my first, crappy, kitchen-side-table date years prior. Pam Brickman was still a senior in high school when we first met. She went away to college, but ended up coming back. We missed one another. Following the script I'd learned from the sitcoms that raised me, the next logical step was marriage.

There was our little bit of an age difference between us. Not a lot, but enough to have her brother admit to me that he didn't even want to like me. But he ultimately did–and so did her parents. Pam and I hadn't really discussed what marriage and family should look like. We didn't talk about so many of the important things: homes, jobs, dreams, or if we wanted kids. (I did. She didn't. She was a kid. I was a big kid.)

Pam's dad was a partner at the Polacheck Company. Bob Polacheck began the company, after working for another firm, when he was fifty years-old, and he became the Vince Lombardi of commercial real estate. He found the site that is now the U.S. Bank building, Milwaukee's tallest skyscraper, amongst a number of other claims to fame.

Polacheck was also one of first people to start thinking about shopping centers. He came back from Texas to put together what turned out to be Southgate, a strip mall that was the first in Milwaukee. He conceived it, found the tenants, and was the broker. The investment came from a man who owned a malt company in the height of the beer industry, but he was looking to make his money for something more important. He invested and Bob got Southgate off the ground, followed by the suburban Mayfair Mall. Because Bob had made a ton of money for the Southgate investor, he was willing to invest again. Ultimately, the investor earned enough money to pursue his own pet dream. The investor's name was Kurtis Froedtert and he donated eleven million dollars to open the private Froedtert Hospitals that today treat thousands through cancer treatments, organ donations, critical injuries, and the most serious medical cases. When I met him, Bob Polacheck was in his eighties and he was so intense, so professional, and so full of integrity. He worked right up until his passing.

Pam's father, Mark Brickman, was very successful in the retail aspect of commercial real estate. He opened my eyes to an industry I never knew existed and he wanted to show me more. I decided to accept his offer of spending a few days observing the work. Keep in mind, I had my days free after ending a morning show at 10:00 A.M. I spent one day with a retail real estate agent looking at land. I spent another day with an industrial real estate agent. It was a different era in manufacturing. We toured through dirty, vacant buildings. Today, you could eat off the floors of most factories.

I also spent a day in the "office group," learning about commercial real estate while being wined and dined. I liked the last one best and kept that in mind for the future. Mark suggested that I get my real estate license during my free time. I knew this opportunity he was offering me could change my life and I went about taking advantage of it.

Pam and I had only been married for a couple of years when I sat down with her dad and said that I was adamant that, if I worked for him, I didn't want special treatment. Everyone respected that. I got to join my father-in-law's company. It was the best of the best and I learned alongside the most respected professionals in the industry.

In my first ten years with Polacheck, I worked my butt off. My first year, I was a total sponge; I learned as much as I could. I didn't watch TV or even listen to music outside of my show. I switched from mornings to afternoons, switched from WQFM to WKLH for six months before joining Polacheck, and ultimately switched careers. I eventually worked my way up to partner at Polacheck at the end of my first decade in the business.

While life at work and with my father-in-law was going great, after a while, Pam and I grew apart. Maturity-wise, we were both still so young. We shared a nice little house in suburban Fox Point, Wisconsin, but we were growing in different directions.

We decided to divorce.

My then-father-in-law Mark could not have been more magnanimous when I told him that Pam and I couldn't make it work. He said he was able to separate the two things and, by his word, he did, and we remained colleagues for years. How he handled it couldn't have been any better. It allowed me to remain on my career path. He gave me that career path in the business world and it changed my life. It would be hard to find a person as good as Mark to emulate and I hope I've lived up to his example with some of the people I've helped along the way in commercial real estate.

Following the divorce, there wasn't a lot of *emotional* pain. That's not to make light of the end. We definitely went into the marriage believing it would last. I felt much more shame than I did pain. Some

▶▶ **I felt much more shame than I did pain.**

of that shame was retrospective, because I know we could have made it work at a more mature place in our lives. I still lived my own life, just with somebody else sharing my home. I didn't know any differently. That's all I'd seen. I was also ashamed because my peers were making it work . . . and I couldn't.

Pam remarried relatively quickly and her new husband, Andy Schlesinger, reached out to me to make sure all was good. Interestingly, his brother became the President of the Milwaukee Brewers. Andy asked me to a Brewers game and we had a guy's afternoon. That marriage didn't last, either and, eventually, Pam married Len Kasper, now the TV play-by-play announcer of the Chicago Cubs. Given my inherent dislike of the Cubs . . . I still wish them all the best.

Before the intensity of the Polacheck Company really kicked in, I enjoyed my life. I didn't set an alarm clock. I got up when I wanted. I'd go out to lunch and get things done for my real estate career. I got into the station at about 1:15 P.M. to be on the air from 2:00 P.M. to 6:00 P.M. Then I'd go out.

As simple as my lifestyle had become, though, it also bored me after a while. I was ready for the business world challenges, but the radio challenges began subsiding. One creative thing that snapped a bit in me was that I was coming from a morning show with freedom and this afternoon show that fit into my new lifestyle was all music. The program director wouldn't allow me the flexibility I desired. I had rock stars like Ian Hunter of Mott The Hoople calling me to talk, and the station didn't want me putting them on the air. Now, I was limited to thirty-second blocks of creativity between songs.

Instead of being in my listeners' living rooms when I worked in the studio, I was on an island.

IN TUNE
Life On the FM Dial

"Blue skies smilin' at me.
Nothing but blue skies
do I see
Blue days all of them gone
Nothing but blue skies
from now on."

▶ *FROM: Blue Skies*
BY: Willie Nelson, Stardust
(Columbia, 1978)
Originally: Irving Berlin, 1926 (32 US Recordings)

*I*F you pushed me, and please never push me to make such a choice, but Willie Nelson's *Stardust* album is one of the albums I would try to take on a desert island ... you know, a desert island with a turntable. As to the other albums, I'll leave them a mystery for now. They may, in fact, be a mystery to me!

I wasn't always revered as a "professor" or historian of music. I didn't have a real working knowledge of the songs on that album, but it was a great American songbook. That album made me listen to, appreciate, and learn about all of these great American songs–so *many* great songs! "Blue Skies" was optimistic and joyful. I listened to it over and over again and—when Rock & Roll Roots came into my life—while I was supposed to play Rock & Roll, my life was feeling all "Blue Skies." Being someone who was moved by many genres of music, I knew there were other people in the audience who would be open to hearing different music too.

▶▶ **While I was supposed to play Rock & Roll, my life was feeling all "Blue Skies."**

Early in my professional real estate career, I'd already had more than a decade in radio studios due to my start being while I was still in high school. After WUWM in high school and WSUW in college, I worked as a stringer covering sports teams. That was followed by those lonely but freedom-filled days working overnights at WQFM and—for a stint—as a production director at WZUU, where I met Larry the Legend. I returned to my on-air efforts when I went back to WQFM for the morning drive time, but 4:00 A.M. wakeup calls were not a natural match for me. When my real estate career was in its early preparation stage, the shift to afternoons at WKLH was a great fit.

Even though I was willing to give notice, WQFM wasn't thrilled about my leaving their morning show to do afternoons at WKLH. So they pulled out my contract and waived the noncompete clause both at my face, and through their attorney, with the threat of going to court. Back when I signed the contract, under some duress, I had stated that I would only agree to the terms on the first page and removed everything between that and the signature page. I gave that back to them (so I could get my paycheck). However, they reinserted all the legalize! They were preventing me from working. I had no money coming in and had to hire an attorney to answer their suit.

WKLH was patient for a few weeks and kept checking back. I checked with my attorney and nobody was budging. About six weeks into the ordeal, I turned on the radio one afternoon and heard a guy on WKLH saying, "Hey, I'm happy to be here from Detroit. I look forward to getting to know you, Milwaukee!"

I admit I cried a little. Then, I got angry and called my attorney. I asked him to inform WQFM that they cost my livelihood and now I had nothing more to lose. He did . . . and they backed off.

I found out that Tom Joerres, the general manager of WKLH, had flown in the new talent as a ruse to fool WQFM, but the job was still mine. It was the single kindest (while nefarious) thing anyone had ever done for me. I did the afternoon shift at WKLH for about six months. Little did I know the relationship would last a lifetime.

I needed to devote all of my energies to learning commercial real estate–the business, the terminology, and the skills necessary to being successful. I was lucky that, from radio, I already had decent articulation and communication skills. That worked for me. From my sports-stringer days, I understood how to read a room. The details would come, but I was spending that first year in the field being a sponge.

I needed to divorce from everything else in life, and that meant radio, too. So, for the first time since I'd cut out my cardboard transistor radio as a child, I gave up the dream, got off the air, and became a career man . . . away from the FM dial.

I was totally immersed in commercial real estate, but WKLH kept coming back to me. "Want to do a show?"

Steve: Do you ever say, "Thank God for music?" You could have been a journalist or worked on roads.

Ian Hunter (Mott The Hoople): I did work on roads. I had forty-four jobs all together.

Steve: Did you just say forty-four jobs?

Ian: Yeah, because you could get work (gigs) in Germany in the clubs, but you couldn't get any work in England except maybe a Saturday night.

Steve: What was the worst of the forty-four?

Ian: Probably washing milk bottles because you had to start at 4:00 in the morning.

"No." Every time. I even had an offer to do TV commercials, but I never bit. WKLH was persistent, though. Tom Joerres would ping me respectfully every couple of weeks.

Finally, I met him for lunch along with the station's sales manager.

"We have a Sunday morning opening. We envision you having a Sunday morning show."

This was different than interviewing for a show. They wanted me. Earlier in my career, when I was doing my morning show in Milwaukee, and before I delved into real estate, I was starting to think about whether I should move to another city.

▶▶ **They wanted me.**

What if I would have gone out to LA and done what I was doing in Milwaukee, but in a major media market?

What if my loyal listeners could have included the Steven Spielbergs of the world?

Should I try to make it in a major market?

The program director of WQFM had moved to Philadelphia, which was the number-five market in the United States at the time. He kept recruiting for Philly, but I was a combination of naïve and comfortable with priorities that weren't in order. I thought, *I don't like the Philadelphia Eagles. That won't work.*

Around that time, I had some friends in St. Louis and someone mentioned a radio station in St. Louis that was becoming a sports station. I was to hop on a plane after my show, do an on-air audition, get wined & dined by them, and feel it out.

"That's cool," I said. "I'm in."

They made arrangements for my transportation, entertainment, a nice hotel, and a nice dinner. I was used to goofiness, banter, stunts, and some music on my morning show; but this was afternoon sports. I never mail it in. I did some preparation, but I didn't do the prep necessary for a totally new genre that required hours of talk.

It was a disaster.

Both interviews I had scheduled during the block ended up falling through. They didn't call in! Here I was taking calls from people in a city that I knew nothing about and I had no guests. I hadn't yet tapped into my confidence or on-air honesty. I shouldn't have tried to fake it.

What the hell do I know about St. Louis?

I don't know that I belonged there. Just because there was an opportunity doesn't mean it was *my* opportunity. Life works out as it should. The worst part, though, was NOT fumbling on-air and dropping the ball . . . sports pun intended. It was not the fact that I could have done better, either. The worst part was that they still took me to a ballgame and out to dinner afterward. There was an uncomfortable awkwardness of obligation. They couldn't have been nicer, but it was a stew of failure.

▶▶ **Just because there was an opportunity doesn't mean it was *my* opportunity.**

I needed the wake-up call that it's not easy, you can't leave preparation to chance, and—if you don't apply yourself—you may as well stay where you are. It's these lessons that I thought about as I was facing another opportunity for a radio show. After all, I was dedicated to a new path in my commercial real estate career. I didn't want to do a show if I wasn't going to be able to bring it my best.

I had a love for Tom Joerres as a leader, but that wouldn't have been enough, until they shared the other details.

"Listen, your name recognition is starting to erode, so it's really now or never. You're a brand and that won't last forever. Second, you'll have total freedom."

Their only suggestions were the name of the show: *Rock & Roll Roots*, and to have a weekly *Root Salute Artist*.

I WAS IN.

THAT WAS JUNE OF 1987.

THE SHOW HAS BEEN

ON THE AIR EVER SINCE.

The new creative freedom I had opened the floodgates of Rock & Roll Roots. I've managed to balance the weekend broadcasts of my show and my commercial real estate career in the three-plus decades since.

Keith Harmon, my radio buddy back from the Reagan inauguration days, talked about the fact that there is synergy and magic in radio when it's all working. When you're clicking with the audience, nothing can beat it. I understood that feeling then. There's something special about being recognized for being on the air. It's funny how you can listen to someone's voice and you paint a picture of him or her. But being recognized for who I was certainly beat the times over the years I got recognized around Wisconsin . . . for looking like Senator Russ Feingold. Not that I don't get the resemblance.

In a lot of ways, it was Steve Eichenbaum, the advertising executive who helped to get Russ into office, as a side note, who helped launch Rock & Roll Roots. I had the opportunity to cross paths with him early in my own career to generate buzz for the new show. He was a true marketing genius who I worked with when Tom wanted to take us outside of our comfort zones. His idea was genuinely unique; he decided to put me into a lot of the iconic rock moments of history. The tag line was that *"Steve Palec was there."*

In a day before Photoshop was commonplace, there was real volume to the campaign he put together. They measured me and put me into exact poses for each picture in the series that would appear in newspapers, marketing materials, and even one on the side of a bus. When the series eventually got national exposure, it ended up in Billboard Magazine.

Steve Palec Was There.

"ROCK N' ROLL ROOTS" WITH STEVE PALEC EVERY SUN 9-NOON. THERE WITH THE ARTISTS WHILE HISTORY WAS BEING MADE. JOIN THIS VETERAN DJ KNOWS SO MUCH ROCK N' ROLL TRIVIA HIM FOR A DISCOVERY TOUR LEADING ALL THE WAY AND INSIDE DOPE, YOU'D SWEAR HE WAS RIGHT FROM THE 60's AND 70's TO THE PRESENT WKLH 96FM /CLASSIC HITS

The most impactful picture had me next to John Lennon and Yoko Ono on the *Two Virgins* album cover.

"Okay, we're ready," they said. "Take off your shirt."

No problem.

"Great. Now, drop your pants."

What?!

Steve Palec Was There.

"ROCK N' ROLL ROOTS" WITH STEVE PALEC EVERY SUN 9-NOON. THERE WITH THE ARTISTS WHILE HISTORY WAS BEING MADE. JOIN THIS VETERAN DJ KNOWS SO MUCH ROCK N' ROLL TRIVIA HIM FOR A DISCOVERY TOUR LEADING ALL THE WAY AND INSIDE DOPE, YOU'D SWEAR HE WAS RIGHT FROM THE 60's AND 70's TO THE PRESENT WKLH 96FM /CLASSIC HITS

I may not have actually stood in the buff with John and Yoko, but I do have some amazing memories, opportunities, and experiences from the years I've spent on the air, both before and during my tenure with Rock & Roll Roots.

> ▶▶ **I may not have actually stood in the buff with John and Yoko.**

Max Weinberg of Bruce Springsteen's E Street Band was coming to Potawatomi Hotel and my friend, Bob Rech, thought it would be great to do a storyteller series. We realized I could be a good host for the program. Weinberg's Jukebox show, wherein he played other band's hits, was already phenomenal. His manager convinced him to do fifteen minutes with me. Max was looking at this as an obligatory commitment.

When Max and I met, I could tell he wasn't sure what to think of me. I'm sure he'd had plenty of experiences in the past when his interviews and media experiences were centered, not around him, but Springsteen. But I'd done my homework, knew how to interest an audience, and it didn't hurt that I was a true fan . . . *of him*. In front of the audience, Weinberg lit up. It was entertaining, fun, maybe even cathartic to him.

We were at about the fourteen-minute mark when he said, "Let's keep going," and we talked for double what was expected.

I really believe audiences connect when there are stories behind the people who bring them their music.

> ▶▶ **I really believe audiences connect when there are stories behind the people who bring them their music.**

I went to California a few times on business over the years, sometimes combining with personal trips, such as when my son was looking at schools out there. I love LA. I remember being at breakfast one morning and looking over to see Carlos Santana next to me. I didn't bother him, but couldn't believe he was just there. It's so different and exciting in that city! I felt like a kid again, going out of my own "neighborhood" to take in a new experience.

I was at the hotel pool in the afternoon on one of my California trips. I was sitting there when I spotted a silver-haired, tanned, fit (for probably about eighty-years old), fun, gregarious, chain-wearing gentleman. I was just having a drink and catching some rays. He was making conversation and it turned to music, so I was all in.

He said "You're never going to know the groups I know."

This man began naming off songs and I named the artists:

He said, "*Green Tambourine.*"

I said, "Lemon Pipers."

He said, "*The Rapper.*"

I said, "Jaggerz."

He said, "*One Toke Over The Line.*"

I said, "Brewer & Shipley."

He said, "*Oh Happy Day!*"

I said "Edwin Hawkins Singers." And on and on . . .

Amused by our conversation, the man shared, "All of those records were on Buddha Records and I was an executive at Buddha Records."

I had worked at radio stations all my life and some songs were played so often that they were ingrained. The knowledge was in the forefront file folder in my head. I even knew the length of each song. (To this day I can tell you Creedence Clearwater Revival's "Fortunate Son" clocks in at 2:23. Funny the stuff that takes up brain space.) This man didn't know that he'd run into the random guy from Wisconsin who actually had a box set from Buddha

Records. I could even describe it to him–the box and the list of artists and songs. I got so much joy out of showing him that his music made a difference and was remembered.

Early in my years of doing Rock & Roll Roots, I got a call saying that Willie Dixon was available for an exclusive interview and would I do it? I just knew his name from a couple of songs in music, but said, "Okay."

As I began my research, though, I learned he had written not a few, but *hundreds* of songs covered by Van Morrison, The Doors, The Allman Brothers, and a bunch of other big names. This wasn't going to just be a phone interview. They brought him into the studio and I did a prerecorded live segment. I had him in the studio for an hour. He had made so many impacts behind the scenes of countless great hits over the years.

When Chuck Berry was recording at Chess Records in Chicago, Willie Dixon was in the studio and said, "Let's throw some blues on this." Chuck did a version of a country song called "Ida Red," which morphed into "Maybelline!"

In that moment, it struck me. Willie Dixon was there at the very birth of Rock & Roll, and now he was here in front of me. Wow.

He said, "I'd like to be remembered as someone who brought joy to the world through the blues."

I said I'd listen to him blow his nose.

He brought a lifelong joy to me in a single hour. I had said, "Okay," to doing the interview, but I should have screamed–just *screamed*, "YES!"

When I was doing my morning show at QFM, every day was spent looking for anything interesting that had audio and would resonate. And sometimes, you catch lightning in a bottle.

This was 1985. It was a Packers-Bears week, the twice-a-year spotlight on the NFL's oldest rivalry.

I had this insane idea. The Chicago Bears would sometimes use William "The Refrigerator" Perry in the backfield and hand off to him to score because he would be able to just plow through defenders. What could stop a refrigerator from rolling downhill?

'What if we collected refrigerator magnets,' I thought.

As the week progressed, we talked about it on the show. THOUSANDS and THOUSANDS of fridge magnets showed up. We drove to Lambeau to present the magnets to Perry. We brought this huge collection of magnets and waited in the hotel lobby for the Bears to get there. There was some local TV media coverage. They arrived (late) and two buses pulled up. The players filed in as quickly as possible. Even though I was a big sports fan and I knew I could recognize any Packer, I assumed Perry should stand out. Instead, I realized that when fifty-six huge guys stream past, four or five abreast, like a moving truck, he couldn't be spotted.

Finally, we just shouted, "HEY, we have something for you!"

Richard Dent called back, "We'll check in and come back."

When he came back and saw our collection, he left. (That was awkward.) Enough press was present, though, that—on the following Monday morning—USA Today ran a story about two Milwaukee DJs who tried to "slow down the Fridge with thousands of magnets."

On the radio, you're always competing for attention. I didn't know how things worked. The only way you were judged was by your ratings. You lived and died for them and they only came out (back then) four times a year. How do you measure buzz?

Newspapers became my source for finding relevant content. There was a story about the Channel 12 news anchor, Jerry Taff. The man had a gaggle of female interns, was a heavy hitter, and the newscast was built around him as the anchor. He always signed off with, "Good Night and Better Tomorrows."

There was an innocuous story in the paper one morning, that his own mom was suing him. She lived out of state. I tracked her down, called her up, and convinced her to go on the air. The second she said, "Maybe," I went on the air. It turned out to be a really sordid, trivial, and unfortunate internal family issue. She started railing.

"That boy didn't do this and that and the other!"

She was unstable and I knew it. My finger was ready on the bleep button. It was compelling radio, but also ugly. I was at a restaurant after my shift and the people in front of me in line said, "Hey, did you hear that thing on the radio this morning?"

People started buzzing on it. That's what I was striving for, but I wanted to do it without the guilt. I didn't mean to insert myself into a family situation. I made it a practice going forward to stay relevant, but also be patient enough to do the right thing.

I hadn't seen the show *Mythbusters*, but a business partner of mine who never asked for anything said, "Hey can you get tickets? My son just loves *Mythbusters*. They're doing two shows in Milwaukee, but they're sold out. I have to get these. Help me out, man."

I called and they said, "Steve, I know you don't ask for much, but that show sold out in MINUTES." Literally every seat had been spoken for, except for the second show on Saturday night for whomever introduced them. If I introduced them, I could have the tickets. For a friend? Sure.

I was let in the stage door and the first person I saw was Carole Caine, then of the Dave & Carole radio show. She looked like she'd seen a ghost.

"You'd better brace yourself," Carole said. "I was asked to introduce them for the first show. You'll be a part of the entire show and you're expected to interview them, too."

I said, "Carole, I've never even seen the show!"

They gave me a few short minutes to run down the program, I took a deep breath, trying to hold onto the few tidbits of information I had, and then we were ready to go!

I got to meet Mythbusters' stars Jamie Hyneman and Adam Savage and I tapped into my ability to just keep the conversation flowing through natural curiosity. I made pleasantries while trying to learn so that I could phrase my next line of questioning. I was so nervous. It turned out to be a forty-minute segment and I'd planned on about forty seconds. We had good banter and I got through it as a genial host, but I came out scared to death and understood Carole's expression.

▶▶ **It turned out to be a forty-minute segment and I'd planned on about forty seconds.**

I was a part of the entire show and I'd never even seen the program!

In the mid-80s, around the height of "We Are The World," someone decided we should do a Milwaukee song for a greater cause. Folk-music legends Peter, Paul and Mary were going to record *Children* for Project: Survival. They came up with the song and did a video with local celebrities. I was in morning radio. My celebrity was limited, but my show was on-air, so we were invited.

The song had Packers, Bucks, politicians, and local media. We were behind Peter, Paul and Mary, this big gaggle of people, and they filmed us (some singing, me mostly lip-syncing) the song. It was a blur, but I do remember a Green Bay Packer standing next to me. I got caught somewhere between not wanting to use my voice and not wanting to totally fake it, so most of what came out of my mouth was spit . . . right into the face of a giant lineman.

▶▶ **Most of what came out of my mouth was spit . . . right into the face of a giant lineman.**

I later had the chance to reconnect with George Thorogood, who I hadn't seen since the on-the-grounds shows at Summerfest, years earlier. We were planning on a phone interview. I had heard he was very cantankerous in other phone interviews; someone from a fellow station had even warned me.

When it came time to speak, I was hanging on for the ride, trying to get some emotion in the interview. Thorogood had covered a lot of songs over the years.

I asked him, "How do you cover songs that are as divergent as country and blues?"

There was an exasperated pause.

"Let me ask you something, Steve," he said. "What do Wayne Gretzky and Hank Aaron have in common?"

"Greatness?"

▶▶ **What do Wayne Gretzky and Hank Aaron have in common?**

FINALLY–he lit up. "Yes! Exactly. It doesn't matter the difference . . . both are *great*. So who cares if a song is blues or country? Greatness is the common thread."

He warmed by the end of our time and even shared some more stories about Milwaukee. I walked out realizing there was a life lesson in that interview. Greatness knows no boundaries. If you're

▶▶ **Greatness knows no boundaries.**

exceptional, passionate, and good at something, it doesn't matter what it is. The common thread is that greatness always rises above mediocrity. I've tried to use that mantra throughout my decades in radio, whether producing a segment, choosing songs, or conducting interviews.

|| ◀◀ ▶ ▶▶ ||

When I conduct artist interviews, I try to highlight greatness. I give them the accolades. I pick the tunes, do the research, and get good cuts, but I want to know what they are interested in. Some of the remarkable guests I've been honored with included:

- Greg Kihn
- Gary Tallent (E Street Band)
- Randy Bachman (Guess Who and BTO)
- David Crosby (The Byrds and Crosby, Stills, Nash, & Young)
- Graham Nash (Hollies and CSNY)
- Dave Mason (Traffic)
- Bob Welch (Fleetwood Mac)
- Jon Anderson (Yes)
- Arlo Guthrie
- Alice Cooper
- Mickey Thomas (Starship)
- Lou Reed
- Lonnie Jordan (War)
- Annie Haslam (Renaissance)
- Ian Anderson (Jethro Tull)
- Martin Barre (Jethro Tull)
- Victor DeLorenzo (Violent Femmes)
- Jenny Haan (Babe Ruth)
- Perry Jordan (Heartsfield)
- Danny Saraphine (Chicago)
- Ringo Starr (The Beatles)
- Peter Frampton
- Les Paul
- Barry Goldberg (The Electric Flag)
- Carl Palmer (ELP)
- Leon Redbone
- Ann Wilson (Heart)
- Ritchie Blackmore (Deep Purple)

▶ Roy Harper (Pink Floyd "Have a Cigar")
▶ John Prine
▶ Steve Forbert
▶ Sam Llanas (BoDeans)
▶ Elvin Bishop
▶ George Thorogood
▶ Willy Porter
▶ Richie Furay (Buffalo Springfield and Poco)
▶ Robin Trower (Procol Harum)
▶ Dr. John
▶ Jim McCarty (Yardbirds)
▶ Sam Butera (Louis Prima Band)
▶ Jim Messina (Loggins & Messina)
▶ Greg Koch
▶ Terry Reid
▶ Willie Dixon
▶ Terry Bozzio (Missing Persons and Frank Zappa)
▶ Trapper Schoepp
▶ Andy Powell (Wishbone Ash)
▶ Justin Hayward (Moody Blues)
▶ Corky Siegel (Siegel-Schwall Band)

▶ John Magnie (The Subdudes)
▶ Dean Friedman
▶ Steve Hackett (Genesis)
▶ Stephen Stills (Buffalo Springfield and CSNY
▶ Chris Difford (Squeeze)
▶ Michael Franks
▶ Peter Noone (Herman's Hermits)
▶ Graham Parker
▶ Don McLean
▶ Warren Haynes (Allman Brothers Band and Gov't Mule)
▶ Kenny Wayne Shepherd
▶ Alan Parsons
▶ Ian Hunter (Mott the Hoople)
▶ David Lindley (Jackson Browne and Warren Zevon)
▶ Roger Powell (Utopia)
▶ Johnny Rzeznik (Goo Goo Dolls)
▶ Jon Herington (Steely Dan)
▶ Robert Randolph
▶ Mickey Dolenz (Monkees)

I hold an annual Christmas special on Rock & Roll Roots. It airs the Sunday before Christmas. One year, I invited friends and notables to join me in the studio for an open house and as an on-air fundraiser for the Milwaukee Public Schools.

My main motivation is to be able to pull out a full case of awesome Christmas CDs, albums, tapes, and 45s I've accumulated throughout my life. I've done all-request Christmases, '70s Christmases, and even created a "do-it-yourself" Christmas album, with songs separated by that crackling fire sound you get from vinyl albums.

Over the years, I've done a number of unique themes. I played Motorcycle Music during the Harley-Davidson anniversary. One memorable show was based on women who have had songs written about them. As I played those tunes, a colleague was posting their photos on social media.

Every week, I include a number of articles for the interest of my listeners. Some of those "articles" have included:

▶ Swamp Rock
▶ Biopics
▶ Same Song Done Twice
▶ Dylan Collaborations
▶ Positivity
▶ Bands that Reinvented Themselves
▶ Mandolin Songs
▶ US Festival
▶ Not Fond of Encores
▶ Big Band Influences
▶ Elevator Music
▶ Lucky Breaks
▶ Groups with Multiple Vocalists
▶ Woodstock Paychecks
▶ Lip Sync
▶ Underrated Guitarists
▶ Songs with Mistakes
▶ Duos
▶ Siblings
▶ Evil Record Labels
▶ Harmonies
▶ Vegetarians
▶ The Summer of Love

▶ Songs with Bach
▶ Bands from Glasgow
▶ Finding Members Through Want Ads
▶ Trumpet
▶ Irving Azoff
▶ High Pitched Vocals
▶ Chanting
▶ CBGB
▶ Weird Time Signatures
▶ Artists Who Started a Label
▶ Vocoder
▶ Bangladesh
▶ Accordion in Rock
▶ Kazoo Songs
▶ Dogs Barking
▶ Tulsa Sound
▶ Played at the White House
▶ Clapton Drummers
▶ Underwear
▶ Slide Guitar
▶ Coconuts
▶ Maracas

I've also had *Root Salute Artists* from household names to the lesser-known people who made a real impact on the industry. My Root Salute Artists are played throughout the weekly show and, over the years, I've enjoyed featuring:

- Red Hot Chili Peppers
- John Prine
- Queen
- Earth Wind & Fire
- Dr. John
- Def Leppard
- Bob Dylan
- Stevie Wonder
- Van Morrison
- Huey Lewis
- Blondie
- Sly & The Family Stone
- Bob Seger
- Stevie Ray Vaughan
- Steve Winwood
- Alan Parsons
- John Fogerty

- The Police
- The Byrds
- Jethro Tull
- J.J. Cale
- Steely Dan
- Bonnie Raitt
- Tom Petty
- George Harrison
- James Taylor
- Linda Ronstadt
- Steppenwolf
- The Beach Boys
- Neville Brothers
- Hollies
- Three Dog Night
- Grateful Dead
- The Rolling Stones
- Dean Martin
- Pearl Jam
- Lissie

- Dave Matthews Band
- Gordon Lightfoot
- The Beatles
- Little Feat
- Frank Sinatra
- The Monkees
- Foo Fighters
- REM
- Bare Naked Ladies
- Subdudes
- Willie Nelson
- Bad Company
- The Blues Brothers
- John Hiatt
- Lyle Lovett
- Rush
- Randy Newman
- Frank Zappa

Occasionally, I've felt some segments and articles were worth more than a feature. They became full three-hour specials:

- Early Beatles Work
- Foreign Language Songs
- Solo Special
- Frequency Modulated Memories
- Unplugged
- Completely 1972

- Lilith Fair of the Air
- Beatle Buddies
- Les Paul
- Beatles Solo Albums
- 911 Anniversary
- 414 Milwaukee Special
- All Drums

- Passing Tributes to Glenn Frey, David Bowie, George Harrison
- Six Degrees (or One Degree) of Separation
- Headphone Special

Besides my three-hour specials, I've done Summerfest specials focusing on the headliners featured. Oftentimes, I'd get to introduce those artists when they put on their shows.

It's a long-standing tradition at Summerfest—and at plenty of other festivals—to use radio station DJs to introduce a headlining band before they play.

It may seem like a five-minute formality, but as usual, there's a backstory to most of what the public sees while standing on the Summerfest bleachers. I can't even remember how many shows I have introduced at Summerfest. The one that sticks out for me was one of those combination nostalgic shows with Dave Mason, Colin Hay from Men at Work, Ambrosia, and Gary Wright . . . who didn't show up.

The just-barely-underage guest I took with me proceeded to hit up the free bar backstage every time I went out to introduce another act. When I introduced Australian-based Men at Work's Colin Hay, I made a reference to Australia-famous Foster's beer, which caused him to laugh uncontrollably. At first, I was pretty proud of myself. Then, when he wouldn't stop laughing, it got downright awkward. Then, when he still didn't stop, I realized it probably had nothing to do with my wit . . . and more to do with the consumption that sometimes takes place at Summerfest.

It's impossible to fully capture more than three decades of Rock & Roll Roots and more than four decades of radio in a few pages. This summary is more than nostalgia; the few lists shared here aren't complete and serve only to remind me of the greatness I've been able to witness through the artistry of others. The various stations, roles, interviews, Root Salute Artists, specials, segments, and opportunities to introduce musicians and artists over the years have kept me in perpetual awe of the opportunities I've been lucky to share during my radio career.

▶▶ It's impossible to fully capture more than three decades of Rock & Roll Roots and more than four decades of radio in a few pages.

Awe is tied to freedom. If there is any secret to the show's success, it's that I never mail it in. I prepare four hours of material for three hours of programming. I inherently believe that my stories aren't good enough . . . so that I have to really work to make them compelling. This keeps me on my toes for every on-air moment. Plus, I have the overriding factor that of the unheard-of freedom on the show to do what I want, take chances, and sometimes cross the line in my music selections with something that is not all that melodic or Rock & Roll-worthy, but it fits into the story. I respect my audience. I never will talk down to them. I never make assumptions that my audience can't follow, even though the essence of a lot of broadcasts today is to play to the lowest common denominator. If I don't find it interesting, neither will the audience. I try to keep the intrigue of my listeners without worrying too much about taking a chance when needed and the result is something that sounds different than everything else.

The Beatles authored the first soundtrack of my life and they made my life better. I'd never purport to be nearly as influential as what I believe to be the greatest rock band of all time, but I do hope that, in now forty-five years of radio, I have been able to connect to people who related to the songs I played.

Given so many opportunities to be a part of great music and musicians over the years, I try to remember my friends' favorite artists, so I can reach out. Tracy Johnson, who runs the Commercial Association of Realtors in Wisconsin (CARW) is a huge fan of Huey Lewis. When I found out that Lewis was coming to Milwaukee, I pinged her to join me at a press conference with him. Anything to make a friend feel the joy I get from music. I've been able to share my love of music over the years with friends, colleagues, family, and clients.

In fact, that is the purpose of my show, too–to share the stories and especially the songs. I treat the Rock & Roll Roots' audience just as I would a friend I have over for a visit.

"Let me put this song on," I'll say. "I want you to hear it."

Why? To keep them there so I can sell some Amway product later? No.

It's to share something that brings me joy. It's to share that irreplaceable feeling of total awe.

Admittedly, there have been a couple of those joyful opportunities that I decided to indulge in on my own, like my friend, journalist Jim Stingl, wrote about in this article initially published in the Milwaukee Journal Sentinel:

"Instant karma's gonna get you, Gonna knock you right on the head."

"It seems appropriate to start this story with rock 'n' roll lyrics from John Lennon's "Instant Karma." The karma in question arises from a lucky break — a rather questionable lucky break — that landed Steve Palec in the front row for The Who in Milwaukee in 1982.

So it's not really instant karma. More like karma that's been lurking for 35 years. So far, Palec hasn't been knocked right on the head, and he has a plan to keep it that way and put the universe back in balance.

In the fall of 1982, Palec left his overnight DJ gig at WQFM-FM radio to be a production director at WZUU-FM. About that same time, WQFM DJ Tim "The Rock 'n' Roll Animal" U'ren announced he would sit on a ledge outside the radio station's studio until The Who agreed to play Milwaukee on its tour. He was out there 16 days and the band finally agreed to come here.

A guy that Palec knew at WQFM — he won't say who — got his hands on two front-row tickets for the hot show, which was Dec. 7, 1982, at the Arena. As the story goes, they were to be given away to a lucky listener.

"Please note, the statute of limitations has passed on the following 'wrongdoing,' " Palec told me in an email. "He said he couldn't bring himself to simply give them to someone at random that may not use them or appreciate them, or may even sell them, so he arranged instead to leave them for me. Awesome gesture. We went to great lengths to pledge confidentiality to each other and enacted layers of prevention to make sure nobody knew."

Palec went to the sold-out show. Loved it.

Here's what happened next, according to Palec's memory. He woke up the following morning and there on the front page of the Milwaukee Sentinel was a concert photo taken from behind the stage that showed him in the first row with his girlfriend at the time, both clapping their hands.

I checked our microfilm archives for Dec. 8, 1982, and found that the photo ran that afternoon in The Milwaukee Journal and on an inside page. The photographer was Allen Fredrickson.

So did the photo mean he was busted?

"I don't know if he/she/it at QFM took any heat. I would venture to guess the other people at QFM were suspicious of me being up front," Palec said. Even his new co-workers at WZUU, including Larry "the Legend" Johnson, spotted him in the photo and asked him about it.

Fast forward to now. In a mix of guilt and self-promotion, Palec will give away two front-row tickets to next

Thursday's Patti Smith concert during his radio show, Rock 'n' Roll Roots, on WKLH-FM this Sunday morning.

He said he paid $100 each for the tickets and later found he has another commitment. So they will go to a listener, just as The Who tickets were supposed to back in 1982.

Time will tell if karma is satisfied."

I'd like to think I've brought more good karma on myself than bad over the years. The artists I've come to know have given so much to me through their music, and none more than John Prine. It is his lyrics that inspired this book.

Obviously, a lot of things have changed over the fifty years I've enjoyed music at Summerfest (and forty-five of those as a DJ). To attempt to list them all would be ludicrous.

Just one of the major shifts in popular music has been how we discover both new sounds and new musicians. As a radio host for much of this half century, I'd like to think it's a format that can still assist in delighting an audience with something with which they are not familiar, especially if the host has the freedom to experiment.

▶▶ **Just one of the major shifts in popular music has been how we discover both new sounds and new musicians.**

I've been around long enough to know that experimenting is now the exception rather than the norm. More and more artists are controlling their own content, their own narratives, and their own music. They have Spotify channels, podcasts, and blogs to communicate *directly* with their audiences, rather than using radios and DJs as a vessel for their messages and brands.

Back in the early days of Summerfest, though, in the late '60s and throughout the '70s, radio was probably the go-to means of discovery for new artists. Sure, television would expose an unknown artist and it's also possible you may have ordered twelve records for a penny from Columbia House and found an unfamiliar gem. Or maybe some of your favorite artists came to your attention from friends, family, and assorted others. In a way, that was also the communal situation of radio in those days. You and your friends had your favorite stations and, when you heard something, you shared it.

When someone asks me to recount my favorite Summerfest memories, I don't hesitate to share the fact that I first discovered one of my lifelong favorite artists by walking the grounds of the festival back in 1974. If it were recreated as a cartoon, I would be shown abruptly stopping in my tracks to spin around like a punching bag. My eyes would pop out of my head toward the stage, bounce back in, and knock me on my head. The bubble above my head would be a collection of stars and music notes. The real-life details are a little fuzzier. What I do distinctly remember is stumbling across a man with a guitar on the Schlitz Country stage. Bear in mind that, at that point, I was a Beatles-influenced, Led Zeppelin-loving teenager. So the country stage would not have been a destination point. But that guy with the guitar told stories in song unlike anything I'd ever heard. That guy was John Prine.

▶▶ **That guy with the guitar told stories in song unlike anything I'd ever heard.**

Prine has gone on to write countless powerful songs. He was the first singer/songwriter to perform at the Library of Congress. He is in the Nashville Songwriters Hall of Fame. Bob Dylan called him one of his favorite artists. He won a few Grammys . . . and I have *every single one* of the many albums he has released.

That warm afternoon at Summerfest in Milwaukee in 1974, I discovered what would become the next soundtrack to much of the rest of my life. At the time, he had released three albums. I went back to not only buy those records but wear them out. I almost felt ashamed that I missed his 1971 debut. He demonstrates one of the most powerful displays of songwriting you can find. And that's the point. I missed it. I discovered a favorite voice that day I had never imagined popping up on the Schlitz stage. Milwaukee photographer

Rich Zimmermann was working for the Bugle American that afternoon and recalled that they gave away free Schlitz backstage from a barrel. I'm glad he took photographs to document not only a young John Prine, but the moment of my personal musical discovery.

John Prine on the Schlitz Stage, Summerfest, 1974. Photo Credit: Rich Zimmermann

Any time Prine comes near Milwaukee, I try to bend his ear, catch a show, get in an interview, and share his artistry with my listeners. Revealing people like John Prine is one of the joys of my life.

Years after first seeing Prine, I had the opportunity to ask him about his affinity for Milwaukee. "I've always liked big little towns," he said and I immediately knew he got it!

Steve: You seem to have such an affinity for Milwaukee

John Prine: I've always liked big little towns. I've got a place in Ireland in Galway. Galway, you can just about park and walk around the whole town. It's still big enough in Ireland to be a big town. And I like working class towns. Milwaukee is definitely that.

He understood the city I loved, where we had all of the amenities of a big city (music, sports, shopping, culture, night-scene, colleges, work of all types and levels, etc.) and all of the warmth of a small town (community, festivals, parks, and local heroes).

The fabric, image, and sophistication of Milwaukee has changed over the years, just as music has. That afternoon in 1974, though, when I first saw and heard one of America's treasures in John Prine, is forever stamped in my mind. The more things change, the more they stay the same. And the more I was grateful to have a vessel through radio to share my excitement about unique artists.

The excitement in media remains even as life on the FM dial has changed and I've been blessed to be a part of it all. People think you're a part of something bigger than you really are and, at the same time, they relate because you're a local celebrity. It's fascinating to be a part of that.

However, two things do irk me about this world. The first thing is something that has changed since I entered the studio forty-five years ago. The red "on-air" light? It used to symbolize something very special; it held a respect I've rarely witnessed; it meant magic was taking place. Now it's just, at best, a warning not to swear.

▶▶ **The red "on air" light? It used to symbolize something very special; it held a respect I've rarely witnessed; it meant magic was taking place.**

The other thing that gets to me is the term "local celebrity." It's just silly. What is gratifying is anything that gets people to listen. That's what it's supposed to be about. I've had a few free meals, a pat on the back, a few shouts, and—admittedly—once it got me out of a traffic violation. But there is nothing better than someone saying, or texting, or emailing, or posting that they like what I did, a song I played, a memory I shared, or a bit of trivia I revealed. That is the reason I do the show.

FM has gone the way of the record–the door was closing and now it's back on the uptick. What had to happen was that the casuals all went away and only the active audience is left. But the active audience is so passionate. The FM signal is physical, has a sense of place, and is in the air.

A few more FM memories – colleagues, Adam West Day, Elvira contests, good friends, and good tunes

Don't let anybody kid you.

Whether it is satellite, on demand, on your phone, or in your car, people are not listening to just devices. They are listening to content. *I have been lucky to be a creator of that content for decades and I've never lost awe of that honor and gift.*

IN MEMORIAM
Farewell To A Legend

"Vaya con dios, my darling.
Vaya con dios, my love.
Now the village mission bells
are softly ringing.
If you listen with your heart,
Youll hear them singing.
Vaya con dios, my darling.
Vaya con dios, my love."

▶ FROM: *Vaya Con Dios*
BY: *Les Paul and Mary Ford (Single)*
(Capitol Records, 1954)

L ES Paul was one of the original creators of and gifts to rock and blues. He absolutely changed the face of music and Rock & Roll forever. It's ironic seeing as he was a jazz, country, and blues artist. But think about it. Can you imagine a Rock & Roll song without an electric guitar? Me neither. Not a whole lot of people outside of Southeast Wisconsin realize that the great guitarist was known, amongst other well-earned titles, as the Wizard of Waukesha, so named for the electric and musical magic he created in his living room laboratory in the city where he grew up. Actually, outside of the Milwaukee suburb itself, I'd venture to say that not a lot of people knew Les Paul, the *man*, at all. He was just the name on their Gibson electric guitars. In the middle-sized, close-knit community twenty miles west of Milwaukee, though, he is remembered, respected, and revered as much as if not more than he ever was in Nashville or New York.

The city of Waukesha, affectionately known as Guitartown, is decorated throughout with electric guitar sculptures created and painted by Wisconsin-based artists. They have a Les Paul Middle School and a crosstown road named Les Paul Parkway (plus a lot of intertwined streets that you can get lost in). The museums have exhibits to the iconic musical genius and even the art district that leans eclectic can't help but make nods to the King of the Electric, who was born and raised there.

I was already a bit of a local radio and music celebrity by the time the Waukesha Historical Society was working on its Les Paul exhibit concept. Sue Baker, who was a part of the project, had been in touch with the legend to do some fundraising, by putting together a show and an exclusive, extensive interview in high definition. She reached out to me over lunch and asked if I would conduct the interview. I didn't know as much about Les as I do now, but I knew enough to make the answer easy. *Would I be willing to interview the father of the solid-bodied electric guitar—the guitar model played by everyone from The Allman Brothers to Eric Clapton to Jerry Garcia?*

"YES. Absolutely!"

Steve: Do you ever just pick up your guitar with no one around and play for yourself or for fun?

Peter Frampton: Oh absolutely. I'm still learning. I still take lessons and jam with people just to pick up new ideas. The reason I started is that I have a passion for it and it's never gone away. Whether I'm playing onstage or not making a record, I'm still playing my Les Paul guitar every day for my own enjoyment. That's how it started.

Then, I began my research. (Preparing of course!) The man invented so much–microphone techniques, the harmonica holder, multi-track recording, everything! The pedal boards that guitarists use today - they didn't exist in Les Paul's day. Instead, he learned how to create all of those effects manually–the effects that took such a high level of skill that they are now programmed into boards to create things like reverb and looping. Even today, the best electric chops don't do it alone; because of this invention, they owe much of their ability to Les Paul.

But I didn't want to overdo my studying. I believed to a certain degree in the Larry King philosophy of doing interviews. King purposely limited his research so that he wouldn't inundate his listeners or guests with facts and figures. Know just enough to be intrigued. If you're intrigued, you'll ask questions that a normal person would ask in a casual conversation. I wanted to be knowledgeable and not naïve, but open to curiosity for asking as many things as I wanted to know, regardless of where the conversation went. I wasn't sure how long our time together would last when the day came and I wanted to be fully present and engaged rather than glued to an arbitrary script.

When he came to town, Les was going to have a show the night before our interview together and I was asked to introduce him.

Again, "YES. Absolutely!"

About a week before the show was supposed to happen, I was called and told that "Steve & Johnnie," radio partners from WGN in Chicago, where they were talk-radio royalty, were coming up to do the introduction and I was asked if I minded sharing the stage with them. Are you kidding? It was a double honor. I had a great deal of respect for Steve & Johnnie, so having them there was just a bonus on the already exciting evening. Years later, Steve & Johnnie included me in a book they were writing about Les Paul, "A Little More Les," by Steve King and Johnnie Putnam[13]. I'm grateful for the mutual respect we shared.

---

[13] *Bantry Bay Books, County Cork, Ireland*

When the night of the show arrived, I turned into the hotel lot where everything was happening. It was intense–borderline chaotic. I don't think they realized the pull the legend would have. Television trucks and vans, as well as print and radio journalists, were there from every station and publication in the area, in addition to the many fervent fans; it was crowded to say the least. It also wasn't planned to every detail; the local DJ was really just an afterthought, so I had to pay close attention for my cues.

As it came time to make the introduction, I realized I needed to get up on the stage. I made my way on stage and, in doing so, had to physically and gently shuffle an older man out of the way with a polite, "Excuse me."

The night was perfect. Les was sharp, cool, and as engaging as anyone I'd ever shared a stage with. He was ninety-years old and still joking, playing incredibly well, flirting like a teenager (from a gentlemanly era), and bantering with and telling stories to the crowd. Then he waited at the end of the stage to meet every single person who wanted to talk to him. And almost **EVERY SINGLE PERSON** wanted to talk to him.

The next day was our interview at the Historical Society. At one point, we had to take a break to change film. We'd been talking for quite a while already. I asked him if he'd mind slipping in my name. (Just asked!) He obliged in a big way in the next segment.

"Steve, Steve, Steve . . . stop," he said, like we'd been friends for ages. "Did you know I was the first human being on television after FDR," he went on. "It was the very first TV broadcast from Woolworth's in New York City. They had a message from the president, then switched to me."

The way he spoke was as if we were just sharing a beer and old tales together. We were two hours into the interview and I was tired, but he kept going, walked me through his whole life telling stories. There's something about hearing a person's experiences, especially when it's later in life and they are more willing to share them so that nothing is lost; it creates a kind of bond. I would end up having only a few engagements with the great man over the near-century he spent on this earth, but I could call Les a friend, almost from the start. I felt like I knew him. I wondered if he made everyone feel that way.

At some point during the afternoon, I glanced over and saw the old guy I had scooted past from the night before. "Who is that?" I asked one of the crew.

"That's Les Paul's son, Rusty." I couldn't believe it.

When we finished the interview, I got a picture with the *original* guitar legend and he signed my Les Paul CD box set.

Les did make it back to Milwaukee a few years later; he did a show at our historic Pabst Theater and threw out the first pitch at the Brewers game. This was 2008; Les Paul was throwing out the first pitch at ninety-three-years old!

I remember asking him, "Les, how do you want us to remember you?"

"What do I care," he said. "I'll be dead." He had such a cutting sense of humor.

He lived a little more than another year. When Les passed away on August 12, 2009, I was called by Dave Luczak at WKLH. The funeral home was looking for someone to help host the funeral, and he thought I would be better suited than he. That was magnanimous.

They asked, "Would you do it?"

Again, "Yes." *For that man?* "Absolutely. I'd be honored."

I showed up at Discovery World Museum in Milwaukee at 3:45 in the afternoon. He was lying in state there, where the exhibit on his life ultimately landed after being put together the year I first got to meet the great musician. There was going to be a procession from Discovery World to his burial place in Waukesha. I rode with another person in the procession and there were people across the whole route holding signs of appreciation and adoration. The respect was shown all the way to the graveside.

I remembered another thing Les had said to me: "If I can still continue to bring pleasure to people after I'm gone," he said, "that's enough for me."

"I'm sitting on top of the world
Just rolling along, just rolling along.
I'm quitting the blues of the world
Just singing a song, just singing a song."

▶ FROM: *I'm Sitting On Top Of The World*
BY: *Les Paul and Mary Ford (Single)*
(Capitol Records, 1953)

I wish he could have seen all of the people who came out to honor him; he'd know the impact he made. His wishes were met.

Les Paul, who was actually born Lester William Polsfuss on June 9, 1915, was a veteran, so his casket was flag-draped in the stars and stripes. The time spent at the burial site was surreal. It's always sad to lose a hero, but he'd lived a long, full, and impactful life, so it wasn't a tragedy. I started introducing the speakers and everybody genuinely loved the *man*, not just the *legend*.

After the last speaker, I said, "I can't imagine a world without music and I can't imagine music without Les Paul." I didn't plan the words. I opened my mouth and that's what came out. I meant them.

I made eye contact with one of the military detail sent for the honors. That was enough. We didn't verbally communicate. That look told them it was their cue. They performed a gunshot salute, folded the flag, and gave it to Rusty.

My life is better for having been in the presence of Les Paul.
"We love you, Les."

In the Suburbs
The All-American Life

"I'm tired Joey Boy while
you're out with the sheep.
My life is so troubled.
Now I can't go to sleep."

▶ *FROM: I'm Tired Joey Boy*
BY: Van Morrison, Avalon Sunset
(Polydor, 1989)

I HAD paternal instincts and a desire to love my own child from a pretty early age. I really wanted to have kids. I had no experience or parenting skills from a sibling or watching kids when I was younger. Maybe it's just that I wanted to do it better than I had experienced, but I think every generation feels that to some extent. By 1991, I was married again, this time with Amy, a woman who shared my itch to build a family.

One little problem in retrospect that probably got us off on the wrong foot. She hated Wisconsin. She was there for one year on business and planned to move back to Colorado. We met one month before she was scheduled to leave and those plans went out the window.

I was unbearable during Amy's pregnancy. I read "What to Expect When You're Expecting,"[14] but she didn't. I was all into it, super passionate to know everything I could. I learned as much as possible while I was an expectant father and I got into trouble for it, too.

"You can't do that," I'd say. "You have to do it this way."

I even committed the ultimate husband *faux pas*. Reading the sports section one morning, I saw the new Packers roster. It listed all of the players, their positions, what colleges they came from, their heights, and their weights. I said, "You weigh more than some of the players!"

BAD!

I had a better filter on the air. I could have used it then.

When my son Joey was born and was literally a minute old, I stuck my finger into his little hand. He grabbed it and it was one of the most powerful moments of my entire life. This was the Super Bowl of awe. Then, after a couple of days in the hospital, it was time to go home. I remember coming up with something I've shared with other parents for years: any male can father a child, but it takes real dedication to figure out how to put in a car seat. It was like NASA wrote the car seat instructions! And this was just the beginning. I was never more nervous in my life than taking my son home from the hospital for the first time. I couldn't believe they were letting us leave . . . with a *human*!

▶▶ **Any male can father a child, but it takes real dedication to figure out how to put in a car seat.**

Parenting to newborns is difficult. At least, it was for me. You have to be responsible and put in pure maintenance with very little in return–no reciprocated bond felt like it was there in the beginning. Thank God I was given an internal joy and responsibility with being

---

[14] *"What to Expect When You're Expecting" by Heidi Murkoff with Sharon Mazel, Workman Publishing Company*

a parent. I don't know how else I would have gotten through. Then, a few weeks in, there was a reaction, at last, a smile that's intentional, and it became a whole different ball game. Suddenly, I was in this life together as a family.

I had such an intensity with wanting to get it all right, not just the car seat, but recognizing the specialness through the difficult times, focusing on the magic moments, the times that brought a feeling of awe. It was like we were living in a bubble for a little while–full immersion family bonding.

Then came a return to normalcy and I plugged back into just how stupid I could be. My buddy Keith Templin and I took Joey to a Brewers game on a ninety-five-degree day. My son was just an infant. It started out bad enough. We . . . um . . . left the house without him at first and had to drive back.

Once we were there, though, we realized our even bigger mistake–blazing sun on a newborn head. Maybe it was a little soon to take him out to the ball game. We moved out of our seats to keep Joey in the shade. Inside, he was a complete magnet for the ladies.

On the other hand....

Left to right: Sam, Joe, and Steve - three generations of the Palec family

Three years after Joey, our daughter Haley was born, in 1994, and so began the traditional husband and father roles in my life, some of my proudest titles I carry. I was still working long hours; too many hours I now know. And, to those hours, I added more. One other thing I did during this time period was transform my body by working out with a trainer three times a week. However, we also found time to do all of the things that you would expect of a young family.

I firmly believe that children are born with an inherent personality that stays with them for life. Haley, from her earliest days, was (as well as an infant can demonstrate) reserved, thoughtful and sweet. Joe was on his way to the unique personality that today has him as an up and coming celebrated artist in Denver.

Back in the late '90s, the WKLH morning show had Brett Favre on as a regular guest. When the Brett Favre Steakhouse opened in Milwaukee, it was a natural idea to host a live broadcast from that hotspot. I was invited as one of the on-air guests. Joe was only about six years old and I took him with me for the event.

When I was called up onstage to sit with hosts Dave & Carole, as well as Brett and (the first time I met him) LeRoy Butler, what I had forgotten was that I had a six-year old with me.

I told Joe to stand in a spot in the crowded bar and restaurant and I would come back for him. He later told me he thought it was really cool that they announced my name and the audience applauded.

Onstage, I bantered for about ten minutes with my radio cohorts and the two NFL All Stars. Then, I hustled down to find Joe at the bar with three of Favre's Mississippi buddies about to do a shot with them!

I circumvented that plan and, moments later, Brett wandered over. At that time I had some disposal income and thought it was pretty cool to order autographed items and sports memorabilia. In fact, a week before, I had purchased a signed Joe Montana 49ers helmet. (I still don't know why; I've only ever been a Packers fan.)

I introduced Favre to my son. He knelt down, shook his hand, and talked for a moment. Something snapped in me. I recognized that the interaction between the two of them was more valuable than any *item* I could ever purchase.

Another event that illustrated Joe's ability to connect with people occurred in Cozumel, Mexico when he was about eleven. He, Haley, and I were walking through a tourist area and found ourselves outside a strip club. I jokingly told Joe to go in. (Let's assume the statute of limitation on my bad parenting has expired.) Before I could stop him, he did!

I thought, *'Okay, I'll teach you a lesson. There will be someone at the door that throws you out in about two seconds.'*

About thirty seconds later, I got worried.

Since I had Haley with me, I sure didn't want her standing outside on the street by herself. I wasted another minute trying to figure out what to do. Since Haley was the responsible one of the three of us, I found a spot where I could trust her to remain.

I was now at the two-minute mark with no bouncer arriving with my son. I went inside the club and had to navigate my way about fifty feet in. There, at a darkened bar area, Joe was holding court entertaining five dancers. I whisked him away, grabbed Haley, and found a safer environment.

We moved to Cedarburg, a city that is every bit the picture you get in your mind when you hear the name "Cedarburg." It was (and is) an upper-middle class community with shops, wineries, festivals, lovely homes, and great schools.

I loved playing softball and I played on lots of teams religiously. My buddy Keith had a team and took it pretty seriously too. He invited me to join. A lot of the guys were older and, through attrition, dropped out. The radio station sponsored us and we played Tuesdays and Thursdays, in a good, competitive league.

One of my real estate colleagues was a gifted ballplayer with great skills. His arm was a cannon! He could throw a ball as fast as anyone I'd ever seen. Everyone wanted to recruit him, but he was a southside Milwaukee guy. They were oblivious to the north and vice versa. He turned down lots of opportunities and never went north of I-94!

I kept trying to convince him. I said, "Come out one night, play with us, and see if you like it."

We had to open up a roster spot because we were allowed only so many out-of-district teammates. Finally, he acquiesced and he easily lived up to the hype. He fielded effortlessly and was a left-handed hitter who sent almost every ball to or over the fence. We went to Village Pub after that and every game. It was a great neighborhood bar that was big enough to accommodate many people.

Because there was an event going on in the pub, something we didn't even realize, the place was packed with beautiful women! His eyes were wide. He walked in, looked around . . . and permanently joined the team!

Our Cedarburg house and acreage were always a good place for a great time and—when we didn't go out into the community—we brought the party home. My joy for an over-the-top party was actually a carryover from my life after my first marriage. Post-divorce, I was living in suburban Fox Point, in a nice house that my first wife and I had picked out together. In those days, boxing was a big deal. When I was a kid, I never had access to fights during the Ali era; it just wasn't available live on regular television and closed-circuit or cable services didn't exist. The big way to watch fights when my generation's first boxing giant, Iron Mike Tyson, gained popularity, was through pay per view. I ordered a Tyson fight, invited friends over, and was planning for the event to be a big deal.

"I've got the fight. Come over," wasn't going to be good enough for one of my events. There had to be something people would talk about so that I could tell the story decades later.

What does a fight have? Card girls every single round who walk through the ring with the number of the upcoming round!

I wanted to hire card girls! I picked up the phone, the yellow pages if you can remember those, and looked up modeling agencies. I talked to the head of an agency and said I wanted to hire twelve models for an event.

I ended up hiring twelve different models—one for each round. Only guys were invited over to watch the fight. I had a nice, finished basement rec room and the girls could be down there in their own space. There was a basement entrance, they could get their cards, be given directions for the evening, and have a private place to change.

As a surprise, a buddy gave a signal and the first girl came up as the fight got started. My guests thought it was awesome. Little did they know there were eleven more models waiting in the basement!

…and little did *I* know that Tyson would win in less than thirty-seconds, against Marvis Frazier!

It was a first-round knockout!

I was speechless.

This couldn't be happening.

Everybody there was surprised by the magnitude of the unusual outcome. I was shocked at the fact that I still had a roomful of eleven other models in the basement.

▶▶ **I still had a roomful of eleven other models in the basement.**

"You're not gonna believe this," I told them, "But the fight is over. You'll all get paid."

Ten of the women decided to come upstairs and hang out with all the guys. When I went to sleep, people were still there hanging out. The next morning, people were scattered around the room sleeping on couches and the floor. One of the guys at the party had told his wife that it was at an all-guy party (which was the initial plan), and his wife found out otherwise. It was hardly the worst thing he'd done, though.

In Cedarburg, I worked alongside my wife to hold gatherings. The fun was still over the top, but we tried to have surprises that didn't get anyone in hot water. We held neighborhood, community, and friend-group parties with themes. I think I could have had a great career as a party planner if I hadn't gone into radio. Sure, I'm okay with the chips in the bag rather than a bowl, but I know that you can add a level to a party with some creativity and a little willingness to tap into your network. If I hold a Super Bowl party, then I want a Super Bowl *player* there! A bourbon tasting? Let's use it to raise money for charity! A cookout? How about we bring in some live music from a national recording artist.

The series of parties that were most memorable when I was married to Amy, though, were our wine parties. We had five acres in Cedarburg and she really enjoyed wine. I could take it or leave it, but I did love her and she wanted to have a wine party. Everybody who came would bring a bottle of wine and fill out a card that explained the bottle. The first year, we had about fifty bottles. The second year, word got around. We had live music from Steve Forbert and threw the party in our yard at the top of a big, long, winding driveway. Guests were greeted by announcements playing on a stereo on a loop in the bushes at the bottom of the driveway.

My kids got a bit entrepreneurial by holding an aspirin stand. They sold packets as people came in. This is another of those times when I wonder if I should be telling this story.

A drug stand.

By my kids.

I thought it was pretty smart.

We held our wine parties for four or five years. About 250 people made it in that second year. At around 2:00 in the morning, it finally cleared out, but there was a woman passed out on our lawn–safe and comfortable, but sleeping.

I walked down to her, noting that the cars were pretty far away. At first, I was a little concerned. There was a body there! She had been a lot of fun at the party–I guessed a little too much. She didn't seem sick, but I needed to bring her in. Amy wanted to leave her there. She was asleep and the weather was fine. She wouldn't let her (this other admittedly beautiful woman) in the house! We went to bed and the guest wound up getting another ride home. That battle? Amy won.

I guess I was becoming really domestic. I even loved to shop. I would get Bed Bath, & Beyond 20% off coupons and those were real currency for me. I loved going through there and looking up and down every aisle for impulse buys. I would get a massage every Thursday after work and, if I got there early, that's where I'd spend my time, walking through the

 I'd spend hours, days, and weeks over the course of years looking for CDs.... that's been taken away from me.

nearby Bed Bath & Beyond. Walmart was my "convenience store." I didn't like to prolong the shopping experience if it was something I wasn't passionate about, but—in the days when I was amassing my record collection—I could spend hours browsing in any store that had them. Then, I went through a period when I replaced vinyl with CDs. This was pre-Amazon–I had to find them in real stores. I'd spend hours, days, and weeks over the course of years looking for CDs. Shopping for vinyl and CDs; that's been taken away from me. I miss those days. Most stores today have only the top new releases.

|| ◀◀ ▶ ▶▶ ||

I lived in Cedarburg for more than twenty years. I was up at 5:00 or 5:30 A.M., went to work for twelve hours, worked out, played softball, prepped the radio show, and fit in my one-hour-a-week massage that I value for my well-being—something I highly recommend after having done it for decades with my massage therapist, Elaine. (I had to roll in the dirt after my massage and before softball on Thursdays to help offset the scents!) After all of that, hopefully there was a little time left to share with the family.

I loved the city's downtown, but was not really ingrained in the community. I wanted to do something in Cedarburg to make a difference and to feel like I was part of this quaint city where I lived. I joined the board for the Cedarburg Performing Arts Center. They had a concert series. If they had seven or eight shows a year, several of them had a local feel, but they brought in a handful of national acts, too.

Roger McGuinn (The Byrds) and John Sebastian (Lovin' Spoonful), were the artists for one of those nights. I came out to kick off the show and reveal some of the history of these two acts.

In my childhood, The Beatles were as big as anyone had ever been, but they were influenced by The Byrds. At one press conference, a reporter asked, "Hey who's that young man with you?"

"David Crosby of The Byrds, a mate of ours," John Lennon answered. "Ahoy, Matey."

They collaborated in the marriage of folk and rock. The Byrds, particularly on the West Coast, really created the foundation for this genre. The Lovin' Spoonful, meanwhile, brought the East Coast feel. It was all just being born. Nothing in music gets born in one place at one time, but multiple places around the same time. Roger agreed.

▶▶ **Nothing in music gets born in one place at one time, but multiple places around the same time.**

"You really nailed the history!" he said.

I met John next and asked him about the things I should share. These guys were icons to me! John had played at Woodstock. It wasn't the highlight of his career because he wasn't prepared to go on initially. He had done the *Welcome Back Kotter* song. I explained the same ideas to John that I had to Roger. I shared my belief that true folk music was morphing from its limited audience. I expressed admiration for what he was doing on the East Coast and for his being an influencer of such an avalanche.

John said, "I'd prefer you just introduce me and not say anything about that history."

He was polite, but he didn't want tangents. He was just there to play the show.

So what did I do? As best I could, I gushed about Roger McGuinn and then barely introduced John Sebastian. To this day, I regret that response. I didn't want people to think I didn't know about or understand his importance. I'll never forget how bizarre it was to me, but I also understand it. I'm sure artists have been burned in the past when introductions aren't articulated well or if the person introducing them doesn't know their topic well. I enjoyed shows like that one, and being a part of the Cedarburg PAC board made me feel like a contributor to my community.

Growing up in an urban area, I missed out on some of the activities that our neighbors and friends enjoyed. I was able to play baseball, basketball, and football. Snow, on the other hand, wasn't for sport. It was to get you off of school, play in, or—if you were lucky—shovel away to earn a few bucks. Skiing on it? That was never even on my radar! Amy was from Colorado, though, and we made multiple trips out there. It even got to the point that I subscribed to the Denver Business Journal and considered starting my real estate career over from scratch.

I'd never even been on skis! One of the times we visited Colorado, I had to ski on the Arapahoe Basin ski area. I was the only one who had never been on skis before. There were no bunny hills. My brother-in-law gave me the ten-second lesson. When you want to stop, snowplow. That was it, before, "Let's go."

Apparently, it's the lift that freaks most people out. I didn't think about that. For me, that wasn't a problem. I saw trees in my path and that was a problem. I put my skis together ... and closer together ... and closer together. I was not stopping. I was not slowing down! Then, the tops of my skis went into the ground.

I FLEW!

Somehow, as I sailed through the air, I managed to keep my skis on. I had the hardest time just standing up and had no interest in doing so. My companions were all well past me while I was on the side of the mountain. I basically dragged myself down the mountain, one skooch at a time. Did I want to go again?

NO!

When we went to dinner afterward, though, a relatively plain Chinese food restaurant, it was the best meal ever. I have eaten in all the best restaurants over the years. But there's something about that first meal right after you think you're going to die. Best. Meal. Ever.

I've done cross-country skiing a few times over the years, but never downhill. We did much better, I think, on the ups and downs of parenting.

Joe would be the first one to say, "My dad is so cool."

He meant it and that made me feel even cooler. There was something special about knowing Rock & Roll when Rock & Roll was at the pinnacle of its popularity. I tried to give the kids fun experiences. We went to Brewers games, more than I could count. I worked to create surprises, sometimes a concert, and other times it was as simple as bringing home a giant sandwich. I liked to keep them guessing.

At one time, Joe had a parent-teacher conference with his history teacher. The teacher was basically saying that everything was just average, but when he asked about Rock & Roll, the conversation bloomed into me standing up, using the whiteboard, creating a diagram of the genre from its early years to the present, and pulling Joe into the conversation. He knew history, just not the history that was on the test. Ten minutes turned into forty-five and the teacher went from being bored to gleaming.

We enjoyed music together, especially anything from John Prine, and we always had great open conversations. Maybe that's why he wasn't afraid to call me on one of those days when a kid has to make a tough call. Well, actually the call didn't come from him. It came from the Cedarburg Police Department. They'd arrested Joe. My son had been smoking pot in a car with friends in a parking lot. Because it was in a school lot, it was elevated to a very serious offense.

They brought Joe into an interrogation room and I thought he was just brought there to be scared straight. My son saw the severity of the situation and was very respectful to them. The detective said they intended to prosecute to the fullest extent of the law unless he agreed to do several undercover buys for them to help them bust others. We had criminals who were selling *heroin* and they wanted to use MY underage son to bust people!

▶▶ **They wanted to use MY underage son to bust people!**

I didn't want to put Joe in a life-threatening situation and I *definitely* didn't want to introduce him to the hard drug. I didn't know how I'd deal with the crisis until I was in it. I was adamant this couldn't happen and, even though I didn't want to be the cliché, well-off parent who fixes things, I brought in a lawyer, something that surprised them. Joe had made a mistake, but it wasn't worth the danger they suggested. Thankfully, he didn't end up with a felony on his record and—more importantly—he didn't fall into the trap of cocaine or heroin. As an adult, he moved to Colorado and now works in the legitimate cannabis industry. No one can say he's not doing what he loves.

Haley was a little less sordid. I got her a cat for her fifth birthday that was just hers–nobody else's. It made her feel special. I also got her a drum set as a little kid, but she was much more interested in being a listener of music than a player of it. So, that's what we enjoyed together. I raised Haley (and Joe, too, of course) on The Beatles. A generation later, they still spoke the same wisdom and growth into a teenager's life–beginning innocent and cute, growing angsty, and becoming worldly. When Haley was in high school, she took a (blow-off) music appreciation class and really thrived in it. She was able to identify every single song and get every question on every single quiz right. I helped her put together a project on Buddy Holly, with old recordings of interviews. In Haley's work, I could see myself in that career-starting, middle-school speech class years ago.

I was great friends with area concert promoter Peter Jest and, through all the decades we knew one another, he would call me and ask if I wanted to interview someone, review a show, pick up some tickets, and so forth. Peter had the passion to promote the artists and I was a legitimate means of doing that. The surprise was when he brought in Ringo Starr and his All-Starr Band.

Ringo came almost yearly, but this was a big deal. He knew how much it meant to me and Ringo was allotted only one five-minute slot for Milwaukee to do an interview.

It was the most nervous I ever was for a phone interview. I remember it as a religious experience. I was also so, so frustrated because I'd had a root canal two days before the interview. I was in pain and there was a deformity in my voice. Nobody else could hear it, but I could.

▶▶ **I remember it as a religious experience.**

Milwaukee turned out to be his first interview of the day and we were minutes out!

"Ringo?" I could hear him, but there was some trouble with the lines at first.

"Hey Steve, what's happening?"

Steve: Hey, what's your favorite decade, Ringo?

Ringo Starr: Well, I can't get away from the excitement of the '60s. I think musically what was happening, what was going on, the band I was in, the music I was making, it had to be the '60s. I was going to start thinking about all the others. The '80s have all their joy, I met Barbara. But the '60s is when I had all my children. You can't say what decade. Then you have to say what year? What tour?

Steve: Joe Walsh almost seems like a permanent member of the All-Stars. I know different people keeps things fresh. Would you like to be in a band again?

Ringo: Sure. The thing about Joe Walsh is he keeps leaving me for that other band. But, the idea that we created in 1989 was a great vehicle for me to not only get out on the road, but to play behind all these great artists. So I have no problem every time we put it together to have a new front line.

It was the first year the Osbournes television show was on the air. I asked if his home life was more like PBS' Shining Time Station for kids or the much more-mature, The Osbournes. He started laughing.

'Oh my God, I just cracked up a Beatle!'

The five minutes felt like five seconds to me and I felt like I'd just run a marathon in those five minutes. I was exhausted. I said goodbye when the promo people wrapped us up, hung up, and completely collapsed from happiness.

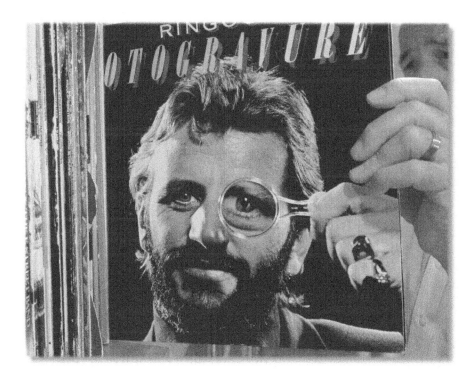

That wasn't all. Peter saved me front-row tickets. I brought Haley. I took her with me to the dinner beforehand and the show. We sat in the first row. Ringo came down from the stage, right to the lip between the first row and the stage. He knelt down and shook my daughter's hand. He said hello to me and my daughter. He picked up the mic and said, "You gotta get 'em early."

I was so overwhelmed with emotion. I had been eight years old when I saw the Beatles on Ed Sullivan and my life changed forever. Here was my daughter, thirty years or so later, shaking Ringo's hand around the same age.

Much like the world got bigger for me on February 9, 1964, the world got smaller for me at that moment. A Beatle. A child. My child. A world in which that can happen is truly inspiring. It can't be described. Only felt.

> ▶▶ **Much like the world got bigger for me on February 9, 1964, the world got smaller for me in that moment.**

Later in the show, Sheila E of the All-Starr Band did a big solo and brought her drumsticks down to my daughter, who still has them today after all this time.

Time is kind.

I hold onto all of the great memories.

But not all of the memories were good.

During a turbulent period in my marriage to Amy, I went to The Hoffman Institute. They taught a self-improvement life philosophy that started with a week-long process during which you cut off contact to the outside world. Their purpose was to take away the distractions of society in order for the guests to focus on being better people. A couple we knew raved about the program and was just trying to help us. It was self-improvement, primarily. You had to totally devote yourself to doing it.

> ▶▶ **You had to totally devote yourself to doing it.**

I went to a cabin out in nature, somewhere in New England. There were three instructors and eight or ten of us in the class. They provided all of the healthy meals (not my typical fare!) and there were no cell phones, no calls or messages, no newspapers, and no TV.

In writing, it sounds like a cult, but that's not what this was. It's no different than going to a retreat or even just off the grid for a few days.

It was time for us to work on us and we were totally immersed in the week-long self-improvement. I remember that I got a roommate and, apparently, I snored. I guess I needed the seclusion. Normally, I couldn't even sleep well because I was so bored by the hours of nothingness. I was given my own room.

During the self-introspection time, there were group activities that were fun and built some camaraderie. There were also some open wounds. I remember feeling pretty good because a couple of people had some really tough issues. They wondered why I was there. I had some scars and wounds they forced me to deal with; but mostly I just wanted to be a better husband. It was great to be detached from the world and begin healing together, as well as dealing with our individual stuff.

▶▶ **I had some scars and wounds they forced me to deal with; but mostly I just wanted to become a better husband.**

One of the guys in the program was an actor and I remember getting caught up when they had role-playing. He and I played two of the parts. I learned a great audio lesson from him. As an actor, he shared that, while we should all let ourselves go, we should never have two people talk at once. I believe in realistic ambient sound, but I never forgot that good advice.

Be it on the radio, in a business presentation, or any means of communication, I need to have one focus at a time! I felt that our role-playing group was the "best." I couldn't turn off my ability to absorb the presentation aspect of the exercises even while we used them to work through our struggles.

The leaders also took us out to a graveyard. We'd been together for days in silence without media, so we were pretty close by this time. In the graveyard, we had to think about mortality and death and think about the song you wanted at your funeral.

At that point in my life, I chose The Beatles' *In My Life*:

"There are places I'll remember
All my life, though some have changed
Some forever, not for better
Some have gone, and some remain
All these places had their moments
With lovers and friends, I still can recall
Some are dead, and some are living
In my life, I've loved them all"

I wanted to put off the actual choice for a few years. I wasn't dying yet . . . but our marriage was.

Haley was ten when my marriage to Amy ended. Joe, being a little older, had a slightly better understanding. I'm not saying it was easy, but it was almost, I don't know, *okay* when the decision was finally made. We'd been under such tension for so long and that permeated everything we did–every action, every thought, every discussion.

I remember the night we told the kids we were going to divorce. We worked to make sure it was as "normal" of a night as possible. We were all *together*, watching a movie, and eating pizza. We wanted to show them that we were both still their parents and we still loved them, even though we weren't going to be together anymore. We were going into a joint custody situation, but we were still a family.

Joe was actually a little excited about the new changes. It was a new chapter. He was looking forward to two Christmases and birthdays. He was also old enough to feel some relief from the tension that had been in the home at the end of the marriage between his mother and me.

Haley got a new cat for my house so that she would have a pet in both homes. The cat was named Katie. Unfortunately, that gray furball was nothing like her first cat. Katie was mean–mean to everyone, except me. (I fed her, after all.)

Then, when Haley was fourteen, Amy decided she wanted to move to Arkansas. She needed the move to be able to go forward on her own life path. Joe was about to be a senior in high school, a tough time to move. Haley was about to *start* high school. Amy wanted to take Haley with her. Joe would stay with me and this meant that his last year of school would feel more like a bachelor pad than a childhood home, for better or for worse.

I should have fought to keep them together–to keep Haley close in my life. But I didn't feel I had a choice about it. I didn't know better, I guess. We had negotiated financial terms that, while quite frankly were a lot of money, even at the apex of my earning years (not to mention losing half my "stuff" – the proverbial cliché). I couldn't risk opening up all the terms–something Amy had the right to do if I questioned custody or living arrangements.

▶▶ **I should have fought to keep them together – to keep Haley close in my life.**

I felt guilty about the marriage ending. I don't know exactly why I didn't fight, but I was being told what would happen and that was it. I didn't think I could argue about it. I didn't think I had a say to keep my daughter near me and it was devastating, though I had to present it supportively for her sake.

The price of that occurrence was huge. My kids were split up and I was split from my daughter!

Also, I had come out of our marriage into a fun but tumultuous relationship with my then-coworker, Tara. She had moved in but hadn't bargained for a seventeen-year-old roommate. It ended.

Haley was really upset about it and confused at first. She spent those first couple of years trying to get back to Wisconsin to see her brother and me more often. We still had a joint custody arrangement, but it wasn't the same. I saw my daughter on some holidays and parts of the summer, a random time here or there. I never visited her down south. We only had time together when she came back home and this situation was a huge emotional gut hit for me. It was hard. Not just hard, I was wrecked by it for a long time.

I felt guilt and regret that I didn't visit her in Arkansas, but I didn't know if I could or should. Joe remembers this transition as the first time he saw me choked up emotionally.

"If I listened long enough to you
I'd find a way to believe that it's all true
Knowing that you lied straight-faced
while I cried
Still I look to find a reason to believe."
▶ *FROM: Reason To Believe*
BY: Rod Stewart, Unplugged...And Seated
(Warner Brothers Records, 1993)

If I'm just being honest, those years after Haley left almost destroyed me. *Something died and it would be a long time before it came back to life.*

▶

IN THE OFFICE
The "Other" Career

"Life is what happens to you
while you're busy making
other plans."

▶ *FROM: Beautiful Boy*
BY: John Lennon, Double Fantasy
(Geffen, 1980)

*B*OB Polacheck worked until he died. We would see his company eventually become part of the international commercial real estate group, CB Richard Ellis. Part of the sale included my working with them for five years.

Our new bosses told us to come to a national convention. It was a big contingent of power brokers who went out to Vegas for the meeting. I got a lot out of it, but it was held in the city of fun and frivolity. A group of us met in Caesars Palace in a steakhouse.

There was a commotion outside the restaurant. A big gaggle of people were surrounding another group of people. It was so obvious something was going on that we couldn't ignore it. It turned out to be six or seven beautiful women who were the "Texas Bikini Team."

They happened to be passing through and they came into the restaurant. I went to the bar to find out what was going on. In the meantime, unbeknownst to me, one of my colleagues who was notoriously frugal went into the mall and bought a disposable camera from the Walgreens. We all enjoyed getting our pictures taken, although some of them weren't exactly publishable.

The women left the restaurant, but on their way out, said they were going to one of the local casinos, so a few of us headed over. They invited us to a private room which was more about avoiding a scene than making one. Nonetheless, one of the guys with us was acting obnoxiously. At about 4:00 A.M., a bouncer came to me to usher everyone out before anything bad happened.

After my five years with CB Richard Ellis, I was ready to create something with the lessons left by the soul I experienced at the Polacheck Company, added to my own style and ideas. I'd already had some pretty interesting experiences in the industry.

In commercial real estate, one of great things you get to do is deal with the highest-level decision makers of companies. But you're also sometimes working on small projects. You can never equate an experience with being jaded. If someone appears to be flighty and unprofessional, you don't know for sure if it's situational. The second you make the decision that someone is not worth working with or helping, you've committed a cardinal sin of business. You just never know what you may be missing.

▶▶ **The second you make the decision that someone is not worth working with or helping, you've committed a cardinal sin of business.**

Some of the smallest deals can lead to companies that end up growing. Wouldn't it suck to know I'd treated them poorly? I don't judge a book by its cover when it comes to business. Plus, you're usually representing a client with a building or need and you owe it to them not to judge.

I got a call once from a guy who said he saw a "For Sale" sign on a building and he wanted to buy it. He asked to meet at Victor's, a nice enough restaurant but considered a pickup joint, as opposed to a business spot. We met at 6:00 at night, which isn't typical for commercial real estate, which usually happens in normal business hours. The guy was sitting at the bar with one of those 80s-style, silver metal *Miami Vice* briefcases. He was flighty and incoherent in conversation. At one point during the talks, which didn't sound like a business transaction, he popped open the cash-filled briefcase and said, "I want to buy this building."

My first thought was, *'WOW! YES!'* but I knew enough to start asking questions. It was a statement I chose to make so it didn't seem too angry or dismissive. "You realize there's some law about paying cash for things, right? You're obligated to report any purchase over a certain amount."

I didn't know what I was talking about specifically, but it was timely. His demeanor instantly changed from cool, eccentric, and intimidating to being on the defensive. It went from an absurdity to great amazement and a true professional encounter. *He* had to convince *me* that he was real, instead of this power move. Although it didn't lead to a sale. I always think back to that guy and how a few calm, well-chosen words can diffuse a potentially tense situation. I don't get mad or defend my position; I simply share facts.

▶▶ **I don't get mad or defend my position; I simply share facts.**

|| ◀◀ ▶ ▶▶ ||

The fact is that Milwaukee, right on one of the world's largest lakes in the middle of a midwestern winter, gets COLD. That was the case on a day that I was showing a potential property owned by Mark Irgens. We had convinced this client to consider the building, but they wanted exterior signage. They acquiesced to taking a look at the building, but it was under construction at the time.

I have this weird idea in me that I think makes Wisconsin winters go a lot quicker. I don't wear a coat unless it's snowing. On that day, it wasn't snowing, but it was about eight below zero. I didn't have a coat with me and there was a short window of time that the client was willing to look at the building, so I climbed through external staircases and this lakeshore construction site to show the building. It wasn't dedication; it was stupidity and youth. It does shorten the winter and it makes you feel a bit tougher.

▶▶ **It wasn't dedication; it was stupidity and youth.**

We made the deal.

Then-Brewers owner, Bud Selig, used to shake his head at me when he passed me in a building we shared with his office. "(Cubs owner) Phil Wrigley never wore a coat either," he mentioned to me.

You'd think I'd be glad when the weather got better and it was time for golf season, but I might be the only guy in commercial real estate who doesn't play. I cared about the major sports as a kid. Golf was not for me. Once I was in the business world, I wished it had been second nature. But I hit a point in business that I figured I should take some lessons, although I didn't want to do it if I wasn't going to be great. It seemed like every spring I'd think it was the year to take lessons.

I've turned down thousands of opportunities that took place on the golf course. One of my best friends, Keith Templin, is a great golfer and he loves the game. He kept inviting me to his club. Finally, I went on a Friday afternoon. It was dead at that time, so I could go out there without feeling the eyes of others and I got a few tips about keeping my head down, how to grip, and so on. I was suddenly, well, at least not embarrassing. I even did well on a couple of holes, although I lost concentration at the end. With a couple of holes left, we stopped so I didn't put on a show at the 18th hole and embarrass him with the people already gathered to eat at that vantage point.

Golf is really important to people who I work with. I've gotten sleeves of balls and even clubs gifted over the years. When I lived in Cedarburg, on my five acres, I thought, *'What the hell.'*

I grabbed a club and balls and turned my backyard into a driving range. I was swinging like a baseball bat, pulling up chunks of grass. Then—one time, one perfect hit—the ball took off at a whistle, in a straight line. It was one of the coolest sounds I'd ever heard and I got it! That combination of swing, smack, and whistle, as it left in a straight line, was beautiful. On the next swing, I did what I thought was the same movement . . . and took out two windows in our gazebo (in and out). Again, I thought, I get it! But this time it was the frustration that I got. I've only played golf a few times since.

> ▶▶ **That combination of swing, smack, and whistle, as it left in a straight line, was beautiful.**

I'm in awe of how often my love of sports, music, and broadcasting intersects with the world of business.

Astute real estate investor, Senator Herb Kohl—a client— owned the Bucks. Major League Baseball Commissioner, Bud Selig, became a real estate investor, as well. I also represented former NBA legend, Junior Bridgman, in a few office space transactions. His involvement in Wendy's and Coca-Cola have led him to stratospheric success. One of those deals was a sublease controlled by five-time NFL champion, Willie Davis, whose business acumen is also legendary. Typically, I would request three fully executed copies of a signed lease for all the parties. In this case, with the autographs of Junior and Willie, I may have asked for a few extra.

Jabari Parker was an outstanding college player drafted by the Bucks (and subsequently subjected to unfortunate injuries). His father also played in the NBA and his strong family ties led him to purchase a home for his parents in a community about twenty-five miles from Milwaukee. However, as a twenty-two-year old, he was looking at more of an urban setting. The team provided residential real estate assistance, but he wasn't getting what he wanted.

We were introduced in 2017 and he described his desire for a warehouse building, in the middle of a nondescript block, near the arena, with high ceilings for a court, a place to park his cars and, a bedroom like (that on the Nickelodeon television show) "Hey Arnold!" We hit it off and it didn't hurt that I had a strong memory of my children enjoying that cartoon. I found a building, negotiated a purchase, and introduced Jabari to an architect and construction company. He turned his dream into one of the coolest little-known buildings in Milwaukee. In 2018, he signed as a free agent with Chicago. Mark my words: that place he left behind will soon house an equally high-profile athlete.

And my Rock & Roll DJ persona found its way into my professional world, too. One afternoon, early in my commercial real estate career, I was walking down Wisconsin Avenue and I waited at a stop light next to a beautiful woman carrying a portfolio. She was looking left and right at buildings.

I asked, "Are you new in town and looking for Cramer Krasselt?"

She was in shock that I had the ability to read her mind and stammered, "Why, yes. How did you know?"

I assumed she was an aspiring model and it so happened one of the biggest ad agencies in town across the street was my real estate client. She told me she was working at a restaurant in the Hyatt and trying to break into modeling.

I took the chance encounter to the next level. Grabbing a portable radio, I glued the tuning knob to 96.5, put it in a box with a note that said, "Please turn this radio on at 9:15 A.M. on Sunday." I dropped the box off at the restaurant.

That Sunday, I was on the air playing songs about journalism and mentioned, at 9:15 A.M. of course, that, "as a former journalism major, I know better than to ever use a 50,000 watt radio station for my own self-indulgence, such as asking a stunning woman I met on the street to call me on the request line."

The request lines lit up!

Line one: "Can you play Led Zeppelin?"

Line two: "What time is the game tonight?"

More of the same . . . and no call from the woman.

The next night, I had a business dinner and told the story. One of the people at our table insisted I go to the hotel where she worked and find out what happened. I declined until he said he was going himself if I didn't. I walked over and found her.

"Do you remember me?" I asked.

"Oh, yes," she said. "I was so excited to listen Sunday that I actually set my alarm to make sure I didn't miss it. In fact, I tuned in early to make sure . . . then—at 9:15—my fiancé and I listened to your message for me."

I can't imagine that did much for her current relationship or for my future prospects for one!

I was ready for my next step of creating my own organization. Cresa would become the commercial real estate agency I helped build in Milwaukee after my time with CB Richard Ellis. I wanted a very different kind of culture.

I wanted our office to reflect a culture of fun and service. I think we were ahead of our time. Our reception area was a living room and we created our own coffee shop within the space. Yet, we had a very formal conference room so our clients could see all sides of us. We also had a nap room, a Nerf basketball hoop, and my dog Luke joined me often to make it a pet-friendly office.

Going from the world's largest commercial real estate firm to building the Milwaukee office of a national organization meant a lot of guerilla marketing. One day, I had noticed a small bank was holding a brat fry in front of their building. I thought, *'what a nice thing to do to engrain yourself in the neighborhood.'* I wanted to emulate the cookout on a bigger scale. So, I asked our building management if we could hold a brat fry on the corner of one of Wisconsin's busiest streets. They said yes!

My friend Beth Weirick of the downtown business improvement district suggested I alert the police and offered to have their street ambassadors promote the event. I had cards printed that said we were new to the neighborhood but had fifty years of experience . . . and we would be cooking out with free brats on the appointed day.

I ordered 1000 pre-cooked brats already wrapped. We set up the grill for the smoke and ambiance, though. It was an event that garnered media attention and made what was ultimately a cost-effective impact.

For months afterward, people said, "You're the guys that gave out free brats."

At Cresa, I wanted that family feeling to be the same in the office as it was at community events. I wanted to show people that they could work hard, be joyful, and also be close with one another. I was building another family, treating the people who I employed as equals rather than minions. And the people I shared the building with were friends.

▶▶ **I wanted to show people that they could work hard, be joyful, and also be close with one another.**

Writer/editor Bobby Tanzilo was one of the other tenants and I asked him, "How much has your life improved since you moved into this building?"

I was referring to the fact that he was swimming at the adjacent Gold's Gym on a theoretically daily basis. "You couldn't swim in anything safe at our old place," he said

I think there was something special in City Center, where we housed Cresa. The building staff took care of everything, from meals, to massages, to dry cleaning, to oil changes, all while you worked in your office. And, in the lobby? Great music overhead, of course.

At Cresa, we built relationships with the other tenants, most of whom I connected with by inviting them over for luncheons or sharing tickets to sporting or music events. And, speaking of music, some of my vinyl selection made its way to the Cresa music room, appropriately equipped with a turntable.

It was a vibrant corner of the city at a vibrant time. I enjoyed watching the entire process of helping clients, not just finding the perfect space, but fitting into it and making it work for their culture. I enjoyed mentoring employees, whether by encouraging their wins or having them find the lessons out of losses.

▶▶ It was a vibrant corner of the city at a vibrant time.

The more you can build your brand and who you are, the more you can make change and make that change for good. That's anybody's end goal. That's how I positioned myself. I was attached to great organizations and had love for my coworkers, and industry, as much as I did my family.

▶▶ **The more you can build your brand and who you are, the more you can make change and make that change for good.**

In the process of growing a brokerage firm from a few people to the top ten in Milwaukee, I was up nights thinking about how to sustain growth. My path was constantly crossing with Scott Welsh and Lyle Landowski at Colliers International. I had known and respected both for a number of years. At Cresa, we only represented tenants, and whenever someone I knew needed other services, I was always comfortable sending them to Colliers. It had been my dream to run Cresa, but the timing was perfect for them to offer a new partnership. We met and discovered a common respect for one another and a shared goal and vision. He says I brought charisma, charm, and relational communications, but Scott was a visionary.

I could take Scott's vision and articulate it. I still pride myself on the ability to bring together teams to construct, engineer, architect, and broker deals that are mutually beneficial.

We did a lot of fundraisers and after-hours bourbon tastings. I got involved in podcasts, growing relationships, and a few transactions. Scott and I became great friends too.

What I never expected after three years as a partner at Colliers was that I would become uncomfortable being comfortable. I had the best of all worlds; coming and going as I pleased, making my own hours, and working only on projects I wanted to work on. That freedom gave me lots of time . . . time to see what retirement in just a few years could look like. I didn't like it.

So, at the age of sixty-two, I told myself that I was ready for a new challenge. Just like going from radio to real estate, I wanted to do something drastic.

I had spent decades working on transactions and creative branding solutions for Mark Irgens, who had formed Irgens, one of the largest development firms in the state. Aside from trust and friendship, we had always seen eye-to-eye on the fact that not enough people in commercial real estate go beyond conduit brokerage; in other words, finding out what someone wants, passing on what the other person wants, and waiting for a meeting of the minds. I had always fervently believed that more effort goes into marketing a $1.00 bar of soap ("Irish Spring® tells you that you'll *feel* refreshed!") than a $100,000,000.00 asset. ("Here's a *picture* of the complex.") Commercial real estate projects should brand based on how a business benefits by being there; it's not just the bricks, mortar, and views.

With Irgens, I'd worked on the largest project of my career, the development of a 500,000 square foot building for GE Healthcare that we ultimately sold for $95,000,000. In a conversation with Mark over lunch, he asked how I was doing. I shared my big-picture thoughts about this approach to marketing and he asked me to describe what I wanted in my career to explore them.

I found myself talking about wanting to give up transactions to focus on branding.

Mark's response was, essentially, "When do you want to start?"

Steve and his step-daughter Jaimie
with Mark Irgens and Tom Irgens

So now, after forty-five years in radio, and thirty-five years in real estate, I am the Chief Marketing Officer for Irgens, a spectacular company. Meanwhile, I could not have left Colliers under better terms. It was mutually beneficial to all of us.

"It is with mixed emotions to announce that our talented and funny Steve Palec has decided to take on a new and exciting challenge outside of Brokerage. After a "storied" 35 plus years in commercial real estate, Steve has decided to use his skills, time and passion to help Mark Irgens and the Irgens team strengthen their brand and community awareness. I have no doubt Steve will be immensely successful with Irgens and will help strengthen the Irgens-Colliers relationship.

Although Steve is only moving one floor below, I will personally miss his day-to-day leadership, insight and camaraderie. Steve is truly a one of a kind and someone I'm proud to always call my friend and business partner"

Scott Welsh
CEO Colliers | Wisconsin

We still work together in the same building and see each other daily. I even visit to bring laughter, malarkey, (and junk food!) from time-to-time. My new role wasn't a case of running to another real estate company. I didn't switch jobs; I switched careers. Commercial real estate has given me the opportunity to expand my horizons and command a stage outside of the studio. There are many transactions I've been able to assist, and I feel joy when I see those ventures making a difference in Milwaukee.

In my thirty-five-year real estate career, figuring out my favorite deal is akin to asking me my favorite album. I've enjoyed a lot of deals and they're not defined just by size. I've been lucky to work with Manpower, MLB, Baker Tilly, OnMilwaukee, United Performing Arts Fund

▶▶ **In my thirty-five-year real estate career, figuring out my favorite deal is akin to asking me my favorite album.**

(UPAF), and thousands of other companies and individuals. Some small transactions have been just as impactful as big ones. I got involved with GE Healthcare when they were growing and that company has been very important to the area. I worked on a number of transactions necessitated by their growth, knowing they'd ultimately come up with a final solution. We had been putting bandages on things and strategizing. When they eventually told me, "You're our guy," that was valuable to me. We were more than business associates; we'd become teammates.

That sort of moment is indicative of what I love about commercial real estate. You get to work with companies at their highest level, or the pinnacle of their growth, and become a part of their path to facilitate those opportunities. I'm careful to leave NO ENEMIES in the wake of a deal, too. I'm very proud of the fact that I build deals that are incentivized and competitive, but non-adversarial.

During the developer's courtship phase of what would become the aforementioned GE deal, one of the developers had invited the leadership team from GE to the owner's box at Lambeau Field. They invited me to join them. I accepted. (*Of course! It was Lambeau!*) While I was in the box before the start of game, I saw a couple of top guys from GE put on coats. I turned into a puppy dog. They were going outside!

"Come here!" was their response as I joined them with the human equivalent of a wagging tail.

I went through the tunnel onto Lambeau. It was momentous and I needed to do something to make it memorable. I pulled up a clump of the grass, put some in my pocket and ate a little of it, too, in case someone took it away. (You're not really supposed to do that.) My hosts just shook their heads.

I learned a huge lesson as a sports fan that day. I still think and talk about it to this day. We were in the end zone. I had just eaten the grass. I assumed we'd be escorted off. Nobody moved us! The other team kicked off. The Packers had the ball and it was 1st and 10 on the

20. I couldn't see *anything* beyond offensive linemen. There was a pass play. How the hell can they see? I thought of all those times fans scream at the TV ('YOU IDIOT!') and realized right then that they're throwing to a spot, not a person, and I don't criticize a QB anymore.

The deals and experiences I've had in commercial real estate have been an awesome honor over the years. I've also been able to help find the spaces for community leaders and local heroes or celebrities. Through commercial real estate, I've tried to make my companies—Polacheck, CB Richard Ellis, Cresa, Colliers, Irgens— better places . . . and I try to make my community a better place, too

Why wouldn't I?

I live here.

IN-DIGESTION
Taking A Bite Out Of Life

"I leave from softball practice
every night
It's getting dark but the golden
arches light up the way.
I turn the corner
at the traffic light.
I count my money and then I
rehearse what I'm gonna say,
'I'd like an order of fries, a
quarter pounder with cheese,
I love the light in your eyes.
Will you go out with me
please?'"

▶ *FROM:I'm In Love With The McDonald's Girl*
BY:DEAN FRIEDMAN
(Universal Records, 1998)

P RIOR to bourbon . . . I basically had to apologize for my drink of
choice; even though I've lived in Wisconsin all my life, I have

never been a big beer guy. For the longest time, it was Malibu and Coke for me or Tequila Rose. I typically had to pull umbrellas out of my beverage at bars—not exactly high-brow.

Bourbon saved me my manhood.

During the famed big game blackout, Super Bowl XLVII in New Orleans between Baltimore and San Francisco, my friend was having a little party and I was having chest pains. It was throbbing. I didn't eat or drink. For me to not eat or drink at a party is inconceivable. I had to be in D.C. the next morning, so I flew to Washington and crashed at my hotel there. I woke up the next morning and I wasn't better, yet. I had meetings all day and went back to the hotel after the strenuous workday. I woke up on day three and it *still* hurt. I hadn't been eating any junk food, again, inconceivable for me; I couldn't figure out why I had this pain.

That night, I had a dinner event and I thought, *'I've paid for this pain for three days; I'm going to order a steak!'* After dinner, the group was going to a bar called Bourbon.

I said, "I have no idea what I want. Give me a really good bourbon, I guess." I felt instantly better. I don't exactly recommend this method of treatment, but it worked for me in the moment. I learned later that it is known as "The Kentucky Hug"—the initial warmth of alcohol descending wherever it is that it goes. The next morning, back in Milwaukee, I went right to a liquor store and picked up bourbon. I've had it every day since.

The chest pain, by the way, turned out to be a pulled muscle from working out. I'd spent all those days with the tension, and because pain makes you even tighter, it only got worse. There is a way you drink bourbon properly, called the "Kentucky Chew." Different from the "Kentucky Hug," the "Chew" begins by rinsing the drink around your mouth before taking a second sip in which you really taste it. The rinse, or, *chew,* helps to get your tongue acclimated to the alcohol so that you can appreciate the flavors in the second sip. Between the Kentucky Hug and the bourbon itself, I became both warm and relaxed. For the first time, the muscles in my chest relaxed too, and my body was able to let go of the pain.

I realized that I really liked bourbon.

Having a drink you can sip is great. It made me feel like an adult–finally. I could nurse it in social situations without judgment for drinking too slowly. I began

> ▶▶ **It made me feel like an adult – finally.**

to experiment and try different ones. I went on the bourbon trail[15]. Now I drink it, understand it, and teach people about it. It's been one of my palate's greatest treats.

The Holy Grail of hard-to-find bourbons is Pappy Van Winkle 23. Once I tried it, I was obsessed with finding it. The face value is about $300, but it is so rare that it goes on the secondary market for anywhere between $2000 and $5000 a bottle.

I kept looking online and never quite was able to justify that cost. But one day at work, I clicked on a site that had it for $2300. I convinced myself that I worked hard and deserved it. So, I impulsively started the purchase steps. I put it in a cart. I entered my information. And—when it came to my choice of payment—check, credit, or Paypal . . . I got cold feet. I chose check thinking that I could still change my mind, but didn't click to finalize the purchase. That was a big check! It timed out and I got kicked off the site.

Oh well.

Two weeks later, the bottle showed up at my office. Not cash(check) on delivery; no invoice. It was just the coveted bottle. I told myself that, if ever billed, I would pay it, but shhhhhhhhh, *please don't say anything!*

---

[15] *The Kentucky Bourbon Trail is a guided journey maintained by the seventeen signature distilleries at the helm of Kentucky's world-famous Bourbon culture*

Despite owning (though not opening) a bottle of Pappy, I've been known for my less-than-refined food habits over the years. When asked to bring a box of chips to my friend's party, I went to the grocery store and bought one bag of every type of chip they had, put them into the biggest crate I could find and arrived with it saying, "Here's your *box* of chips."

Another party had me picking up all the famous items from different fast-food restaurants . . . McDonald's, KFC, Arby's, Taco Bell, and the Culver's ButterBurger (a Wisconsin specialty). I cut them into bite-sized pieces, threw a toothpick into each quarter or sixth of each famous item, and showed up with my version of a "gourmet sandwich tray." Let people say what they will; those sandwiches were the first things gone!

That wasn't the case when I made my Big Mac Grenades, though. I always loved Big Macs, but they have way too much bread. So, I bought ten Big Macs, threw out the buns, blended the rest of the ingredients (yes - blended), and put it into crust-less Wonder Bread pockets pressed together and sealed as only Wonder Bread could do. I was the only one who ate them . . . and shouldn't have. They were disgusting.

At Brewers games, they occasionally hold one-dollar hot dog days. I love one-dollar hot dog days, even though they probably cost the club about twenty cents apiece. A buddy and I went to the game and the challenge we had was to eat a hot dog every half inning–eighteen in all. Around the bottom of the 7th inning, I just couldn't do it anymore. I bought another ten hot dogs and put them into an accordion folder I had with me. As it turned out, the first person I saw on an elevator when I went back to my office after leaving the game early was Bud Selig.

He said, "Steve, you don't look right." He assumed it was because the Brewers were losing, but I confessed to my gluttonous sin and what was in the folder. You can fit so much into those! He just shook his head

I once ordered the full McDonald's menu to review it and, another time, the EVERYTHING sandwich from the Arby's Secret Menu which has, well, every item they sell on it, just as the name implies.

Even once after a formal, legendary Pappy Van Winkle bourbon tasting event, I was busted by a good friend as I turned into a Taco Bell right after a much-more refined night of bourbon tasting and fancy appetizers.

My love of food from the cheap and fast to the aged, fine, and refined hasn't gone unnoticed by the community. Maybe because I often wear that food, but also because I treat others to it, talk about it, and write about it. I've been a go-to for restaurant recommendations and, most honorably, a multi-time judge for the Wisconsin State Fair Sporkies, its annual anything-goes food competition.

I always put together a list of food I need to find at the fair. This list started innocently as a handwritten reminder to myself of the voluminous choices I could no longer leave to chance. The fair goes way beyond the Dairy State's flavored milk stand. And Wisconsin offers way more than cheese, sausage, and beer. (Not that we don't do those things amazingly well.) My fair-food plan has evolved into a formal checklist that I am happy to share with others.

There are two things I need to also share with possible fairgoers. The first is that, as an honored Sporkies judge, I was privy to try and anoint the best new foods. It is a day I look forward to every year, not only to tantalize my senses, but to interact with the crowd and my fellow judges. In fact, having judged for four years in a row with former Packer great LeRoy Butler, we have become close friends. The fair, governed by state by-laws, frowns on judges becoming too entrenched.

LeRoy may be mistaken for believing that I, too, was a professional athlete, given my ability to tackle massive amounts of food. I sometimes have to remind him that we are not peers. Butler is *Hall-of-Fame-* worthy. I am *Haul of Food*.

▶▶ **Butler is Hall of Fame-worthy. I am Haul of Food.**

The second disclosure is that, while it takes some time to set up the list, I love sharing commentary on the new choices each year as much as I love trying them. One year had such delectables as: French Onion Soup On-a-Stick; Deep-Fried Turducken On-a-Stick (or chicken stuffed into duck stuffed into a turkey . . . on a stick); Bourbon BBQ Brisket Egg Roll (minus the stick); Wisconsin Hot Chicken Bombs; Deep Fried Spinach Lasagna Bites; Ants On-A-Stick (I accept the challenge!); the Bacon Jam and Brie Burger; Sheboygan Brachos (a sort-of walking brat taco) Flamin' Hot Corn on the Cob; Flamin' Hot Asian Burritos; Vegetarian Wings-On-A-Stick; and the Desert Heat Burger–the alleged World's Hottest Camel Cheeseburger.

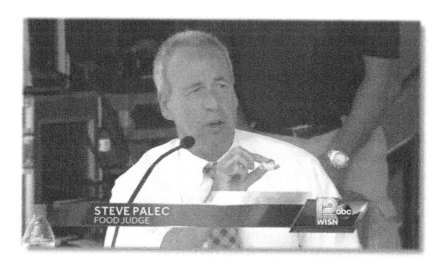

I've met an even bigger burger lover than those brave enough to tackle camel meat. He's Don Gorske[16], the man who had eaten 29,000 Big Macs at the time we crossed paths.

He is obsessive compulsive.

He knows it.

He admits it.

Gorske is in the Guinness Book of World Records for his obsession with two all-beef patties, special sauce, lettuce, cheese, pickles, onion, on a sesame seed bun.

His adventures have also resulted in appearances in the movie "Super Size Me," on talk shows with Jimmy Kimmel and Rachel Ray, and on "Good Morning America." He's been the subject of a joke on "Saturday Night Live" and a question in Trivial Pursuit. And I met him at the McDonald's on 66th and North Avenue in Milwaukee, where he was handing out limited editions of Big Mac sauce in bottles, as well as to interact with admirers. I became one.

I couldn't help but like his polite and appreciative demeanor. Somehow, the man had a cholesterol level under 160 milligrams and deciliters, the common measures in your blood, but his dedication and loyalty to the one sandwich he says comprises ninety percent of his diet is off the charts. I had to know if there was anything else in his life that rivals that focus.

Ian Anderson (Jethro Tull): I grow hot chili peppers as a hobby. They do say that music is good for the generation of plants. So I tried playing to my peppers a couple of years ago and I had the most bountiful harvest imaginable. There is truth in that rumor that music will help grow plants.

Steve: I know you're quite a connoisseur of food. You grow your own; you raise salmon; you grow chili peppers. Have you ever tried a steak quesadilla at Taco Bell?

Ian: (Laughing) No. I do like Mexican food, but I'm not big on fast food. My son bought a book that was an expose' on the world of fast food and the terrible things in it like preservatives. If you're into that, that's fine. But don't waste time with food. Just have the preservatives neat. Be a man.

---

[16] *As of the printing of this book, Mr. Gorske's Big Mac consumption stands at 31,000 and climbing*

"My car," Gorske said. "And, of course, my wife, Mary. But I guess I am what people would say is obsessive compulsive about Big Macs."

Gorske started eating Big Macs when he drove his first car to McDonald's in 1972. He ended up having nine that day. He hit 25,000 on May 17, 2011, and then 29,000 on December 8, 2016. On the day I met him, his count was 29,099. I'm not sure where he stands today. But I do know that he stands with me as a lover of food.

I've created my own set of tongue-in-cheek rules that my wife would likely tell you to not follow under any circumstances!

1) Calories are a myth. Don't count them. I'm no expert, but you can't tell me I'm better off eating 10,000 carrots versus only one McRib.

2) Always eat free food. If you eat the maximum amount of free food offered to you, then you will eat less food that requires payment. And since most food requires payment, ergo you eat less.

3) DO NOT avoid fast food. Now you may have to train your body over time to process it correctly, but once you get the hang of it...since it contains few nutrients, your body will not recognize it as food and while you may feel bad, you won't gain weight.

4) Buns are bad for you and generally unnecessary. Whether used for burgers, hot dogs, subs or just sandwiches, they are simply edible meat holders. You may discard them or bite around them but either way you'll save valuable stomach space.

5) The single best way to stay slim is to worry. If you constantly worry about everything, I've found you burn so much energy that it offsets eating.

6) Feel free to spill. I buy T-shirts in packages of six and use them as wearable napkins. Even when ultra careful I get so happy, excited and distracted when eating that I inevitably spill. Spill more=eat less.

7) Try to remember to chew. I recently inadvertently swallowed an entire cream puff. Had I eaten it incrementally it would have taken a longer period of time hence avoiding the second cream puff I ate since the satisfactory TSE (time spend eating) equation was thrown off.

8) Drink bourbon. Sipping this magical elixir during meals not only replicates the flavor satisfaction of food but also allows you to focus on the entree and offsets the need to habitually consume unnecessary things that come on plates like green beans and broccoli.

   (Unfortunately this doesn't work well at breakfast. But all breakfast food is great so there's nothing to avoid.)

9) Get married. Having a spouse or two or three constantly shaking their head or raising their eyebrows will cause you to eat less AND force you to sneak in extra meals when they are not around. Of course, the exercise of moving to another location to eat offsets the food intake. Make no mistake, there are no easy fixes. You must exercise.

10) Fruit is God's candy. Think about it...almost every candy (cherry, apple, orange, banana, etc.) tries to replicate the flavor of fruit. Eat lots of fruit and stick to only treats that have flavors not found in nature (Twinkies, Tiramisu, Kit Kats, etc.).

11) As much as possible, eat in the car or watching TV. The energy you burn by moving the steering wheel, using the turn signal, poking the TV remote, yelling at a fumble and/or squinting at a flickering picture in the middle of the night will ALL use energy that offsets the consumption.

12) Let corporations control your portions. Whatever is put in front of you in a restaurant or in a bag from a grocery shelve is exactly what you should finish. This does not apply to items purchased at Costco.

I live to eat, not eat to live (obviously). *All joking aside, food has been one of life's joys to me and even soothed the heart.*

▶

IN THE STANDS
The Parks We Play In

"Stand on hills of
long-forgotten yesterdays
Pass amongst your memories
told returning ways."

▶ *FROM: Tales of Topographic Oceans*
BY: Yes, Tales of Topographic Oceans
(Atlantic, 1972)

*N*ICOLE Koglin, a good friend from Fox 6 News, has enjoyed a number of baseball games in the stands with me over the years. Our schedules both have the kind of flexibility that allow a day game from time-to-time and we're both true fans. Apparently, I've ruined her daughter, who expects the close seats that I've been blessed to have as I've gotten more successful, enabling me better ticket hook-ups throughout my career. Nicole has also brought station colleagues occasionally and I enjoy messing with them.

When meeting her fellow news anchor, Jessob Reisbeck (now working at WJLA in Washington, D.C.), I greeted him with a handshake, leaving behind a handful of Spree-like hard, colored candies. He was all too surprised to discover they were all covered in crude and risqué phrases which he then passed along to the servers. Here he was, a television anchor, handing out obscene candies at a ballgame (though he insists he only gave out the tamer ones).

At the end of the day, baseball stadiums are grown up playgrounds where you can goof off in the outdoors and act a bit like a foolish kid. In other words, they are the perfect environment for me. When Nicole brought her colleague, Cassandra McShepard, another TV personality from Fox 6, Cassandra shared that, as a former fashion designer for music artists, baseball wasn't really her thing, but I assured her I could change her perspective in just a few minutes if she'd let me try.

▶▶ **At the end of the day, baseball stadiums are grown up playgrounds where you can goof off in the outdoors and act a bit like a foolish kid.**

A group of us had brunch and drinks and then I got to the business of baseball. "Listen," I said, "baseball's been around for around 150 years, so you can't understand the intricacies, but going to a game is not about the regulations and rules. Don't think about those things. Understand that, unlike a basketball game in an arena, where that is your focus and reason to be there, and unlike a football game in a stadium that occurs only eight times in that city in that year, for baseball, you are in a park. This is a ballpark. You're not obligated to watch the full game. You can talk and hang out; you can walk around; you can watch or not watch; you can even check out the backside on all-star outfielder Christian Yelich if you want. You are in a park right now. Relax and enjoy the atmosphere."

"If you want a basic knowledge to have an appreciation for when people are cheering," as I continued explaining to her, "let's equate this to your music background. There's home plate; everyone is trying to get there. It is the Grammy. Each label—each team—wants as many Grammys as it can get. In Miller Park, Grammys come with a home-run celebration that includes our mascot riding down the slide and fireworks . . . every time. How do the teams get those Grammys? Through hits, just like in music. A one-hit wonder? That's a base hit. Maybe not a Grammy, though. You have to work your way toward that. But an infectious song or a full album of hits? That's an over-the-wall home run! By contrast, a recording career isn't one album, even with a Grammy. That's where innings come in. Imagine it's a nine-year career and the industry is hard. They're not handing it to you. There will be some artistic or business decisions (like balls), and some misses (like strikes). All in all, the most Grammys over the most years with the fewest wrong turns and misses equals a win."

With all that said, Cassandra said she felt the ballpark that day. She understood what was going on in the game and enjoyed the park for being a park. We watched the Brewers, their famous racing-sausage feature at the bottom of the sixth, the seventh-inning stretch with not just, "Take Me Out To The Ballgame," but the Wisconsin staple, "Beer Barrel Polka," and she may have even checked out Yeli a time or two. I love sharing *my* love of sports with others.

Steve with Fox 6 News Team's Nicole Koglin, Cassandra McSheppard, and Carl Deffenbaugh

It would have been harder to *not* be a sports fan than to relish in and enjoy the athletics when you grew up in Wisconsin in the '60s. It was the Lombardi era. Every fall Sunday meant the Packers and sports deeply permeated the state's culture. Coke caps used to have a Packers player featured underneath them when you opened the bottles and, if you collected the whole set, you could get an authentic Packers football. As you might expect, it was close to impossible, even though—as a youngster—I refused to drink water or milk that wasn't chocolate. I lived on Coca-Cola. (Years later, I was gifted a full set.) It was in my DNA to be a "Packer-Backer," which was what we were called long before we were Cheeseheads. The glory-years, Lombardi-era, championship Packers were so dominant.

▶▶ **It would have been harder to *not* be a sports fan than to relish in and enjoy the athletics when you grew up in Wisconsin in the '60s.**

Winning was everything.

But also, I loved the Milwaukee Brewers, the Milwaukee Bucks the Wisconsin Badgers, and the Milwaukee Admirals (hockey).

Wisconsin was always progressive, too. We didn't just have the Milwaukee Does of the short-lived Women's Professional Basketball League, we also had two All-American Girls Professional Baseball League (AAGPBL) teams during the '40s, called the Milwaukee Chicks (like the birds!) and the Racine Belles, filling the gap for the military-depleted Major Leagues. AAGPBL was the organization made famous by the movie, "A League Of their Own." I once took my son to an exhibit of women's baseball at the Milwaukee County Historical Society Museum and, thanks to the movie, he could relate to the importance of the AAGPBL . . . and so could I. Today, in addition to Wisconsin's great professional teams and college teams (which also include Marquette and UW-Milwaukee in basketball), the state hosts minor-league baseball teams, plus professional soccer and minor-league hockey. It's also home to a number of Winter Olympics sports training centers. Sports can't be separated from the culture of Wisconsin any more than music can.

#THISISMYCREW

#GOPACKGO

#JUMPAROUND

#MKEADMIRALS

#FEARTHEDEER

When I was doing my morning show at WQFM, '60s-era Hall-of-Fame Packer Jerry Kramer, was, by happenstance, on a book tour. His publicist out of New York set up an interview with us, not knowing we were a  rock show–a music station, but I devoted an entire no-music hour to Jerry Kramer and the Packers. I snuck in some music in the background and got some audio from the era. I really did my homework. Bob Long, who was a reliable receiver in those years, and later a successful developer, had a real estate office in Milwaukee. Hall-of-Fame quarterback Bart Starr had recently been fired as Packers coach and rumor was that he was going to coach an expansion team in Arizona. I had arranged for Long to call in (and knew that Starr was at his office).

Starr heard the respectful conversation with Long and knew it would be serious enough for him to join in. The coolest moment of the day was being handed a note that said:

"BART IS ON LINE 4."

Part of me was a kid and the other part of me was a journalist. Nobody could get Starr on the phone. He was doing NO interviews. Was he going to get back into coaching? We were forty minutes into the show with good, gritty, Lombardi-focused stuff, which to Starr showed legitimacy.

"Jerry, guess who this is," our bonus caller chimed in. Jerry couldn't identify Bart's voice.

"Can you get your footing?" he asked. Bart's voice shared the words before Jerry's most famous block in the Ice Bowl championship game against the Cowboys, sending the Pack to the Super Bowl.

"BURT!" Jerry lit up! (I assumed that was an inside joke–something he used to call Bart in jest.)

The two of them were just talking as old friends when Jerry, very innocently, asked, "So you gonna take that Arizona job?" Bart Starr was so controlled. He immediately pulled himself out of the friendly moment, answered politically, and then plugged back in to the friendly tone of the interview.

That interview was one of my greatest honors and I was able to reflect on the moment and all of those remarkable players gifted to Wisconsin fans by the Packers over the years.

Jerry Kramer: In desperate situations, really critical moments, you reach down for something. I have a thought that what we found were Lombardi's principles. Our fundamental values. Our preparation. Our consistency. Our commitment. Discipline. Perseverance. Character. Pride.

Steve: What was it about that man, day in and day out, that made people follow him?

Jerry: It's a multi-faceted question. He was a multi-faceted human. He believed in commitment. Not just sometimes when it's convenient. Total commitment. Steve, a lot of his philosophy has lived with me for many years. I didn't want to just get by. Like coach said, "You don't do things right once in a while. YOU DO THEM RIGHT ALL THE TIME!"

When Starr passed away in May of 2019, I shared that, "The future will always remember Bart Starr fondly. I know I will."

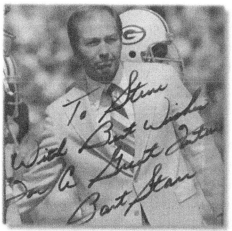

While I may have been hopeful for a moment with Bart Starr, one of my greatest sports memories is from a time I never planned on and with a man I also admired.

Bud Selig became the commissioner of Major League Baseball and he owned the Brewers. He asked something that was unheard of at the time. Bud insisted he'd stay in Milwaukee if he chose to take the commissioner job. There have only been eight commissioners for Major League Baseball in a hundred and fifty years! And Bud wanted his office, not in New York City, but Milwaukee. This was real history!

It was such an honor to be a part of the transaction to represent Major League Baseball in opening up a commissioner's office in my city. I tried to treat it as any other transaction. Bud's heart was set on being in the US Bank building, but there was only a vacancy of about 2000 square feet available in that whole million square foot building, so it didn't work. When another organization in the building was willing to move out, we were able to make it happen for Bud.

> ▶▶ **It was such an honor to be a part of the transaction to represent Major League Baseball in opening up a commissioner's office in my city.**

We negotiated the terms of the entire lease and somebody at the bank in Minneapolis had to approve the deal. We were told, "We can't approve this without MLB's financial statement."

WHAT? This was around the time when there was some real controversy on what MLB and the different teams were worth, so that information was not something that was available for consumption for the players union ... or a bank in the Midwest. The bank wouldn't approve the lease.

We finally asked the bank to stand by the fax machine and MLB sent ONE PAGE with so many zeroes on it that the bank would have been ridiculous to turn it down.

Bud's assistant was Lori Keck, who had been Vince Lombardi's assistant. Bud hired her unseen. If she was good enough for Vince, she was good enough for him. The day that Bud moved into his brand-new thirtieth-floor office, I got a panicked call from Lori.

"We can't get radio reception! If we can't even get the game in here, he's not going to be happy!"

Mistakes were okay, but excuses were not. I got in my car, drove to Best Buy, and bought a $250 desktop radio with a walnut finish. It took an external antennae, so I hooked it up, got an antennae, and ran it along the windows in time for the game to be heard in the office.

I got a letter saying, "You saved the day!" but it took the space of only about a week for MLB to upgrade from the desktop radio to a $10,000 audio visual package in the office.

I officed in the same building as the commissioner. I was headed to a meeting for which I was running late. I saw Bud coming some twenty steps behind me. Part of me thought, in a split second, *Do I keep going to make sure I'm on Lombardi time or wait for Bud and walk with him?* It was the commissioner of MLB ... I waited.

We were walking to our cars and Bud asked, "What are you doing this afternoon? Do you want to go to the game?"

He said "THE game." The only game that day was a playoff game in Detroit. He said, "meet me at Sterling Aviation."

I called the office from my car phone. This was before actual cell phones. I cancelled my other meeting and told someone to shut down my office. I didn't even know where Sterling Aviation was! I started to go toward the airport. I saw it, went in, and said that the commissioner told me to meet him there.

"We need your driver's license and car keys," said the woman who greeted me. Whatever. I was in. I was sitting there when Bud showed up a few minutes later. Earnell Lucas, his bodyguard, was with him and, the next thing I knew, I was in a private jet.

Bud had newspapers and magazines all over the place. I engaged as little as possible. I assumed we'd land at an airport and go through the terminal to another waiting car. Nope. We got off the plane and were met by a motorcade with a police escort straight to the game. I never thought I'd have a police escort unhandcuffed.

When we arrived, someone said to Bud, "You'd better do a press conference."

"Can I tag along?" I asked.

"Sure," he said.

There were fifty cameras and I was standing there behind him craning my neck to be seen. Nobody at home even knew where I was. I watched the game in the owner's box and enjoyed every moment. In the middle of the 7th inning, Earnell said to me, "I can't believe we're still here." Apparently, Bud usually left by that time, but he was enjoying watching me as I took it all in.

As a kid, I'd had an Al Kaline glove. Now, walking down the hall, there was Al Kaline. The guy on my glove! I may as well have been at Disneyland. When we got back to Milwaukee, the plane went right into the hangar. There was Bud's car washed, running, and waiting for him. That's his life, I thought. That's the only way to efficiently run his job. To my surprise, though, there was my car right behind his, washed, running, and waiting for me! That's when I realized my jaw literally ached. I had a smile on my face from ear-to-ear, from the time I ran into Bud, until I was home.

A year later, during the playoffs, I got to go back again. This time, I was on the manifest; it was planned. Mark Irgens, Earnell, and I went to Cleveland. Even though this one was planned, it was still cool, but for different reasons. I remember talking to the owners of the Indians. When they heard I was from Milwaukee, they thanked me for what I did. That year, Cleveland had a game snowed out and the Indians used Miller Park. The owners were grateful to me for just being a part of Milwaukee.

"You're welcome," I said, as though I was the maker of that plan!

When I was at Cresa, I was always looking to bring decision-makers together. I was always looking for something that would be a draw. I found out I could get Jonathan Lucroy for a lunch; this was just as the Brewers were starting to get good and he was an All-Star catcher that year. We had a restaurant near Lucroy's house where we did the Q&A, and it was successful and entertaining, but what I was most excited about is that my dog, Luke—who was only one-year old at the time, was going to be in the room with Luc. I wanted to have a picture of Luc and *my* Luke, who, unfortunately, had just gotten a haircut–basically a shave. He looked so goofy. It was an awesome opportunity, but my Luke didn't look like my Luke, so I couldn't enjoy the picture as much as I'd wished, but I truly appreciated Lucroy's willingness to be a good sport!

I'm still appreciative and in awe every time I get to do something in the sporting world with my heroes. Such was also the case when I was invited to take batting practice at Miller Park and thought, *'that's the coolest thing in the world. Hell yeah!'*

Over the course of the five weeks leading up to the batting practice, I realized I should be prepared because I hadn't picked up a bat for years. I thought, just one day in a batting cage would be a prudent thing to do. Before I knew it, though, I was in the week leading up to the honor. Every day I meant to get to the cage. Next thing I knew, though, the event had arrived and I hadn't practiced.

Twelve of us were invited and it was such a first-class experience. We were given jerseys and caps; we were being wined and dined; we were seeing our names on the scoreboard. Six of us would hit first while the other six shagged flyballs in the outfield, and then we'd swap. I was the second person up. There was a bullpen catcher throwing batting practice.

On the first pitch, after not having held a bat for at least a decade, I had an expected swing and a miss. The next pitch–swing and a miss. I thought, *'uh-oh.'*

But, on the third pitch, I made contact. Base hits followed on the fourth, fifth, and sixth pitches. I was spraying the ball around and I felt pretty good. What I figured out later was that the batting practice pitcher was so good, he figured out my swing and threw the ball onto the bat. Thank God I had the confidence, because shagging the balls in the outfield was really exciting. By the time I was in the outfield, the nerves were gone and I was in awe. Two hard-hit balls magically went right into my glove.

What an experience!

 **What I figured out later was that the batting practice pitcher was so good, he figured out my swing and threw the ball *onto* the bat.**

|| ◀◀ ▶ ▶▶ ||

Another experience I've had the pleasure of taking on is serving on the board of the Wisconsin Athletic Hall of Fame. It was a role I was lucky to share with former Super Bowl Packer and Dancing With The Stars Champion, Donald Driver. What a picture of perfect health. I was once at a lunch meeting with him when I didn't eat at all . . . and he still ate healthier than me!

Not only was our work on the board something to feel proud of, but I got to experience the kindness of "DD."

At an event one evening, my wife was duly impressed when we walked into a room in which Donald was holding court. He saw me and said, "Hi, Steve."

We went over to him and, as we were speaking, my wife mentioned it would be great to send a photo to her son. Donald said, "Let's just FaceTime him." The next thing I heard was the Green Bay Packers all-time reception leader having a conversation with my stepson, Ben.

My wife was touched, but Donald told her he makes it a point to do something kind for someone every single day. Now that's character, and it's one of the most impressive goals I've ever heard. The fact that it came from Donald, somebody who always went beyond expectation, doesn't surprise me at all.

ESPN-Milwaukee radio is owned by a well-healed individual who wanted to go beyond being a radio station. Craig Karmazin also has phone stores and bought up homes near Lambeau Field in Green Bay. My friend, Shane Blackman, who works with Craig, would offer interesting sports opportunities to me during my Cresa days.

One thing that came my way, as a result, was a very last-minute experience that I didn't understand being passed up by anyone. I was shocked.

I went to Kohler, Wisconsin—myself and a client—where we would have had two rooms for the night, attendance to a live radio show, golf the next day on courses used on the PGA tour (yes–I know the irony, given my golfing inabilities), and a private dinner with the Packers quarterback, Aaron Rodgers.

"Do you want two of those spots?" he asked.

Rodgers wasn't as nationally known then as he is now and it was before he or his agents elevated his national appeal, accompanying his rise to super-stardom. Rodgers wasn't massive yet, but we knew he would be and this wasn't something I was going to miss. I invited my buddy Kevin Kennedy from Northwestern Mutual. Lucky for me, he didn't want to play golf the next day.

We met for the radio show portion, but Aaron was not part of that. I had personally autographed photos of Bart Starr and Brett Favre and brought along a picture of Aaron I hoped to get signed.

We had a few beers and appetizers and I shared with Shane that I had brought a gift for Aaron, a collection of 8,000 songs, all hand-chosen, on an iPod. This was when such a digital collection was rare. Shane was pretty adamant that this was an intimate dinner opportunity with no autographs or anything like that.

Jason Wilde, a Sportswriter of the Year who would be doing a show with Aaron that same week, overheard us and offered to pass it along. Aaron arrived, stayed for dinner, mingled, had a scotch, answered questions, and was incredibly personable.

▶▶ **Rodgers wasn't massive yet, but we knew he would be and this wasn't something I was going to miss.**

Steve: If you were playing Jeopardy with your Packer teammates, who would give you the most competition and who would be the most likely to cheat?

Aaron Rodgers: Let's see. John Kuhn would have given me the most competition and, the most likely to cheat? I'd say John Kuhn.

Before he left, Shane addressed us all with the intention of letting us know a signed football had been placed in each of our rooms.

"Aaron left a surprise on your bed," he said. Even Rodgers raised an eyebrow at that choice of wording and we all cracked up.

From my early days listening to Ted Moore to a lifelong fan of the Green Bay Packers, I never take for granted the honor of having crossed paths with Starr, Favre, and Rodgers, some of the greatest quarterbacks, not just of my favorite team, but of all time.

The greatest honor, though, is sharing the sports I've enjoyed for all my life with those I love. I've shared this love with my children – Joe and Haley–who I brought to games, even when they weren't women-magnet adorable babies. (I imagined Luke would be a magnet, too! He has been in Miller Park a couple of times on non-game days.) I've invited my colleagues in the industry; I have friends out on the field, including photographer Scott Paulus, whose lens has occasionally caught my crew in the stands. And in moments like the Brewers playoff loss in 2018, nothing removes the emotional disappointment like looking around and realizing—at the end of the day—*I'm surrounded by people and things I love . . . in a ballpark.*

In between

Working On A Dream

"Just hold on loosely
but don't let go
If you cling too tightly
you're gonna lose control."

▶ *FROM: Hold On Loosely*
BY: 38 Special, Hold On Loosely
(A&M Records, 1980)

*T*o "hold on loosely" to love is the best relationship advice I ever got. Over the course of two failed marriages, counseling, seminars, friends pouring into my life, and seeking out help in meetings, nothing was as impactful as the lyrics to that song.

In all of my relationships, I had been jealous, paranoid, and either checked out, or—the opposite—had been too clingy. I tried everything to do relationships better, but (no surprise) it was music that finally got through.

What did serve me well after I divorced the second time, was that I consciously decided against internalizing the experience.

I didn't want to talk about it the first time. The second time, I felt better opening up.

> "I ain't nothing but tired
> Man, I'm just tired
> and bored with myself
> Hey there baby,
> I could use just a little help
> You can't start a fire
> you can't start a fire
> without a spark."

▶ *FROM: Dancing In The Dark*
BY: Bruce Springsteen, Born In The USA
(Columbia, 1984)

When I was back in the dating scene after my first marriage, I didn't want to spend a long time sitting with the guilt. I wanted to be okay with feeling joy again. I decided to go out to LA with the girl I was dating at the time, because I loved Hollywood and thought it might be nice to have that "movie star feeling" for a few days, staying in the best place I could, driving a fancy rental car, and enjoying some events.

▶▶ **I wanted to be okay with feeling joy again.**

We planned to go to an Arsenio Hall TV show taping when he was at the height of his popularity, but I got lost; we were supposed to be there at 2:00 P.M., but we arrived at 2:40. There was a huge line. Against my personality, which would have been to find something else to do, I went to the front of the line and notified the person in charge I had arrived! My name was on the list, just in time to get in before the people waiting for overflow seating were turned away for our two saved seats.

We sat down on the aisle and there was an "X" on the floor next to me. There was a man across the aisle from me who was constantly being approached. Arsenio came up into the crowd and stood on the X! It turned out the man across from me was one of the Commodores.

During a commercial, he came back to introduce the musical performer, Three Times Dope, and stood on the X again. He was holding an album.

He said, "This is one of the hottest young rap groups in the country. Taking the charts by storm."

He looked down at me and, interacting with his audience, he said, "You got this album, man?"

I said, "Yeah, I have the 8-track." He laughed. (The perfect answer from the Midwestern white man in his crowd.)

I cracked up the King of Late Night! Here I was in LA, convertible outside, beautiful woman with me, I was just on national TV (and had even called my brother back home to make sure he set the VCR to record it). I was on cloud nine!

▶▶ **I cracked up the King of Late Night!**

As the show let out, the crowd was being escorted left to exit. I just had a whim to walk to the right rather than get herded out. We stepped out on the grounds of Universal Studios and nobody stopped us. If you walk somewhere and look like you belong, usually, nobody bothers you!

▶▶ **If you walk somewhere and look like you belong, usually, nobody bothers you!**

We walked into a building and a man in a director's chair looked back and saw me and said, "Hey, how ya' doing?"

It was Gary David Goldberg, producer/writer of Family Ties, and just like that, I was on the set of the show he created. I was well-read on pop culture and knew who he was. He looked at me like he was trying to figure out how he knew me. (He didn't, but awe and confidence can go a long way!)

While the relationship with that woman didn't last, the movie star feeling helped seduce me back into the dating world.

**"Let's slip off to a sand dune,
real soon
and kick up a little dust."**

▶ FROM: Midnight At The Oasis
BY: Maria Muldaur, Midnight At The Oasis
(Reprise Records, 1973)

I remember hearing *Midnight At The Oasis* long before I could even spell seduction. I never really had a type. I had an appreciation for beauty and drive. Then, I would just have to work on myself to be able to approach that when I saw it in people.

So, after my second divorce, I went through an interesting period. My transition began with the three people who saved my egotistical insanity. I had an intern over the summer who let me hang out with her two roommates; It was nothing romantic, but it helped

▶▶ I *didn't want* to be a cliché, dingy, apartment-living guy who gave away his paycheck to children he couldn't see.

me to just have fun friendships; People called them "Steve's Angels," after the TV show, Charlie's Angels. I *didn't want* to be a cliché, dingy, apartment-living guy who gave away his paycheck to children he couldn't see; so the Angels helped serve as a bridge to finding vibrancy again.

After that, I was strong enough to get into another relationship. It didn't last, but it did serve as another bridge . . . this time to a realization. I *didn't want* to devalue myself over my failed relationships. I realized that I had some

▶▶ I *didn't want* to devalue myself over my failed relationships.

good assets as a person: health; financial security; a career; and passions. I'd made some mistakes, too, like getting too wrapped up in some of those personal assets, sometimes at the expense of connecting with others, but I'd learned those lessons. I also had a part-time personal assistant at that time who was a lot of fun.

During that same time period, I discovered "Embracing Uncertainty[17]" by the late Susan Jeffers. It not only allowed me to see that I could be an extroverted introvert, but it gave me tremendous comfort in understanding

▶▶ I *didn't want* to be paralyzed by the hundreds of things I enjoyed worrying about.

that I *didn't want* to be paralyzed by the hundreds of things I enjoyed worrying about. I sent her an email after I read it and cherished the reply I got. (I'll do the same if you find anything valuable from this book!)

---

[17] *"Embracing Uncertainty" by Susan Jeffers, St. Martin's Griffin*

I also read self-help author Rhonda Byrne's *The Secret*[18], I realized I could get whatever I set out to get. I put it out into the universe that I wanted a real relationship. I didn't want to do it connivingly, or like a business deal, but with respect for the universe. I wanted the mystique that comes with love. I wrote out my own attributes so that I could hold onto them while seeking to share them with someone else. I was focused and spiritual, but still me and still a bit mischievous.

I saw a story about Jennifer Aniston coming off of a relationship and the story was about how she was fed up with the traditional means of meeting someone, so she was going to hire a matchmaker in LA. I tracked down that LA matchmaker and, against my better judgment, I sent them my list of attributes. They got back to me and were selling me on their matchmaking, so apparently, I wasn't a great fit for Ms. Aniston. Back to *The Secret*.

It was perfect timing to have read the book, but it was something that I had subconsciously and instinctively believed in beforehand. I still have a philosophy that, out of every 100 people or so, only one or two are consciously making efforts to make something happen with their lives, skills and talents. I don't have anything to back that up other than my own observations and experience. But, I truly believe tapping into potential is what sets people apart from the majority.

Besides the authors of *Embracing Uncertainty* and *The Secret*, the "Angels," and my assistant who helped me to rediscover fun, the other person (or people, really) who got me through were my two dearest friends, Susi and Keith Templin. I'd known them for years. They affectionately joke that they "got custody of me" after each of my divorces. Sometimes it was sad, always it was hard, but they understood me. They believed in my goodness.

I really do believe I'm motivated by love and sincerity and, almost in a poetic way, maybe that doesn't come to the surface. People don't necessarily think that's who I am. I've always believed in

▶▶ **I really do believe I'm motivated by love and sincerity.**

---

[18] *"The Secret" by Rhonda Byrne, Atria Books/Beyond Words.*

love–not just the euphoric feeling of the emotion, but in the partnership of a loving relationship. Every time I was in a relationship that didn't culminate in marriage, when all was said and done, I realized that the true connection of our souls wasn't there. They were nice people, but not the right match. As much as they didn't fit me, I didn't fit them. I was stuck in between and needed to find my next journey.

I was reading a music publication and came across a four-day Cayamo Cruise which intrigued me because I don't mind cruises; all-inclusive food options and music *did* fit me. This was an Americana music-themed cruise that was headlined in 2010 by Lyle Lovett, John Hiatt, Brandi Carlile, Emmylou Harris, and others.

Cruises are interesting. You're living closely with a few thousand people in a moving hotel and the first thing you do when you get to your room is a fire drill. It was so bizarre to me to see Lyle Lovett's shock of curly hair next to me sticking out of a life jacket. Every night, there were headliners and other performances everywhere you turned: Buddy Miller, Shawn Mullins, Robert Earl Keen, and on and on. I walked through the buffet line and battled Steve Earle for the last Crab Rangoon!

▶▶ **It was so bizarre to me to see Lyle Lovett's shock of curly hair next to me sticking out of a life jacket.**

At one point, I went to the restroom and next to me was James Taylor and Carly Simon's son, Ben Taylor. The ship was rocking quite literally and we shared a short conversation about nausea.

After the drill portion of the cruise, I went up to the pool deck and said, "I can drink whatever I want. I'm going to pick an official drink for the cruise."

Two girls standing nearby thought that was an awesome idea and the group of us ordered the same thing.

That night, heading to see John Hiatt, I heard some music from a bar area: I stopped in my tracks.

▶▶ **I stopped in my tracks.**

I was blown away by a voice, guitar work, and songs. It was one of the girls I'd met at the pool. After she finished, we started talking and I told her, Lissie (Maurus), that the last time I was that amazed by an individual performing was when I first saw John Prine.

Lissie and I bumped into each other a few more times on the cruise and, when I got back home, I discovered she had been signed to a major label. She's since released a number of albums and become a major star in the UK.

I played her music on my show and always got a good reaction. I reached out to her management to do an interview occasionally, but it never seemed to work. I even booked her for my wedding. About three weeks before the big day, though, I got a call from her management saying nonchalantly, "she can't do it."

I finally interviewed her a few years later and learned it was legit. She had been invited to a prestigious overseas music festival. Good for her and good for music. And . . . it was good to even imagine the singer for my own wedding; it meant I was ready to get there.

Music, sports, and radio had served as my rudders for so long. I had a lot of turns and changes in my life, but that was my faithful passion. It was the only thing in my life that remained strong when I had trouble with other things.

> ▶▶ Music, sports, and radio had served as my rudders for so long.

My first marriage was a starter marriage; we were young and unprepared for what marriage was supposed to be. I couldn't work it out with my second wife and it tore me up when we divorced.

It was to music I turned to find my inspiration to find the long-lasting love I'd always been seeking. Every morning, I would start my day in the car, cranking up a Bruce Springsteen song, because I was on a mission. I had a dream I was willing to work on. I wanted something real, with the feeling matched equally.

I wanted the love of my life.

"Out here the nights are
long, the days are lonely
I think of you and I'm
working on a dream
Now the cards I've drawn's a
rough hand, darling
I straighten the back and I'm
working on a dream."

▶ FROM: *Working On A Dream*
BY: *Bruce Springsteen, Working On A Dream*
(Columbia, 2009)

▶

In and around Milwaukee

IN THE CITY
The Community I Love

"How the hell can a person go
to work in the morning and
come home in the evening
and have nothing to say?"

▶ *FROM: Angel From Montgomery*
BY: John Prine, John Prine
(Atlantic, 1971)

I 'VE worked in the heart of downtown Milwaukee for most of my
life. I'm just a few blocks from one of the largest lakes in the world
on one side and tall buildings on the other–not New York City tall,
but I've worked in the U.S. Bank building, which reaches forty-two
stories high into the Southeast Wisconsin sky. The diverse city of
Milwaukee has a downtown that is home to museums, offices,
theaters, a world-class dining industry, shopping, sports stadiums,
one of the world's largest multi-stage music venues, a beach scene,
two Division I universities, numerous ethnic centers, unique districts
and festivals, public markets, and traditional Wisconsin companies,
such as Harley-Davidson, Milwaukee Tool, and Northwestern
Mutual.

The city is a genuine mix of blue-collar staples, unexpected arts and entertainment, sports, education, professional industries, and a lot of

▶▶ **It's always been a great city.**

well-deserved city pride from people too humble and hard-working to say as much. It's always been a great city. And in 2020, it will be the national spotlight for the Democratic National Convention. Admittedly we have issues like segregation and public education to tackle, but we also have no shortage of willing participants to manage those issues.

I drive into my office each day and I've had some exciting vehicles over the years. Like any good Milwaukeean, I've had my Harley experience. One of the point guys for a company I represented in a real estate deal was a big Harley guy. He had to sell his bike. This was a guy who had a garage where you could eat off the floor. He treated his motorcycle like a child.

He said, "I really want you to own this, have this, buy this."

It was a big deal to him, like finding a new home for a beloved pet, so I listened intently. This wasn't about trying to make a sale. He actually wanted me to care for his long, wide, soft tail deuce *child*. We arranged a fair deal and he brought it to my house. I signed up for a week-long riding class. At the time, I was putting in ten-hour real estate days, working out, playing ball twice a week, and running a short-lived-five-night-a-week-plus-the-Sunday radio show. When I signed up for that Monday-through-Friday, 9:00 A.M. to 2:00 P.M. class, it completely *derailed* my life, so I probably went into this supposedly relaxing hobby with much greater stress than I should have had.

I learned a lot in the course and, conceptually, I knew everything that would be on the test. I could tell the instructors *what* I should do and could even articulate the *how*, but I struggled in actually implementing the lessons. Shifting on the bike did not come naturally to me. I was having the hardest time. I was barely getting through the test and I screwed up the very last maneuver. Somehow, though, I passed and they licensed me.

That beautiful Harley, after I passed the test, got a total of eight miles on it. It was just so massive that I never felt in control of it. I liked the concept of a motorcycle, though. I went out and, against my Wisconsin pride, bought a Yamaha. Now the Yamaha has been sitting in the garage!

The vehicle I truly loved was my Jeep Wrangler. When the doors and roof were off, it was *like* a motorcycle . . . but attached to a La-Z-Boy recliner. To me, it was the epitome of cool. It had everything I wanted and the only thing about it was that it was older.

There wasn't much to go wrong on my old Jeep, but I found the one thing that I couldn't manage. I'm not technically proficient or mechanical. Just inserting "Tab A" into "Slot B" sets me fumbling. I had trouble getting the doors back on after I took them off, so I was very cautious about when it would come out of the garage. I woke up every morning, checked the news, and only took it on the days when no rain was in the forecast. It was a treat to take my Jeep. Running errands was fun. Just dropping off a plan to a client was fun.

One day, when I brought it to work, I was in a suit on the interstate in the middle of a crawling rush hour. All of a sudden, out of the blue, a summer thunderstorm deluge began to drop *buckets of water* on me. Every time I turned my head, people were pointing and taking pictures. I looked out of place in it even on the best of days, but this was something that turned into a spectacle . . . and the radio never worked the same after that day.

I made the decision early in my adult life that, once I'm at work—unless it's precipitating heavily like my Jeep Wrangler memory—if any meeting is within seven blocks, I don't want to drive there. I'll walk in my city. I don't know why I picked seven blocks. It was just some arbitrary number I decided upon that seemed to make sense and it's served me well for decades. I don't want to move my car, for sure.

▶▶ I walk a lot downtown and I really enjoy it because it gives me some time to not answer my phone, get into my head, think about meetings I'm headed into, and observe what's going on around me.

That's a pain in any city. But it's more than that. I walk a lot downtown and I really enjoy it because it gives me some time to not answer my phone, get into my head, think about meetings I'm headed into, and observe what's going on around me.

Real estate legend Bob Polacheck used to tell me, "When you are driving somewhere, if possible, take the city streets, not the highway. Notice opportunities. See businesses that could be exploding soon or that are in an under-marketed area where you could be helpful."

Working downtown, I was able to intensify that "noticing" by walking. Some people are intimidated by walking near perceived dangers or unfamiliar city realities that may make them uncomfortable, but I had a little experience that broke those fears in me. I once served as host of a panel on homelessness. It was a group that was working to eliminate this harsh human reality. The district attorney, the mayor, the county executive, the police chief, and other high-powered people from the area participated and I was there to moderate. It was an honor and awe-inspiring to be a part of the conversation to make the city I love even better.

I remember learning—and I think it was the police chief who explained this—how to recognize the difference between danger and just discomfort. If you're in a big city and there's somebody you would traditionally perceive as a "crazy person" on the street wearing eighty mismatched, misfit layers, standing on the corner, it might be your instinct to associate him with harassment. If he's there talking to a group, though, he's just a character, one of those who give a city its eccentric flavor. Now, if it is just you and he standing there—and he's still having that conversation, that could be a red flag. Not always, but you need to learn to read, not just people, but the full scene. City dangers aren't about specific people, locations, or even situations; they're about who or what stands out as a sore thumb. If something is not an aberration, it's probably not a problem.

▶▶ **City dangers aren't about specific people, locations, or even situations; they're about who or what stands out as a sore thumb.**

So, fearlessly—though with awareness—I walk. Just as I did when I was a kid coming into the city, I walk. I people- and scene-watch for positives and negatives, for whimsicality and waywardness. I've even found myself stopping to admire a piece of art or a street performer. I observe – noticing all the things I would miss from behind the wheel of my car.

In my car, it's just the vehicles around me, the road beneath me, and the radio. The radio debate one afternoon was about immigration reform, the hot news topic of the day. Instead of listening to extreme opinions on that day, though, I ended up walking by the federal courthouse downtown.

A large group of newly anointed citizens were exiting the courthouse at just that moment. I was swept up into a wave of them as they all flooded out at once, maybe thirty or forty people. They were there with family members and friends. The new citizens who had just taken the oath stood out from the rest of the group of well-wishers with them. They each had a little American flag that they'd received as part of the ceremony.

So here I was amid America's melting pot of people, beaming with what I can only describe as ecstasy at becoming American citizens. There were family members with tears in their eyes and pride in their postures; a glow was over every person on that square; the rush of emotion that filled me, even without saying a word; from simply observing that scene; has stuck with me; I didn't have the outlet to share or express or do anything other than take it in; a tweet couldn't capture it; a photo would have seemed contrived.

Don McLean: I've tried to be a pure artist and tell the truth with the songs that I write. I don't like to grasp at straws to get attention. Everything just came from the heart.

Steve: So that explains why you don't like to explain everything, right?

Don: Exactly.

Steve: Do you think Madonna's version of American Pie resonated with people?

Don: Definitely. Oh yes. There was a period for about three years after that came out when I was signing bras and getting picked up again.

A couple of weeks later, I did a show with the theme "Songs About America," but even that couldn't do it justice. The lyrics to that moment could only be felt, not spoken or even put to music. I've walked through angry mobs before ... aberrations; this was the antithesis to that. It was a mob of joy and it was indescribable. I still think about it today.

▶▶ **It was a mob of joy and it was indescribable.**

When you walk down seven blocks of any major city in the United States, you'll see consumerism, obliviousness, and probably a few sore thumbs. But if you look, if you notice, you're going to see beauty, whether in a piece of art or in the eyes of a single person in a swarm of many people bursting with indescribably ecstatic joy at something the people behind the wheels may take for granted.

Milwaukee is unique because not many cities of this size are on a body of water like we have here. The lake is big and active, but the city has just more than half a million people–enough to offer everything you could want while still having a close-knit community, neighborhood familiarity, and a small-town feel. It's growing in positive ways as part of a one and a half million people metropolitan area. There is a lot of great history and charm to be seen and taken in, but it's also staying relative and current. It's an attractive city for business and entertainment, with a great music scene *and* a great sports scene. Sure, it's cold for too long, but that's the only drawback.

▶▶ **There is a lot of great history and charm to be seen and taken in, but it's also staying relative and current.**

Like any city, Milwaukee has some shady elements of history. I almost became closely tied to one of its worst. I was a full-time commercial real estate broker already when I was called to jury duty for serial-killer Jeffrey Dahmer's[19] approaching trial. I went in and quickly discovered that the prosecutors had seen to it that they could not screw this up. They were on top of everything with every potential jury member and there were what looked like 1,000 people there to be considered for the twelve peer spots, although I can't imagine anyone was considered a peer to Dahmer. Everyone knew what they were there for.

This man was an aberration to humanity. I was sitting there thinking to myself, *'On one hand, this is going to be history. Everyone is talking about it. Imagine being there in the fold as this trial happens. On the other hand, I know it is to be long and sequestered in addition to being horrifying. Do I really want to be in the room when we hear about his atrocities?'*

It would take a naïve person to not get kicked off of a jury selection if they tried. I needed to decide if I wanted to be truly considered or if I was going to "allow myself" to be disqualified. I made the choice that, given the opportunity, I was going to be a part of the jury. They randomly assigned each jury pool member a number and brought us in by groups, a handful at a time. I had a really high number, so my concern and worrying was for nothing, as I was ultimately dismissed before my group went in. They had their jury.

"The Monster's" trial was broadcast *live* on the radio and I remember hearing it, uncensored, as I was driving around. After days and days of gross and unimaginable details, it became so disturbing that I had to turn it off. I didn't want that poison in my head. Though I had made the choice that I

▶▶ **I would not have been able to turn off the live experience.**

---

[19] *Jeffrey Dahmer was termed the Milwaukee Monster–a serial killer who first killed in Ohio before he murdered and cannibalized sixteen more young, male rape victims over thirteen years. After pleading guilty to most charges, he was sentenced to multiple life sentences. He was later murdered in prison.*

would serve if asked, I was glad not to have had to be a part of it. I would not have been able to turn off the live experience and it's hard enough to remove the memory of it from my ears.

I did serve on a jury later. Someone had been beaten up by a bouncer at a bar and he was suing the bar. He didn't win. The assault to my own senses was far more manageable in such a simple case.

I care about this city and get upset about the black marks on its history. Rock & Roll Roots makes me somewhat well-known, but my personality in the business world is just as good a fit. Sometimes I meet other DJs who love music and know it as well as I do, but I'd like to think I'm a connector outside of the studio, too. People hear me on the radio, but can experience what I'm like in person too.

Whenever there's an announcement for a new project, I want to talk about the positive impacts to Milwaukee and the area. I remain excited about the Milwaukee I grew up in, but am just as engaged in new projects. I want to absorb every moment of life and this city is an extension of my life. I try to go full force into any development or any project. As long as there's a good impact to be had, I want to be a part of it. And that means that I connect with all of the people that can make a project happen, regardless of their philosophies or politics.

If anyone tried to label me politically, well–I can't even do it, so I don't know how someone else could purport to try. My parents were Democrats. They were very typical Kennedy-era working folk, although they actually wanted Adlai Stevenson to win the nomination and become president. My folks believed that Democrats were the party of civil rights.

> ▶▶ **If anyone tried to label me politically, well–I can't even do it, so I don't know how someone else could purport to try.**

So, politically, I was kind of a Democrat, but never labeled myself even then. Later in life, when I started having some success and giving what I could to charity, I started steering toward the right in fiscal responsibility. I guess I had gone from idealism to realism.

That's where I still stand now. I'm still conservative fiscally; I believe in an individual's rights and I don't like changing things that are working just for the sake of having a cause. That's mostly conservative or Republican stuff. At the same time, some would call me ultra-liberal (using today's definitions) in terms of social justice. Honestly, I would think that most Americans shouldn't wholly identify with any one party of today's extremes and if so, we can all be grateful for that.

Where the line gets really weird is in the area of drugs. In the '70s, they were prevalent. I'm so thankful no one ever put heroin before me. But today, I find it abhorrent that someone would tell a cancer patient that they can't have cannabis if it is causing them relief from pain, or a PTSD victim can't have it to calm his or her nerves, or someone with concussive syndrome can't use it to manage symptoms. Those aren't the same things as using hard drugs for a high that could lead to addiction. And that's before you even consider the tax revenues that result from the cannabis industry.

Steve: I know you get to Milwaukee often.

Alice Cooper: Wayne's World was one of those things where Mike Myers came along and said we needed somebody iconic. He knew I was an actor on top of being a rocker. He handed me all the dialogue. I had dinner with him recently and he's still funny as hell. It was pivotal because it introduced me to a '90s audience. The best TV thing I did was probably not seen by a lot of people. I did the Gene Wilder show. I played his next-door neighbor. I did about a ten-minute comedy scene with him in front of a live audience. It's probably one of the things I'm most proud of. Having to time it and knowing when to wait for the laugh and wait for the mug. So to work with Gene Wilder was like jamming with The Beatles.

Steve: And you know where he's from, right?

Alice: Yeah. Milwaukee. And the sweetest guy in the world.

The love I have for Milwaukee means it doesn't matter who is in office. I appreciate the willingness for leaders to serve. I see the personal connection more than everybody's talk about ideological beliefs. Like personalities in the media, or in business, politicians have a need to interact with people of all different backgrounds and I have a healthy respect for anyone willing to do so in such an ugly political climate.

I remember interviewing iconoclastic rock-star Alice Cooper, a Midwest native, who has his own love for Milwaukee. When I asked if he'd ever vote for himself in a political

▶▶ **And first of all, who would ever go to a rock star to ask who to vote for?**

race, he said, "Oh, I would never vote for me. I would be the worst thing to ever happen to this country. I would give away the baby with the bathwater. I'm so extremely unpolitical. Rock & Roll and politics are just so far away from each other, I think–at least they should be. I think it's a little bit wrong to shame your audience into voting for who you're voting for. 'If you're my fan, you better vote for blah blah blah.' Now you're treating your audience like sheep. Now you're telling them that they don't know who to vote for. And first of all, who would ever go to a rock star to ask who to vote for? The guy that's working in my yard in the backyard knows more about it than I do; why would you ever ask me who to vote for?" Laughing, he finished with, "Are people forgetting that we're rock stars?"

The short of it is that I am so lucky to live, work, and be involved in such a vibrant town and I don't think any powers that be are powerful enough to change the culture of the community as much as the new generation has for the better. Milwaukee is diverse in a way that you wouldn't expect. That diversity makes it a city for arts, food, and entertainment in great variety. You can't get sick of any one thing, because the people aren't any one thing, so neither is what they bring to the city and what they've been able to bring to me for my entire life. I think back to my early college regrets about not going further away and realize that things have reason and purpose. For me, in this lakeshore city, that purpose has so often been awe.

This city is part of the fabric of my being.

IN THE FEEDS
My Online Life

"Know you got to run
Know you got to hide
Still, there is a great life
engrained deep
within your eyes
Open up, open up
Baby let me in
You expect for me to love you
when you hate
yourself my friend."

▶ *FROM: Everybody I Love You*
BY: Crosby, Stills, Nash & Young, Déjà vu
(Atlantic Records, 1970)

S OCIAL media has become part of the fabric of today's society. It's not going anywhere anytime soon.

Every time I tweet something, I think about the risk/reward equation . . . and then I do it anyway. That equation is so absurdly stacked against you that it's stupid! The chance of something being substantive and positive is so slim compared to tweeting something that will ruin your career. You could have a lifetime of relationship-building with your followers and a single word that is taken out of context can cause offense and exodus. It's a tightrope on the best of days, but there is something that I love about walking that tight rope. I could fall to my career death, so I'd damned well better walk it well.

I remember when the Eagles' Don Henley was preparing for a possible Storytellers tour. He was considering going out on the road to tell stories behind iconic songs, take audience questions, and play some music. He did a one-off show in Dallas to an audience of just 220 people and I was lucky to be one of them. The day of the show, I couldn't have been more excited. I was sitting down waiting for the show to start when Don Henley came out. He asked for no pictures or recordings because he was trying something out. He said he'd do a song later that we could record, knowing everyone was dying to do so.

The Eagles are notorious for protecting their work. If every musician deserves the right to decide what happens, how to profit, and retain intellectual property, the Eagles believed anyone who violated it should pretty much be shot on the spot. They went after almost everything. They sued and later settled with a place that called itself Hotel California, so we respected Henley's request and kept our devices away.

The show he put on was spectacular–phenomenal. True to his promise, toward the end of the show, he said, "Okay. One song. You can bring out your phones."

He played "Hotel California," told the story behind the song, a journey from innocence to experience, and he answered questions. He was gregarious and warm. Everybody was thrilled, filming, and taking pictures. He stayed behind to meet and have a picture with every single person who wanted one.

That night, I tweeted a little twenty-five-second clip of the song we were allowed to record. Likes and retweets were piling up quickly. A week or two later, I got a letter from a law firm with a cease and desist order asking for its removal.

I recognized the difference between trolls and people protecting legal rights. They didn't ask for any sort of financial damages. There wouldn't have been any to give unless they wanted to withdraw from the bank account of words in the comments. They just wanted the video down, so I removed it.

For years, I didn't want to do anything with social media. Anything I did do, I wanted to be for sincerity. I consider myself quirky, goofy, irreverent, and straddling the line of good taste, but hopefully not stupid. I question myself every day, *'Why do I tweet?'*

▶▶ **I consider myself quirky, goofy, irreverent, and straddling the line of good taste, but hopefully not stupid.**

I've had tweets I thought were brilliant that were totally ignored to the tune of one or two likes and innocuous things that went viral. I've had innocent things that were taken as anything but and passionate moments that passed without a second glance. Tweeting has become my second creative outlet after radio.

▶▶ **I've had tweets I thought were brilliant that were totally ignored and innocuous things that went viral.**

At my first radio job in the '70s, there were grammar nuts out there who would send written letters about my spoken grammatical slip-ups. Today, anything goes. There are a lot of times people totally don't get what I'm saying. Sometimes a subtle cleverness vocalized on the air may or may not be interpreted correctly in writing. But, again and again, I walk that tightrope.

I never know when something is going to become viral. One time, a tweeted photo of Adrian Peterson being walked through a restaurant after an injury because it was the straightest path out of the stadium during the Packer/Viking matchup. That tweet got picked up by national media. A similar thing happened with a tweet about Jim Kelly's cancer revelation. It was retweeted and then viewed over a million times. Those didn't compare in impact to my biggest buzz, though (pun intended).

There's no question I'm a Brewer fan, so my followers were very engaged during the last four weeks of the 2018 season and pennant race. That was some of the most fun I'd had in my online life.

▶▶ **That was some of the most fun I'd had in my online life.**

Right around when we were pretty sure they'd make the playoffs, I created the coupon that offered to share a toast of bourbon if the Brewers won the division and fans caught me at the game. I tweeted it and got a lot of responses, laughs, and fun. Then, the magic happened. The Brewers were on a winning streak! The Cubs lost. The Brewers in position to TIE! We had a one-game playoff. I reiterated the tweet and, all of a sudden, the click counter was going crazy. I was so nervous for game 163; I wanted the Brewers to win as a fan, but also thought, *'HOW EXPENSIVE WILL THIS GET?!'*

In retrospect, it helped me remain safe. If the Brewers lost, I didn't have to spend hundreds and hundreds on bourbon. If they won, I couldn't be happier for my team. They won and my friends at Bell Ambulance printed 250 copies of my coupon and handed them out. When the playoffs began, people were walking up to me with coupons! I started reaching out. If doing it, I wanted to do it right. So, I started making videos with celebrities and pushed the offer to even greater popularity. I bought hundreds of bourbons over those weeks. I carried it around in my car with plastic cups and I'd serve people wherever I ran into them! The cost was nothing compared to the joy of sharing a toast with fellow fans.

In all the years I've been using Twitter, I've connected with people and built friendships from it. There have been times when I've learned or confirmed breaking news and instances where I felt rewarded by impacting somebody with a tweet that made a person smile, or laugh, or relate. Just as in my radio show, the checks are a bonus, my payment for social media is the words from followers. I have joy when people reference something I've posted. But I have also angered people, deleted posts, and even regretted things that I couldn't truly take back. It comes with the territory.

I remember one day wanting to be clever (too clever). The Brewers had a giveaway of a starting pitcher Matt Garza Russian Nesting Doll. It would be absurd even as Babe Ruth, but Matt Garza? I googled Matt Garza, found his wife's name, and tweeted, "I would think the only person wanting a Matt Garza Nesting Doll would be his wife." I got a few likes and comments. Then, Matt Garza followed me.

'Wow! Cool?'

But, wait a minute. He was following me to direct message me. I got a very powerful message from him that I respected. "You can say whatever you want about me—criticize me—but do not dare bring my wife or family into it."

My heart sunk. I didn't really want to hurt anyone and he was right. I got back to him and said, "You're right. It was not my intent and I truly do apologize." I sent him that and I kind of looked away and thought to myself, take the lessons out of this:

▶▶ My heart sunk. I didn't really want to hurt anyone and he was right.

- Every joke affects somebody.
- Creativity that forces research may be something you shouldn't do at all.
- If you have a platform, use it for good.

I looked back at my phone and, the second Garza read my direct message, he unfollowed me.

Unfortunately, I've also had times when a misinterpreted tweet has gotten negative attention. I was at a game by myself and, to my right, was a young lady scoring the game on an old-fashioned scorecard. I looked at it and thought that was the best thing I'd seen all day. I tweeted about being encouraged by this nostalgic show of fan interaction. The picture, which didn't show the girl's face because she was angled away from me with her hair in front of her (and a baseball cap on) got a lot of likes and engagements and snowballed from there. Then, someone in Madison took offense and posted, "Did you have this girl's permission from her parents to take her picture?" Then, someone else chimed in and called me "creepy."

The insinuation was that I was perverted or stalking! A few people replied in agreement and I made the stupid decision to engage. They all came at me, then. So, I had to just stop. The lesson I took is to never engage in negativity. Instead of the negative, I walked away with the awe. I didn't look at others' words again – I looked instead at the picture and found joy in its simplicity. In a world where there are problems everywhere, this was hope.

What didn't have any hope, according to social media, was my singing skills. I was excited for the opportunity to catch an Adam Sandler routine when he was in town taping his *Netflix Special*, but I had to take a bathroom break at one point. When you do that in the midst of a comedy act, not only are you fair game, but I had no way back to my seat other than to walk right in front of the stage! Coming back to my seat, Sandler had me sing along on one of his signature comedic

songs. He stopped playing and said, "That was terrible, man," which I tweeted about later! That night, though, I laughed all the way back to my seat.

I always try to stay open-minded and young at heart, Most of the internet and time-saving technology that exists has my full endorsement. I love ordering food from restaurants without talking to a human, feeding a parking meter without standing in the rain, and only asking a mostly infallible GPS system for directions rather than a very fallible stranger at a gas station.

I love that we carry computers in our hands the way people in the Wild West days had their firearms always with them. I am not one to look around and count how many people I see on the street are looking directly at their phones (except that there were eleven out of thirteen in my two-block downtown walk one day) because I sometimes do it myself.

Stephen Stills: There's no texting allowed in the first ten rows at one of our concerts. Even if my eyes are closed and I'm really into it, it's not like I'm not going to notice. From the stage, you see this "moonlight" that's shining up on you and people are obviously not paying attention. Use your phone to stream songs . . . for pennies on the dollar.

Steve: That's so pertinent to point out how addicted our society is to electronic devices. It's important to note. It's sickening. And, can I get you to follow me on Twitter?

Stills: (Laughing) Actually, they are all forming one conglomerate. It's called "YouTwitFace."

What does impact me is that it seems increasingly systemic that I can't just do something in one step without being redirected to an app. I realize those entities tell me it will be easier in the future and I do know that they are looking for repeat business. But every once in a while, it would be refreshing if the person next to me would just hand me the document they want me to see for five seconds, without having to go to my Dropbox app first.

Can I hear a song, get a paycheck, buy tickets, get my hair cut, change the temperature in the house, buy a hat, find a burger, or read an article without first adding a specific app? Even some of my favorite sites and blogs demand apps.

I enjoy blogging as an outlet, but I am so used to the radio, where I can say something dumb and it's forgotten seconds later. This internet stuff keeps your mistakes in some permanent sphere where they can come back to haunt you. Some of my mistakes have definitely haunted me.

I once wrote that it was Dave Marsh that was the music critic who called Bruce Springsteen the future of Rock & Roll. Somebody *kindly* corrected me that it was Jon Landeau in the comment section of my blog . . . by also making sure to point out that I was no Dave Marsh or Jon Landau.

I made the mistake and all I could say was "whoops-a-daisy." It's the phrase I heard almost every day as a child – my mother's very British term for "I screwed up!"

Everybody makes mistakes, but the internet keeps a record of all of those wrongs. Being digitally put in my place reminded me of some miscues over the years from some of my favorite musicians, and I shared them in another blog, fully aware that somebody could claim I was no Mick Jagger, Ringo Starr, Lou Reed, or other musician worthy of being forgiven for my "whoops-a-daisy."

▶▶ **Everybody makes mistakes, but the internet keeps a record of all of those wrongs.**

The Rolling Stones used the British version of the Hells Angels as security at one of their European shows. That went well since those motorcycle enthusiasts wore sweaters and had meerschaum pipes. Mick and the boys figured the U.S. version would work just as well at their Altamont, California, show. Those guys had leather vests and lead pipes. It didn't turn out very well.

Ringo Starr forgot the words to his own song at the fundraising, rock star-studded "Concert for Bangladesh," and decades later it is still there for all to see and hear. I feel for you Ringo, although I have a feeling there will be no movie made of my latest tweet or blog.

Sinead O'Connor tore up a picture of The Pope on Saturday Night Live. There went her Supercuts endorsements.

David Sancious quit the E Street Band.

Decca Records rejected The Beatles.

In 1989, The Grammy Award for best Heavy Metal album went to Jethro Tull . . . over Metallica and AC/DC.

In the movie The Rocker, they are in a bus going past the Rock & Roll Hall of Fame and the driver says, "It's on your left." I have been there four times. The street they are driving on is a dead end, and it can only be on your right.

Mick Taylor quit the Stones.

Lip-syncers Milli Vanilli didn't quit when they were ahead.

In 1958, the Esso Research Center came out with a study that said it was not smart to listen to Rock & Roll on the car radio because it caused drivers to unconsciously jiggle the gas pedal and waste fuel.

Dennis Wilson of The Beach Boys befriended Charles Manson. They actually collaborated on a song that made it to the B-side of a Beach Boys single in the '60s.

Lou Reed was once so mad at his record company that he released a double album that was all grinding noises. Really! It was called Metal Machine Music.

Mistakes in music and media happen. Mistakes in social media? They happen, and are highlighted, and commented on, and archived, and made to work against a lifetime of non-whoops-a-daisies.

Okay that's three whoops-a-daisies, sorry.

It's love, and it's hate, and it's here to stay. Social media has completely changed the media industry. People have so many ways to get their news and entertainment. We have to tailor our

▶▶ **It's love, and it's hate, and it's here to stay.**

communications and be multi-dimensional. We want to be prevalent and present on all of the platforms where we can make an impact in a way that has, hopefully, more reward than risk. Social media has completely reformatted how audiences consume.

For better or for worse, though, I choose to walk the bittersweet, 280-character tightrope to reach another unseen audience.

IN THE END
Remembering A Friend

"And this love
Is like nothing
I have ever known.
Take my hand, love
I'm taking you home
I'm taking you home."

▶ *FROM: Taking You Home*
BY: Don Henley, Inside Job
(Warner Brothers, 2000)

*M*Y mother was dainty and proper and—to my children—she was sweet. She made all sorts of little finger puppets for Haley when she was a little girl. She must have knitted 100 of those things. She had always been thin and lanky, like me, so I still see her in the mirror sometimes, but she never said, "I love you," to me until the day she was on her deathbed. A few days after she died, I was at a Don Henley concert with Joe and Haley's mom on my right and a family friend on my left. Henley's lyrics hit me.

"I had a good life
before you came
I had my friends
and my freedom
I had my name.
Still there was sorrow
and emptiness
'Til you made me glad
Oh, in this love I found
strength I never knew I had."

The great thing about music is that it can affect people differently than even the writer or performer intended. It doesn't have to be the same for everyone. I had long ago decided that, for me, *Taking Me Home* was about taking a child home for the first time. I remember that feeling of completeness and love when I brought Joe home, and then

Haley. When I heard it that day after my mom died, this song of fulfillment said something different to me. I could feel the tears start to come. My friend noticed and comforted me with a simple hand to my shoulder. There's something about human contact that gave me this immediate sense of comfort. In this case, it was the human contact of my friend and, at a deeper level, of the song.

I love that music can reach the parts of ourselves that we don't even want to show or know are there. The lyrics of Henley's *Taking You Home* could be about meeting the love of his life; it could be about bringing a kid home from the hospital; and—on that day—it made me think of taking my mom eternally home. That's the essence of music.

My dad died shortly after my mom. It's odd for me to think about the fact that my father was in the Holocaust. It really is incredible and I know there's honor and a tremendous survival instinct I believe he passed on to me that goes with his experiences. This book wouldn't be here if it weren't for that; I wouldn't be here; and I choose to be grateful for him.

Everybody loses people and the lucky eventually lose their parents. Not that losing parents is a good thing or that it isn't hard. It is definitely hard. I say it's lucky because I can't imagine the pain when it happens the other way around. And, for me, losing my good friend John Rausch, was just as hard as losing my parents.

Early in my adulthood, the two of us worked briefly together at WAUK (more on that stint to come). We ended up becoming roommates in a duplex in suburban Whitefish Bay. It was very unusual to find something in that upscale area that two goofy radio guys could afford. It was on a corner with a nice yard and was being used as investment real estate for a man who was much more well-off than the two of us were. For us, it was a magnet for our friends. We had full use of the garage, basement, and yard with no one upstairs. Every once in a while, the owner would run an ad for the upstairs part of the home, but that's it. We realized we could sabotage anyone looking at it. If he called us to let us know that someone was

going to look at it, we'd be the worst neighbors! (I'm not proud of all of John and my stories.) We'd blast our music and be loud. We would go to Arthur Treacher's Fish & Chips, where one of the side dishes was hush puppies. We would put them into the toilet.

They'd see the toilet backed up. Together, we were very successful at keeping people out.

There was one couple who was not dissuaded by our shenanigans, so we eventually had to share "our" house. We were working in rock radio and they were a preppy couple with no children, perfectly manicured nails, and a golden retriever. Not that there was anything wrong with manicured nails, but it was the '70s and to see that on a man was so foreign to us.

When John and I lived together, whoever woke up earliest got to choose the first album of the day. We carried our shared love of music into the studio with us.

After all the time in high school at WUWM and after college radio, while I was employed with the bank and trying to break into radio by working as a stringer, there was a small but real station, 1510 AM (WAUK). The station had a strong signal, owned by a Chicago company. I called the program director, and he agreed to see me. The interview went great. He said he liked me and could give me a chance in the 6:00 to 7:30 P.M. slot. I was to start in a week.

I was told to listen to the afternoon guy because he was the epitome of what they wanted. His name, John Rausch, was familiar. There was a John Rausch a year behind me at John Marshall High School. The next week, I went in and discovered it was him! I didn't really know him well since we ran in different circles as teenagers. John had been into muscle cars and music by Little Feat. I was more into Taco Bell and The Beatles.

I did my hour and a half. The format was adult easy listening. Every once in a while, we could sneak a Fleetwood Mac into the mix next to Barry Manilow. We relished those moments. That's where I learned one of my best lessons in radio (and life): it was always easier to ask for forgiveness than permission.

As a daytime-only radio station, they went off the air at sunset. One day, as summer was waning, the program director said, "Sign off at seven." We had to shut down so that our signal didn't interfere with other stations.

Back then, we had to take meter readings in a back room to make sure we had the right power and the right frequency at the right time. We had to do it hourly. I had done enough to pass the test, but didn't really know what I was doing. I had all this power at my fingertips. I could have gone in, jacked the knob up, and taken over national stations, but that would've been a one-time-only bad decision, so I lost half an hour of my show.

As the daylight hours shortened, I had to shut down at 6:45.

Then 6:30.

Then 6:15.

At that point, I had a fifteen-minute show!

So, I quit.

But, due to my short time as a colleague at that station, John and I became and remained good friends.

There was no competition between us. I couldn't tell you why. It just wasn't there between John and me. John—the voice that graced thousands of announcements and who spent time at WQFM, WMYX, WAUK, WISN and WTMJ—and I never fought. Not once.

Everything we ever did was in support of one another. Some people you run across in life, you go years without seeing and everything falls right back into place as if no time has passed. I think back to being roomies,

▶▶ **Everything we ever did was in support of one another.**

working together, being involved in each other's lives, kids' lives, and significant others . . . I can't think of one single time we ever had a cross word or disagreement. We had perfect chemistry. We never had a chance to be partners on the air and he didn't stay as an on-air personality for his whole career.

When radio stations switched from vinyl albums to CDs, John and I fought that. Then, when CDs gave way to digital files, we fought that, too. John fought harder than I did. In fact, long before those technological changes, he fought really hard to get the radio stations we loved to open their playlists to emulate the days when we were lucky enough to grow up hearing all the artists we loved being *introduced* to us on air. Man, he fought for that.

He moved to Colorado eventually and that's where he continued to have the real fight of his life. It started with a dreaded cancer diagnosis. And he fought that in a way that taught me about dignity, tenacity, optimism, attitude, and the importance of family.

I mentioned, though, that WE never fought. While most of the blurry pay-per-view-worthy stories of our times together are not shareable, as I eventually made it full time into radio and we both enjoyed the perks of our Rock & Roll lifestyles, there is no doubt in my mind I must have been annoying as a roommate. But never once could I recall a harsh word from John.

▶▶ **Never once could I recall a harsh word from John.**

We also never once shared the air together, but I witnessed the most important show of his life: the start of the thirty-seven years he spent with the love of his life, Kim. I had the honor of being the best man at their wedding, and he was best man at my first and second weddings, but that doesn't

John with his wife, Kim, and their two children.

help the longevity of our story. John was one of those friends that you could not see for years and immediately pick up where you left off. And that is what we did for three decades.

We shared music, and crazy stories, and laughter. One of the times we spoke toward the end of his life, though, John asked me to stop making him laugh . . . because it was making him cough. I knew that he was coughing all the time then, and he was starting to suffer, and there was nothing funny about that. I loved him for leaving me that memory, though–the memory of a conversation that needed to hold off the laughter of a lifelong friendship. It was the last time we spoke.

Our conversation was indicative of every interaction he had with all of his friends throughout his life and over the length of his fight. He was optimistic and always focused on what is important: family and friendship. I also love him for leaving me that lesson. And I know he left it with Kim and their children. It will be there every day.

I'm not sure this is the right word, but it was "poetic" that I heard about John's passing on a Sunday morning while I was on the air. I don't know that the words I used did him justice, but I knew that he would have wanted me to play some Little Feat.

So I did. For John Rausch. My friend.

He was a huge Little Feat fan. He just fought tooth and nail for all this great music that he knew, but wasn't able to share, because they weren't money-earners. He fought for those marginal bands to get exposure. I played the song . . . it wasn't enough, but it was right.

When John passed away, his wish was not to have a traditional woe-is-me funeral, but a party. He dictated the aspects of that party. They buried him in Colorado and waited until summer to hold a celebration of his life in Milwaukee.

It was the best celebration I'd seen in my life. He had a playlist of music that probably was about five days long. His motorcycle was there. He loved candy; he wanted a big table with all sorts of candy. I offered up our home, despite all of the other venues available and it was such an honor to have the celebration. The weather couldn't have been more cooperative. Saz's Catering donated massive amounts of food. It was a '70s and 80s Milwaukee radio reunion with hundreds of people. And my favorite part? Everyone just told stories.

"We all loved John. I spent more time in their apartment than my own. They had a wall the size of a garage door of record albums. I'd never seen so many; it was more than the local record stores. It was a cool place to hang out and I made myself home there." (Jay Filter)

"John was a friend to all of us–wonderful, funny, full of life. He approached life in a positive way, even though he was snide as hell." (Susi Templin)

My second favorite part of the event involved Popeye's Chicken. The last thing John had searched for on his laptop was, "closest Popeye's Chicken." So, I ordered dozens of Popeye's drumsticks and we all held them in the air as a toast to John.

The music was great, the speeches were heartfelt, and there was an outdoor screen set up to share pictures and video. There was no sadness in that event. In fact, 911 was called three times to our house! One woman fell and broke her hip. Then, we had someone pass out who was at first not revivable. He wouldn't go with the EMTs. They had to come back to get him when it happened again.

I know John was up there looking at it all and laughing (but not coughing).

"I'm taking you home.
I'm taking you home,
where we can be with
the ones who really care.
Home, where we
can grow together.
Keep you in
my heart forever."

In Love
Security, Freedom, And Aleta

"Meet me in
the middle of the day
Let me hear you say
everything's okay."

▶ *FROM: Romeo's Tune*
BY: Steve Forbert, Jackrabbit Slim
(Nemperor, 1979)

I WAS not in a relationship at the time I first heard Steve Forbert's song, "Romeo's Tune," in the late '70s. It had just missed the Top 10, so it wasn't as familiar as a lot of music from that era. But I remember wishing then that I had somebody with whom I could say that line. I wanted the kind of relationship that had his daytime love description, as well as words for the night: "Meet me in the middle of the night. Let me hear you say, 'Everything's alright.' Let me smell the moon in your perfume."

There's a dichotomy of freedom and security in the song. He says, "Hold me tight and love and loving's free," and that's a feeling I'd spent my life longing to feel. I wanted to hear the "I love yous" because they should be free. I wanted the home that people could come to and feel welcomed and joyful and encouraged . . . the things I always tried to create around me . . . things I didn't have when I faced out toward the alley. Instead, I was a twice-divorced, two-career man without a truly *serious* prospect for a future relationship.

Meanwhile, for about five years before meeting me, Aleta Norris was known by her friends as a one-date wonder, in search of her forever guy. She wanted to meet someone with whom it was the real deal.

My assistant at the time, Kendall, knew I was on the search. She had met Aleta and thought I'd like her. I googled Aleta, saw an image and admittedly thought, *'Works for me!'* based on the beautiful picture, alone. But I didn't know anything else about her.

I had a business team meeting at the Milwaukee Club soon after when a gorgeous woman walked by and my assistant said, "I think that's her!"

"THEN DEFINITELY!" I confirmed.

Kendall reached out, but Aleta was uninterested at first as she actually was in a more-than-one-date relationship at the time. I never forgot the image of her, though. A few months later, my assistant had heard the update that Aleta was no longer in the relationship and she asked if I could reach out to her; yes. The set-up may have made it seem I was more of a gentleman than the goofy kid I would prove to be.

I called her on the day her car was getting serviced to add Bluetooth capability. Apparently, my voice came booming out over the speakers in her car while the salesman was getting her system set up. That seems a little more accurate for the way we began and still continue today. I provide the "malarkey" while she's busy doing the serious stuff of life.

Aleta's daughter, Jaimie, was home from college and needed to use her mom's car when our first Starbucks chat arrived. "Absolutely," Aleta told her. "No problem, but I'm meeting someone for coffee downtown, so if you could drop me off and pick me up, that'd be great!" So, my future stepdaughter actually drove her mom to her first date with me.

I had just had a meeting with the mayor, so I was feeling confident. I even left Aleta a voicemail that said "I just wanted to confirm when we'll be getting together. I'll be coming straight from meeting with the mayor. I'm not sure why I said that; I just wanted to tell you I was meeting with the mayor."

She'd later tell me that when she saw me in the Starbucks, she was in from the start. Apparently, the pale blue suit I had on is still her favorite.

I did well enough to earn a proper date and her daughter didn't even chaperone. My office is only a couple of blocks from the art museum, so I met her there and actually waited in the guard's booth of the parking garage to get a laugh out of her. She liked the surprise, but wasn't giving in that easily. She could be happy and calm at the same time. I didn't know her steady nature yet.

▶▶ **She could be happy and calm at the same time. I didn't know her steady nature yet.**

As for the museum, I like realism. Abstract art really doesn't interest me. I love people who can paint realistically and I appreciate the patience it must take. After that, the next best thing is photographs, but I don't enjoy those as much as painting. We walked over to the museum and the whole date almost didn't work for me. I was trying so hard to be humorous and funny and witty and clever and I was getting nothing . . . *nothing*!

After I made a handful of comments that I thought were witty and charming, while getting no reaction, I thought, *'This isn't gonna work."* Since it wasn't going anywhere, I didn't care what I said anymore.

She asked what I thought at the next picture and I said, "It's my favorite."

"Why?'

"I see my reflection."

Finally! A laugh. I needed that!

We went from the museum to dinner at a place I'd been to before where I knew they would fawn over me and my date. Then, we took in a Bucks game.

We made arrangements for another date. I was going to take her to the zoo. This was back to my old dating habits, in a way: have a distraction if necessary and make sure there's a little bit of a scare opportunity to open the door for me to comfort her. That was the plan, anyway, but I got the first scare.

I rang Aleta's doorbell and there stood a seven-foot guy who opened the door. It turned out Jaimie was dating a basketball center at the time. Then, this tiny little dog started attacking me. I met Aleta's other daughter, Steph (whose twin, Ben, I'd meet later). The entire thing was a little chaotic.

Introductions to Joe and Haley didn't go very smoothly, either. Haley saw us on the television screen when we were at a Milwaukee Bucks game.

▶▶ **Introductions to Joe and Haley didn't go very smoothly, either.**

"Who are you with?" she texted me.

"Aleta."

"Who the fuck is Aleta?"

And this was also the time that I was basically in a bachelor pad with my son, Joe. I was totally frustrated by his falling into bad things and I was in a bad spot, too, yet I started bringing Aleta into that mess.

Joe had and still has a welcoming and fun nature to him, so there wasn't animosity from him. Aleta walked into having a maternal role. She doesn't remember it being that way, but she made meals for us to have in our fridge and spent time to just be present around the home. She started coming on Friday nights, sometimes when I would still be at work. She'd do her work at the house and prepare food for us to have in the fridge during the week.

Who does that? I didn't deserve her!

One night, she was over watching a movie when Joe came in before heading out with a friend.

"I'll see you guys later and, oh, by the way . . . today is my birthday."

Aleta leapt up so fast to hug him and, from that moment forward, she made sure I always paid attention (and she continued paying kindness and attention better than anyone I'd ever known).

A typical date in our early days was Sunday Brewer games. On the very first game we went to, we passed the people selling the 50/50 raffle tickets, so I stopped one of them in the aisle.

"Oh, wait! This is for charity, right?"

I whipped out a twenty. Then we went to the dessert cart in the club. Those aren't our normal game day experiences anymore, but I didn't want to leave anything to chance early on. I wanted her to know that I gave to charities and—contrarily—that I liked and wanted to share indulgences with her. Everything was planned until we were truly comfortable with one another.

Aleta still tells me my humor is stupid, but she talks about how much others think I'm funny. Something in her tone always made and makes me feel like she's actually my greatest fan. She's pretty even-keeled. It's hard to get her off of her seriousness. "Malarkey" was how she described me. And the times we spent together became her "Moments of Malarkey."

I guess that meant I was truly comfortable and that's when we'd mix it up on our dates–we'd be in Cedarburg where I lived or in Wauwatosa (Tosa) where Aleta lived. We were okay just being together. We settled into comfort.

The hardest thing for me, always wanting to be together, was when Aleta would come to the studio on Sunday mornings and sit through the whole show. At first, when it was new for her, she had a lot of questions and interest, but then it was just her working on other things while she was with me. I have to say it was a little disconcerting when I 'd thought I'd said something brilliant or funny on air and I'd look over at her and she was oblivious, with her face down, typing on her laptop. I realized we didn't need to spend *every* moment together, but we still wanted to be a part of each other's lives in every way. We would have one to two "dates" a week and each morning, before coffee, we would text "good morning" to one another.

After our first year of dating, our Christmas Eve tradition began. We would all go out to dinner, Aleta and I, our five children, and our children's significant others. Like a lot of traditions, it evolved into what it is. Some dinners were just spectacular, others, not as notable. The conversations and company was and is always fun.

One such dinner, at The Five O'Clock Steakhouse, was like a Supper Club from the '60s. We also liked to go to Rare Steakhouse, Carson's Ribs, and Capital Grille. As anyone who knows me can attest to, I love cheap fast-food *and* white tablecloth restaurants. I've never been accused of being a food snob. But, Christmas Eve was different. I wanted it to be special and at the best steakhouses and restaurants we could find. We wanted to be fawned over and coddled for the holiday while enjoying the uniqueness of the atmosphere, incredible food, and one another's presence.

The second year we held the dinner, Aleta volunteered to make the plans and chose Outback Steakhouse. As she tells it, she wasn't thinking. Not that I dislike Outback, but its Bloomin' Onion was not part of our typical, high-class, dressed-up, white-tablecloth, Christmas tradition.

It became a family joke for us and Aleta was a bit embarrassed by it. Fast forward to Aleta's birthday years later, I picked her up and drove her to dinner at Outback Steakhouse. She was so confused, because we were all on record that it wasn't our thing for a special evening. I stopped at the door, let her out, parked the car, and came in to meet her in line to put our name in. I was all in on this, even spending some time on the waiting list. Finally, I offered, "Should we go somewhere else?"

Enthusiastically, she said, "That would be *great!*" We walked outside . . . where a stretch limousine was waiting. I opened the door and the limousine was filled with all of our kids! She called it her best surprise ever.

As our dating started to progress, before our first Christmas, and with all of our kids in town, I suggested renting a cabin in the Wisconsin Dells for a two-day trip. We were in pretty cool cabins with seven people, but it could have been awkward. You didn't know what would really happen.

Aleta and I had been doing fine, though, so I was fine with the get-together. I used to take my kids to the tourist-oriented Wisconsin Dells all the time. Famous Dave's would bring out a huge feast . . . on a garbage can lid. Aleta's kids were more refined. We had dinner there and everybody was a bit tense and strained. It was only 6:30 P.M. We had the rest of the night and the next day. How were we going to bond?

There was an outlet mall near the Dells. It hit me as we were having dinner that we needed to find a way to get our kids to interact.

"Here's what we're going to do," I said. "We're going to the outlet mall." (Eye rolls all around.)

When we got over there, though, I handed each kid fifty bucks. I said, "You each have thirty minutes to go through this mall and whoever, with their money, buys the most creative, fun, and cool thing will win an additional prize."

They scurried like mice, while Aleta and I hung back. We walked and watched them, comparing notes and collaborating before we went back to the cabin for an unveiling.

Joe showed his personality right from the start. I remember giving him money to spend at a Brewers game once when he was younger and he bought a pencil and pocketed the rest. This time, he had found a "Magic Ball" that levitated . . . and pocketed the rest. I was really surprised, though; he might have chosen another pencil. Ben bought Nikes; he didn't care if he won—he wanted the shoes. Steph

had an extremely fancy candy apple. Haley and Jaimie bought clothes, but the actual objects weren't the real point of the exercise. It was goofy, but it was a bonding adventure and instant fun. Plus it showed each of the kids' characters a little bit. It couldn't have gone better. That was the beginning of what seemed like a pretty cool family. I tried to make sure that everything we did with the kids was just fun. I wanted to bring a lot of spontaneity to the family.

Before me, Aleta didn't have a relationship with a guy interested in her kids . . . ever. It's a big part of why it didn't work. After we'd been dating for about a year, we were watching the Wisconsin Badgers in the Sweet 16 of the NCAA championship bracket. The kids came home after the game. Aleta's daughter, Jaimie, was dating a Badger at the time and she ran in saying, "Oh my God! We have to go to New Orleans."

I opened up my computer, asked, "who's going?" and booked the trip.

Then, one night, Ben came into the room and asked, "Hey Mom do you have twenty bucks?"

I reached in my pocket and said, "Here."

In my mind, and I expressed this to Aleta, it all came from the same place. I think that's when she realized I saw us—ALL of us—as a family. Aleta, and me, and my two children, Joe and Haley, and her three children, Jaimie, Ben, and Steph; we were all one family.

Left to right: Haley, Aleta, Steve, Steph, Jaimie, Joe, Ben

I implemented a bi-annual family trip. Mexico was a really fun one. Each kid got to bring someone. Most of us them were in relationships at the time, so it worked out well. They could do whatever they wanted during the day—me learning to "hold on loosely"—as long as we all came together for dinner. Ben's friend, Jaimie's date, and I did shots of Patron tequila one of the days we were there, and one of us, not me, didn't make the meal, but I stayed true to my word and meals together kept their place of importance.

Getting to know Aleta's kids was a priority for me. Ben and I went to a Bucks game. Jaimie and I went to a Pink Concert. As of this writing, Steph and I haven't done anything one-on-one, but that will eventually occur. About three years before Aleta and I married, Jaimie started calling me her stepdad and Joe and Haley were her stepbrother and stepsister.

We truly knew each other.

We truly accepted one another.

Aleta and I kept a journal for months that we would hand off during the day. We posed questions to one another back and forth; we spent a lot of time getting to know one another in a really vulnerable way through that journal.

An early entry I shared said, *"We're looking for the exact same thing. Someone to love you. Someone to love me. We can do that."* We moved forward with the assumption that we were going to work.

▶▶ **We moved forward with the assumption that we were going to work.**

The journal was BRUTALLY open and honest with soul-baring aspects. In retrospect, the motivation, passion, and attraction was obvious, but the honestly of the expectation was in that book: *"Someone to love you. Someone to love me."* That expectation allowed us to jump start what a lot of relationships need grinding and time to do. It allowed the meshing of our lives.

Our friends became connected to our joint life, too. My closest friends Susi and Keith claimed that, if this relationship didn't work out, they'd take custody of Aleta this time. I don't blame them, but I'd fight them for her, so I guess that means it's worked out. Aleta and I let each other have friendships and lives outside of one another while also being in each other's lives.

Like a lot of relationships, minutiae starts coming in. We had a strong foundation in honesty, made even clearer in our shared journal, and that's where the hiccups may have come in.

Aleta tells me she wishes she had met my mom. She wants to know how I was raised to be very complex in that I'm loyal to a high degree in adult relationships, but—in terms of social graces and chivalry—I'm more known to act like a seventeen-year old. That's the sort of "malarkey" that drove (and continues to drive) her crazy. I always wanted the fun, the laughter, the goofiness, and—sometimes—she just wanted (and deserved) to be treated with refinement and class. She occasionally wanted the gentleman that asked to call on her and not always the goofy kid who liked his own reflection at the art museum.

> ▶▶ **I always wanted the fun, the laughter, the goofiness, and— sometimes—she just wanted (and deserved) to be treated with refinement and class.**

I showed the world my exterior, funny-guy persona that most everybody loved–the guy whose purpose in life was laughter and music. Everyone thought I was funny, creative, or clever, but Aleta would get frustrated and her reactions then revealed the fragile side of me. I needed safety, love, and approval. I needed to know I mattered. And when I felt like I was still alone staring out at an alley as a detached little kid, I'd shut down . . . and shut *out* everybody– including her.

Aleta was and is a communicator. I never had been. At least not outside of media. If she tried to talk with me about something difficult, I'd want to go away and shut down for three days to avoid the conflict. I wouldn't respond to phone calls or text messages. I wouldn't even eat and you know how I love to eat. If I avoided the conflict, maybe it would just go away. This clash of Aleta the communicator and me the processor happened intermittently over the course of five years. She used to say I was "going into the cave."

I'd come out of the cave, where I had been thinking and working on myself, but she really didn't like the cave. The difference with Aleta was that if I took her kindness and her patience, the cave dwelling was a bit different than it had been in past relationships. I still had to have my own time and terms, but I would actually change. She was patient and full of grace. So, I didn't keep her fully out of my cave. Today, I'm in utter amazement that I can be in the "cave" for as little as an hour.

Then, we incorporated the "reset" button. Sometimes, it was the only way out. We would agree to hit the button and move forward, sometimes without me having to have alone time at all. Still, Aleta was getting tired of everything needing to be funny and entertaining.

'I get it. Women get tired of me and leave.' I thought. I didn't think it was anything I had a say in. I never did, before Aleta.

One night, we went to a really nice dinner with another couple. Aleta was dressed up beautifully, but there was nothing I did for her that would have suggested we were on a date. I didn't hold the door, pull out her chair, or hang up her coat. I went first when the bartender took our drink order and made her open her own doors on the way out and into the car home, too. Nothing about that night made her feel special.

On the way home, she said, "I am SO mad at you."

I was oblivious, but the straw that broke the camel's back was that my response to her being upset was to go into my cave. While I was out, Aleta gathered all of her stuff from my place, put the garage door opener at my closed door and left. She was done. She was going to let me live in the cave and go on and live her life.

> **"I knew someday that you would fly away, for love is the greatest healer to be found. So, leave me if you need to, I will still remember Angel flying to close to the ground."**
> ▶ *Angel Flying Too Close To The Ground, Willie Nelson*

In the first few weeks after the breakup, the kids found out, of course. Jaimie reached me when I was coming back from a Packer game. It caught me off-guard, I had all sorts of game-related texts and, in the midst of them, were words from the girl I already saw as my step daughter.

"I'm disappointed in you. You didn't just do this to our Mom. You did this to our whole family. You know—I consider you family."

Her words broke through like a bullet.

At that point, several weeks away from the initial pain, I was steeling myself to *not* come around. I didn't want to do the work. I was figuring out how to get back to enjoying my life without Aleta and without the expectations of our journal promises. I was just starting to be okay with it all, but Jaimie changed that.

I had a family and I needed them back.

Shortly afterward, I had lunch with Susi Templin and she asked, "Do you want me to get involved or not?"

I said, "YES."

Susi reached out to Aleta and said, "Aleta, most women never have a man in their life love them the way Steve loves you. You should hear him talk about you. He loves you so much."

Aleta and I met for a drink and I remember that I was focused on having a sort of pep talk, bringing the fun as always. She came back two days later with a nine-page letter, harkening back to our journal days. She wasn't having the fun. Instead, she told me the kind of man she needed and asked, "Can you be him?"

I'd had a lot of women in my life tell me what was wrong with me (and therefore any kind of "us" that might exist with me) but Aleta actually wanted to help fix it. This was new.

Much of my and Aleta's breakup was based, not on heart intentions, wishes, or soul, but my actions. I had no experience with truly being committed. How can you truly be committed if you think the other person is going to walk away. That leaves the exit strategy open. It's like an emotional pre-nuptial agreement. The single biggest change was in my responsibility of being present. I needed to not disappear for days into the cave, but also accept that she wasn't going to disappear when I frustrated her. It was back to that original promise: "Someone to love me. Someone to love you."

Back together after the breakup, I'd never had so many rules in my life . . . and I'd never been so happy." I'm still me. At times, I'm intellectual, and other times I'm an eight-year old. With Aleta, somehow, I hit a balance of feeling comfortable with myself, and also accepting rules for—really—the first time in my life. The most important thing to me, though, is the confidence that I'm not on trial.

We moved in together after five years of dating, making what was Aleta's Wauwatosa home into OUR home, renovating every room. We turned the dining room into a pub. It opened onto the patio that we made into another entertaining space, and I put in my studio upstairs, the walls lined with the soundtracks of my life, as well as a gym in the lower level.

I waited to propose until about two years after we got back together. For a good year, Aleta surely thought every special occasion was going to be when I asked. We went to Costa Rica on a trip with the kids while Steph was there with the Peace Corps.

I handed Aleta a box and said, "See? I told you I'm not going anywhere." She opened the box and it was a ring.

"Are you asking me to marry you?"

She said, "YES!"

Aleta put the ring on and we went down to the pool. She was playing it kind of cool, talking to her daughter Jaimie while holding a drink in her left hand, waiting for the ring to be noticed.

"Mom," Jaimie said to her, "We all kind of thought you'd get engaged in Costa Rica."

Aleta turned her hand toward her daughter and Jaimie let out a scream! She ran over to the rest of the group and everybody was screaming and hugging.

Steph yelled, "Oh my God! I'm glad you're going to be my stepdad," and then she hit me . . . HARD . . . but playfully, of course.

We immediately facetimed Haley because she wasn't able to be with us in person.

When we began going to the Brewers games early in our relationship, Aleta had an open attitude toward understanding the game. She embraced the intricacies of watching and all of the moving parts. Aleta did those things and it was really enjoyable for me! She now knows the game. At some point, I wasn't just going with a "girl," on a date, I was going with a fan! Baseball time together has life of its own and, as a place where we both are ourselves, it made sense to be the place where we would choose to hold our wedding.

While our engagement didn't have specifics, our wedding had to be special. I flippantly mentioned one day at lunch in Colorado with some of the kids that we should get married at Miller Park. Before Aleta could even react, they jumped all over it. To my amazement, we picked a date and were able to reserve the ballpark! The planning was intense and could have led to some heated disagreements. At one point, we discussed the number of guests. We were all over the board, so I suggested we each write down a number. Aleta had 100. My number was 20,000. We compromised at 100.

I insisted on utilizing every aspect of this unique venue and suggested numerous ideas for the show, at which point Aleta reminded me that it was a wedding ceremony . . . and *not* a show! Our compromise was perfect. She handled all the arrangements for the reception, from flowers, to food, to dancing. I handled the . . . uhh . . . ~~show~~ wedding ceremony.

All the guests walking into the stadium were handed a hot dog and a beer, then seated behind home plate. Rob Edwards, the longtime Brewers Public Address Announcer handled the introductions of the wedding party. The ceremonial first pitch were footballs thrown by LeRoy to me, my son Joe, and my soon-to-be (official) stepson Ben. The Mayor of Milwaukee, Tom Barrett, shared a few words. We flew in Steve Forbert who sang those meaningful lyrics I'd always desired to live in my life:

**"Meet me in
the middle of the day
Let me hear you say
everything's okay."**

Our great friends, Jessob Reisbeck and Wisconsin State Fair CEO Kathleen O'Leary both got ordained to perform the ceremony. Strings were pulled so that our dog Luke could participate on the field with the famous racing sausages in a Miller Park tradition. The giant scoreboard in center field continuously rotated our family photos. Sammy Llanas, formerly of the BoDeans, put together a band to play another meaningful song for us, *Still The Night:*

"If I can hold you tonight, I might never let go."

Each of our five kids spoke and it was the highlight of the "show." My friend Keith ended up being very sick that day, so Susi also pinch hit on a speech. She almost felt bad because they'd known me forever and yet she realized this was the first time she'd ever seen me so happy. She didn't want to say as much in front of the children, but to her, there was truth to what she saw. Aleta answered the call of my soul. She's brilliant, independent, capable, and somehow still laughs at my jokes and adores me.

The next thing I knew, I was married and Forbert played a song as the wedding party and guests made their ways upstairs to one of the clubs at Miller Park to enjoy the reception.

Steve: Do you remember that you were supposed to play at my wedding at Miller Park? And you deserve to be playing stadiums!

Lissie: I'm not sure I want that. It's funny all the little rooms in your brain that exist. I totally remember. I had to go play Glastonbury. I'm so sorry. I would have loved to play at your wedding at the Brewers stadium. Glastonbury is a big deal, so I'm sure I was pressured to go, but I hate letting people down. I missed my cousin's wedding, so I'm sorry I wasn't there.

All wedding photos by and used with courtesy of Kyle Kelley

"Kisses that come all the way
from China
Kinda remind her of
memories of Spain
If I get lost, you can always
find her
Standing right beside me in
the rain.
She is my everything."

▶ *She Is My Everything, JOHN PRINE*

Aleta is my whole package. I've worked at becoming the whole package for her, too. One of the things I like to do is bring her things that she loves. She loves red velvet cake and chocolate of any kind. It was not unusual for her to arrive home at the end of a day to find a full-on red velvet cake sitting on the counter. She finally had to ask me for help.

Aleta said, "It is so nice that you do this, and it means the world to me, but you have to understand, if it's in the house, I'm going to eat it. And I don't want to eat it."

I reluctantly stopped buying sweet treats for Aleta and switched to flowers. Perfect, because she loves flowers. And she doesn't eat them.

In the city, in the stands, and in my life, I have Aleta. Even in the studio, every week during my radio show, there is a secret song I play for her. She knows when I'll play her "message." *It reminds her that this life—my life—is better for having her as a part of it.*

And in the end
the love you take
is equal to the love you make

▶ *The End,* THE BEATLES

IN PICTURES

Thousand-Word Stories

"Picture book, of people with
each other, to prove they love
each other a long ago."

▶ *FROM: Picture Book*
BY: The Kinks, The Kinks are the
Village Green Preservation Society
(Pye Records, 1968)

*T*o say there was some editing out of parts of my personal history
and stories in this vast work would be an understatement.
There is more I want to tell: more encounters, more adventures, and
more things learned; more laughter, more joy, and more . . . awe.
There simply aren't enough pages or words to keep you here, but I
hope that this picture book will give you a glimpse into some of the
life I've been lucky to live. These are in no particular order–REALLY!
With each picture worth a thousand words, these pages make up at least a
few more cool anecdotes.

"I ain't as good as I once was,
but I'm as good once
as I ever was."

▶ *FROM: I Ain't As Good As I Once Was*
BY: Toby Keith, Honkeytonk University
(Dreamworks, 2005)

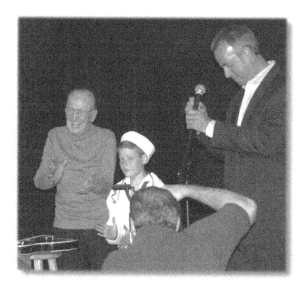

In awe

An Epilogue

"After years and years of
writing story songs I've
learned one thing. If you're
writing a story song you
better have a darn good
ending. And if you don't then
you better have a good moral
to the story. *So here's the
moral to the story.*"

▶ FROM: *The Bottomless Lake*
BY: *John Prine, In Person & On Stage*
(Oh Boy Records, 2010)

I AM known as the cool and crazy uncle to a few of my friends who
have children. Maybe it's because I'm this twelve-year-old kid
stuck in a grown man's body. I brought a boxed gift to the boys of my
good friends, Susi and Keith, one day. I hung out near them until
their mom passed it off to them to open. It was a stack of Playboys! It

wasn't really for them; it was for me. The gift of the reaction on my friend's face as she snatched them back is what I really wanted

"What the fuck are you doing, Steve?! Oh My God!" You are the WORST-HUMAN-EVER!" she said. But then she laughed—and I laughed—and I live for the joy of laughter from others.

I waited back like the Cheshire cat in the corner until her laughter came. I love doing stupid things like that. I guess I want to be unexpected. I lived off the goofiness of that moment, the laughter – not the gag gift, for probably a week. The truth is I love those kids and have even been a mentor to them in some ways, much like Nicole's daughter at the baseball games, or my own kids–both Joe and Haley, as well as Ben, Steph, and Jaimie.

Susi and Keith took care of me a lot in the days before Aleta by having me over and sharing their house and family. I'd show up all the time with ridiculous gifts like a whole case of Fun Dip or something else unpredictable. It should both terrify them and warm their hearts that I can be so much myself with them. Like in my studio and in my relationship with Aleta, I am at home with them.

I didn't have that feeling of "home" much growing up, but I think the life experiences I've had since then have given me tools to maximize life and to maximize the feeling of awe within that life.

I've learned to balance humility and ego. I've learned to tap into creativity, be appropriately motivated by fear, and find humor where it lives (and sometimes where it hides). I express admiration for others and also accept myself . . . including all of the flaws that come with me. I value what history can teach me and am aware of the constraints of time in the short moments and the long haul. I have gained an attitude that allows room for sarcasm and skepticism, without allowing those things to interfere with my optimism. And I keep asking for the life that brings all of these things, no matter where I think I can find it.

Just as I hear all of the layers of a soundtrack, I look for the unnoticed to find opportunities to connect. Let's say I see a rock that is maybe just some plain old stone with a speck on it. While everyone else is seeing the rock, I want to see the speck . . . and also know why it's there. If I can't figure it out, I can tell a story that will hopefully be creative and funny for those around me. I'm giddy about finding those types of opportunities.

I want to share that the baseball stadium is really just a park, that seven city blocks contain the whole scope of life from ecstasy to aberration, that even a toilet seat handle can make a person smile, that a Big Mac with a toothpick in it can be as fun as a formal hors d'oeuvre when shared with friends. I want to look for ways to make an impact and an impression. I want to live life larger than most people do, but not because they can't or because I have something in front of me that others don't based on the fact that I am on the radio. Rather, because they can—and I want to help them discover awe in the spectacular and simple stuff of life.

People don't always think to ask for all that life has to give and it has so much to give in even the most ordinary of things. A glass of bourbon in my hand, Packers logo on my hat, a conversation about an athlete or musician, The Beatles playing in the background, tweeting at the same time with some ridiculous or random picture, and talking about a separate shared experience with loved ones: does it get any better than that?

It so happens that I made my name in radio and commercial real estate, but I want to remind people to enjoy those things that are out there to be indulged in during this great American life–enjoyed by *anyone* who wants them. Humility, creativity, fear, humor, admiration, confidence, respect for history, an attitude of flexibility, and pausing to truly recognize important moments all can come alive for you when you ask for life. And all of those things can lead to joy.

When joy is evasive, it's as empty and cold as dead air. This life is a song whose notes and words are ours to play. And like any lyrics, they can be lived and interpreted differently for every single person.

This life isn't about lingering on the air or in the spotlight. It's full of high volume, unexpected cuts, and segues to the next notes we're to experience.

It's about seeking joy.

For me, food brings that.

Sports bring that.

Success brings that.

Friendships bring that.

Family brings that.

Radio brings that.

Aleta brings that.

I don't hold myself down, anymore.

If I were to float above myself, I'd see it all.

I've learned, if I just let go, I can live my life ... *In Awe.*

▶

A Note To Readers

I've been told I look at life a little differently.

I agree.

*This whole book experience started with my sharing a bunch of stories–some I'd told a hundred times and others that I'd never before revealed. Many of the stories came from being in the right place at the right time during a lifetime of broadcasting. I've had access to musicians and athletes and—through my real estate career—business and community leaders. I almost stopped writing before I started. I didn't want this to be a collection of name dropping or "look what I did" vignettes. I've read those stories and I needed to know that there was something more that could come from these pages than self-aggrandizing. Through the journey of reminiscence, **I discovered that there was one thing all of my stories had in common: AWE.***

At heart, I am just a regular guy who happens to see awe in almost everything. I am in awe of the people I encounter and the things going on around me. I seek out big things and I appreciate little things. I like to think that maybe I've tapped into that "power of awe." Awe is at the root of all of my stories as I tried to find inspiration, and hope, and – sometimes – simply cope with what life brought my way. It's been a fun way to go through life and handy when life hasn't been fun.

In John Prine's 2010 live album, In Person & On Stage, toward the end of a song called The Bottomless Lake, he said, "After years and years of writing story songs I've learned one thing. If you're writing a story song, you better have a darn good ending. And if you don't, then you better have a good moral to the story. So, here's the moral to the story."

Well-said, John.

Awe has been my moral to the story . . . to this story.

I've been in awe of the simple things like combining a McDonald's double cheeseburger with an Egg McMuffin.

I've been in awe of the big things like getting up every Sunday morning to play music for thousands of people for more than thirty years.

I've been in awe of playing basketball in an alley where my full court was two hoops on garages that didn't line up and also in awe sitting courtside during the NBA finals.

And I'm in awe that, after even the roughest of nights, the sun comes up in the morning and brings me another chance to find even more awe.

These have been my stories, and some song lyrics, and a few insights, but – most of all – it's been my moral to the story:

The reason I look at life "a little differently" is because I look at it from the powerful perspective . . . of AWE.

▶

Steve is available for speaking, reading, and events to talk about the stories in this book, a lifetime of radio and real-estate, and his cornerstone life experience-influenced tips on maximizing awe.

1) Balance Humility and Ego
2) Tap Into Creativity
3) Respect Fear
4) Just Ask
5) Find Humor
6) Value Respect and Admiration
7) Don't Compare
8) Honor History
9) Don't Run Out The Clock
10) Have Kindness With Any Attitude

Visit **www.stevepalec.com** to get the tips in a free, downloadable e-book, complete with even more awesome stories.

About The Creators

STEVE PALEC's friend, LeRoy Butler, may have said it best. The capital of Wisconsin is not Madison, it's Steve. Born and raised in Milwaukee by immigrant parents, Steve is a first-generation American who began his love of music on February 9, 1964. The Beatlemania that encompassed much of the world also grabbed the attention of the then seven-year-old and never let go. Steve was obsessed with the exciting new music he heard on the radio daily. In addition, his love of sports had him fascinated with the legendary sportscasters he listened to intently. Between music and sports, he found himself from a very young age practicing for his lifelong career in broadcasting long before he even knew it would happen.

Unable to make up his mind between sports and music, he chose both. Steve began his on-air work in his high school days and has been a Milwaukee radio personality since the '70s, even winning a national ADDY award. He has worked in the music industry and interviewed artists, as well as radio broadcast journalism covering Milwaukee area professional sports teams. In

June of 1987, Rock & Roll Roots, a Milwaukee institution, was created and Palec's baritone has provided its voice for all of its thirty-two years, missing only one live show in the three plus decades. His weekly Sunday morning history of music show is one of the longest running programs on Milwaukee radio.

In addition to his now total forty-five-year career on the air, Steve has overlapped a second successful profession in commercial real estate for the last thirty-five years. He's worked for multinational firms, run his own company, brokered deals with high profile corporations and individuals, and today serves as the Chief Marketing Officer for Irgens, a large and respected real estate development firm in Wisconsin and Arizona.

As such a prominent Wisconsin personality, Palec has used his network and talents to better his city and state through personal, professional, and philanthropic movements as often as possible. He has served on the boards for respected institutions including the Wisconsin Athletic Hall of Fame and the Hunger Task Force; served as a contributing blogger for OnMilwaukee; participated as a judge at the Wisconsin State Fair Sporkies; held fundraisers for numerous worthy health and community causes; and emceed important events for organizations and non-profit enterprises.

Steve's personal experiences in radio and real estate have provided a lifetime of amazing stories, relationships, and experiences that truly do read like the lyrics of a great American song. Despite his life of awe and famed friendships, though, it is the simple things that continue to bring him the most joy: his amazing wife, Aleta; their five children, Joe, Haley, Jaimie, Steph, and Ben; his dog, Luke; and his good friends. It is with these loved ones you can find Steve taking in a great game at Miller Park or Lambeau Field, often with a bourbon in his hand. It is his hope that, through this book, others can learn to experience joy, laughter, and awe in all that life has to offer.

Learn more about Steve at **www.stevepalec.com**.

286

Reji LaBerje

After more than two decades in writing, editing, layout, publishing, co-authoring, teaching, marketing, and author coaching and consulting, Reji is retiring from the industry to rediscover a time when her art was done for the sake of the art, rather than as a business. She is thrilled and honored to have worked on *"In Awe"* as her final biography and co-author partnership and is immensely proud of what she and Steve, her now-friend, were able to create in these pages.

While the power of words continues to be a personal passion, Reji—a wife, mother, pet-lover, and veteran Air Force linguist—looks forward to enjoying her Wisconsin life through service, travel, music, languages, and time spent taking in sports, nature, arts, church, and home life with family, friends, and loved ones.

Though Reji intends to return to her roots in playwriting, children's books, and fantasy fiction (as a hobby!), plus whatever other writing draws her imagination, she also wants to continue helping people find fulfillment and connection through story and she desires her lessons, processes, and unique creative methods to remain available to prospective authors. To preserve her approaches, the same tools that earned Reji 10 personal #1 Bestsellers (so far) out of nearly 60 publications, led another 70 authors to their #1 Bestsellers, managed more than 80 projects with independent and traditional authors and publishers, and coached thousands of writers over the years, will be available for free on her website (**www.bucketlisttobookshelf**) or in bargain-priced book resources. Those resources can be picked up on Amazon and other online retailers, along with many titles from her extensive new releases and backlist of books across a wide variety of genres.

LeRoy Butler

LeRoy Butler played his entire career with the Green Bay Packers, from 1990 through 2001. As a member of the Pro Football Hall of Fame 1990's All-Decade team, a 4-time Associated Press All-Pro selection, and a 4-time NFL Pro Bowl selection, his work on the football field has been widely recognized. He was the first player in NFL history to record 20+ sacks and 20+ interceptions in a career.

At the time of this book's printing, Butler is a nominee for the Pro Football Hall of Fame Class of 2020. (He already is a member of the Green Bay Packer Hall of Fame—Class of 2007.) Famous for being the player who invented the Lambeau Leap in 1993, LeRoy's celebration is still used today, but he leapt well-beyond the field in his post-NFL career.

LeRoy leads an anti-bullying crusade, Butler vs. Bullying, and he's available for speaking to schools, sports teams or clubs, and other youth organizations. From a crippled childhood to leaping in the stands, few have triumphed like Butler.

LeRoy and Steve Palec became friends through a shared affinity for food, football, laughter, and radio. Steve stood up for LeRoy's 2019 wedding to his wife, Genesis and LeRoy was part of Steve's wedding ceremony when Steve married Aleta. The two men support one another in all of their career and creative endeavors. It was an absolute joy for Butler to create the foreword for *"In Awe"* and he imagines it's just one more leap tallied in their enduring and endearing friendship.

Learn more about LeRoy and pick up his book, *"The LeRoy Butler Story"* on **www.leroybutlerinc.com**.

Steve's Acknowledgments & Gratitude

And now, although it is counterintuitive to my selfish nature, I'd like to follow the (**directions**) provided to me by my co-author, Reji Laberje, for writing about the appreciation I sincerely feel:

1) **(Who are your children, biggest cheerleaders, closest friends, etc. that need mentioning?)**

I actually really like my kids. Each and every one of them. Biological or not. That means Joe, Haley, Jaimie, Ben, and Steph. My brother Andy, too, who I've known all his life. Same for my loyal-and-always-glad-to-see-me dog, Luke. And my always-there-for-me friends, Keith and Susi Templin, plus my brother from another mother, LeRoy Butler

2) **(Express gratitude for radio and real estate career inspirations, supporters, and contributors.)**

Heck yeah! I don't know where I would be without the people that came before me to lead the way to doing things the right way. That starts in commercial real estate with Mark Brickman at Polacheck as well as Gary, Max, and my former teammates, Bill and Kevin. Also, the late Jeff Siegel, who was so ultra-competitive that he raised my game without knowing it. Danielle Maletzke, my right hand at Cresa. Scott Welsh and Lyle Landowski at Colliers. And, of course, one of the most creative problem solvers I've ever met, Mark Irgens.

On the radio side, it was Dr. Ruane Hill at UWM who responded to my original letter asking to do anything . . . even sweep the floors. Dave Edwards is who helped me out there. Robert Marsh, Brent Alberts, and Andy Bloom at WQFM. Paul LeSage at WZUU. Bob Bellini and Annmarie Topel at WKLH. WE Energies and Potawatomi Hotel & Casino for sponsoring my show. The Brewers and Bucks PR departments during the '70s and 80s that let me eat . . . with the "real" working press.

3) **(Give special thanks to those who were interviewed to help write this book.)**

Dozens were interviewed to provide hundreds of pages of content, quotes, words, and pictures to be refined and added to my own hundreds of pages of stories and hundreds more pages of researched material for *"In Awe."* Even more friends were willing. Know that even the kind words that did not end up in this book will be with me forever. I thank each and every one of you and will probably say so again in person.

4) **(Don't forget the many people who helped bring this book to fruition.)**

It wouldn't have happened without the aforementioned Reji Laberje. She not only listened to all my stories (imagine how painful that is being subjected to the ones that *didn't* make it in), but she translated them into English that you all would understand AND was first to recognize the common thread of awe. We battled over everything but made this a thing. It wouldn't be without her.

Thanks to Jay Filter and Scott Paulus, two amazing photographers who I've been proud to call friends long before I envisioned needing their photographs. And thank you also to the editors, designers, videographers, and publications that stepped up to help.

5) **(Express personal appreciation for fans of you and inspirations to you)**

Obviously, anyone who has ever given me a bottle of Blanton's, my favorite bourbon. You know who you are! Thank you.

Oh yeah, all the friends that I've been lucky enough to share laughter with. Yes, that's you!

Also, food delivery drivers, concert promoters, The Beatles, and creators of TV content.

In all seriousness . . . my ex-wives and ex-girlfriends. The truth is that, at one point in my life, I was lucky to share your warmth. It was me; not you.

6) (Last but certainly not least – your most important thanks to Aleta....)

Thanks.

(....or others that warrant a distinguished acknowledgment)

There are no others.

(....with a personal note that is genuinely affectionate)

You're hot . . . and the kindest, most supportive soul ever in my world. You fill my life with awe.

"I want to share that the baseball stadium is really just a park, that seven city blocks contain the whole scope of life from ecstasy to aberration, that even a toilet seat handle can make a person smile, that a Big Mac with a toothpick in it can be as fun as a formal hors d'oeuvre when shared with friends. I want to look for ways to make an impact and an impression. I want to live life larger than most people do, but not because they can't or because I have something in front of me that others don't based on the fact that I am on the radio. Rather, because they can—and I want to help them discover awe in the spectacular and simple stuff of life."

"In Awe"

Made in the USA
Monee, IL
03 December 2019